Living Wages, Equal Wages

"This book addresses an issue that is particularly timely after years of growing income inequality and draconian decreases in welfare support for single mothers which is likely to work increasing hardship as unemployment rises. The authors deserve credit for making it clear throughout that their concern is not so much with economics, as practiced by neoclassical economists, as with political economy. The difference, as they make clear, is that the latter takes full cognizance of the importance of social conditions and government policies, not merely market forces, in determining wages. This is an important lesson for an economics profession that has tended to resist any efforts to improve upon a wage structure that rewards some with riches beyond the dreams of avarice and leaves others destitute."

Marianne Ferber, Professor Emerita, University of Illinois

"Moving from early twentieth-century struggles over minimum wages for both the women worker and male breadwinner and post-World War II attempts at equal pay through job evaluation and legislation onto recent battles for comparable worth and the living wage, Figart, Mutari, and Power unmask wage setting as a central vehicle for institutionalizing gender and race inequality in the United States. Their focus on the wage as a living, as a price, and as a social practice demystifies the labor market process at a time when employment has replaced income assistance as the goal of welfare policy. Full of theoretical sophistication and historical insight, *Living Wages, Equal Wages* is feminist political economy at its best."

Eileen Boris, Hull Professor of Women's Studies, University of California, Santa Barbara

Wage setting has historically been a deeply political and cultural as well as an economic process. This informative and accessible book explores how US wage regulations in the twentieth century took gender, race-ethnicity, and class into account. Focusing on social reform movements for living wages and equal wages, it offers an interdisciplinary account of how women's work and the remuneration for that work have changed along with the massive transformations in the economy and family structures.

The controversial issue of establishing living wages for all workers makes this book both a timely and indispensable contribution to this wide-ranging debate, and it will surely become required reading for anyone with an interest in modern economic issues.

Deborah M. Figart is Professor of Economics at Richard Stockton College, New Jersey. **Ellen Mutari** is Assistant Professor of General Studies at Richard Stockton College, New Jersey. **Marilyn Power** is a member of the Faculty of Economics at Sarah Lawrence College, New York.

Routledge IAFFE Advances in Feminist Economics
Series editor: Jane Humphries

1 Living Wages, Equal Wages
Gender and labor market policies in the United States
Deborah M. Figart, Ellen Mutari, and Marilyn Power

Living Wages, Equal Wages

Gender and labor market policies in the United States

Deborah M. Figart, Ellen Mutari, and Marilyn Power

London and New York

First published 2002
by Routledge
11 New Fetter Lane, London EC4P 4EE

Simultaneously published in the USA and Canada
by Routledge
29 West 35th Street, New York, NY 10001

Routledge is an imprint of the Taylor & Francis Group

Typeset in Goudy by RefineCatch Limited, Bungay, Suffolk
Printed and bound in Great Britain by
T. J. International Ltd, Padstow, Cornwall

British Library Cataloguing in Publication Data
A catalogue record for this book is available from the British Library

Library of Congress Cataloging in Publication Data
A catalog record for this book is available from the Library of Congress

ISBN 0–415–27390–0 (hbk)
ISBN 0–415–27391–9 (pbk)

Contents

PART III
The century ahead   177

Illustrations

Plates

Figures

Tables

Series editor's preface

The International Association for Feminist Economics (IAFFE) was formed in 1992 in response to several critical concerns. Economics is a conservative and narrow discipline. Many issues pertaining to the experiences, well-being, and empowerment of women have received little attention. Scholars undertaking feminist economic research and policy advocacy typically experience a lack of support from their colleagues and institutions. Researchers and activists on women's issues often work in isolation, and feminist researchers in different parts of the world face difficulties in finding out about each other's work.

IAFFE seeks to combat these problems and to advance feminist inquiry into economic issues. The organization aims to increase the visibility and range of economic research on gender; to facilitate communication among scholars, policy makers, and activists concerned with women's well-being and empowerment; to promote discussions among policy makers about interventions which serve women's needs; to educate economists, policy-makers, and the general public about feminist perspectives on economic issues; to foster feminist evaluations of economics as a discipline; to expose the gender-blindness characteristic of much social science and the ways in which this impoverishes all research, even research that does not explicitly concern women's issues; to help expand opportunities for women, especially women from underrepresented groups, within economics; and, to encourage the inclusion of feminist perspectives in the teaching of economics.

IAFFE pursues these ends through a variety of publishing and networking activities. These include: the publication of the scholarly journal *Feminist Economics* to present theoretical, empirical, policy-related, and methodological work on economic issues from a feminist perspective; the holding of regular summer conferences where feminist work is presented and discussed; and, the organization of panel sessions at national, regional, and international meetings of economists and researchers from related disciplines. The IAFFE book series pursues the aims of the organization by providing a forum in which scholars have space to develop their ideas at length and in detail. The series exemplifies the value of feminist research and the high standard of IAFFE-sponsored scholarship.

Living Wages, Equal Wages: Gender and Labor Market Policies in the United States by Deborah M. Figart, Ellen Mutari, and Marilyn Power is a fitting volume to inaugurate the IAFFE series. Written for a wide, interdisciplinary audience, this fine book argues that wage setting is a political and cultural as well as an economic process. Figart, Mutari, and Power identify three different but coexisting approaches to wages and the process by which they are set. Wages are a price, so supply, demand, and market adjustment must play a role. Indeed orthodox economics would stop right here with wages market determined. But wages are also a living and so socially acceptable living standards must play a role. And finally wages are a social practice. They grade the labor of workers by gender, class, race, and ethnicity so the relationships between types of workers in families, unions, and workplaces must influence where differentials stand. The three interpretations are not mere theoretical constructs. The authors show how all three were appealed to, mobilized, contested, and referenced by social reform movements for living wages and equal wages in the U.S. in the twentieth century. The market mattered, but so did the other interpretations of wages and wage setting.

Debates over wage regulations and practices at key junctures in the development of U.S. labor market policies are examined to cast light on changing ideas about what should matter in setting wages. The key historical moments, all milestones in the campaign for equal wages for women and living wages for all, are state minimum wage laws, the federal minimum wage introduced under the Fair Labor Standards Act of 1938, the National War Labor Board's promotion of equal pay for equal work, and the Equal Pay Act of 1963.

The central theme of the book is that wage setting is a human story. By demonstrating the importance of perceptions of wages and wage setting, manifest in political and cultural movements, *Living Wages, Equal Wages* provides a richer understanding of how wages are really set. There are lessons on many levels for students of the labor market.

Jane Humphries
October 2001

Acknowledgments

In developing a feminist economics or, as we prefer, feminist political economy of wage setting, we began by posing two questions: (1) What can we learn from the range of perspectives in political economy, from classical to marginalist? (2) What additional insights can we offer as feminists? For the latter, we turned to feminist theory outside our own discipline as well as the legacy of feminists working within heterodox political economy.

Colleagues from various disciplines who generously read and commented on one or more of the chapter drafts or work-in-progress presented at professional conferences include Randy Albelda, Nancy Ashton, Heather Boushey, Jan Colijn, Penny Dugan, Robert Drago, Susan Feiner, Mat Forstater, Mary King, Edward O'Boyle, Paulette Olson, Janice Peterson, Steve Pressman, Dawn Saunders, Diana Strassmann, and Myra Strober. We especially appreciate the careful attention to conceptual analysis and detail that legal scholar Elaine Ingulli, economist Ann Jennings, and historian Nancy Robertson gave to the entire manuscript. Of course, we retain responsibility for any errors or omissions. We also had helpful discussions about specific topics with Paula England and Robert Gregg. IAFFE book series editor Jane Humphries and *Feminist Economics* editor Diana Strassmann championed this project. We received support and assistance from the staff at Routledge (Taylor & Francis), especially economics editor Robert Langham as well as Heidi Bagtazo and Terry Clague.

Our historical research has been aided by assistance from library staff at Richard Stockton College, Sarah Lawrence College, and the Hagley Museum and Library in Wilmington, Delaware. Research was partially funded by a Distinguished Faculty Fellowship from Richard Stockton College, a William Waters grant from the Association for Social Economics, and a Research and Professional Development grant from Richard Stockton College.

We received permission to draw upon and extend parts of our previously published work, and gratefully acknowledge the following:

"Equal Pay for Equal Work: The Role of Job Evaluation in an Evolving Social Norm," *Journal of Economic Issues* 34 (1): 1–19, by special permission of the copyright holder, the Association for Evolutionary Economics.

"The Fair Labor Standards Act of 1938 and Competing Visions of the Living Wage," *Review of Radical Political Economics* 32 (3): 408–16, by special permission of the Union for Radical Political Economics.

"Implicit Wage Theories in Equal Pay Debates in the United States," *Feminist Economics* 7 (2): 23–52, by special permission of the International Association for Feminist Economics.

"Wage-Setting Under Fordism: Job Evaluation and the Ideology of Equal Pay," *Review of Political Economy* 13 (4): 405–25, by special permission of Taylor & Francis Ltd. (http://www.tandf.co.uk)

Still photographs were provided by the National Archives and Records Administration, the Franklin D. Roosevelt Library, the John F. Kennedy Library, and Albert C. Krawczyk, Member of the Vermont House of Representatives (with assistance from the National Committee on Pay Equity). Special thanks to Ken Parks for creating the photograph prints in Chapter 7.

The lengthy collaborative process that resulted in this volume has been fun for the three of us, especially when we managed to combine intense discussions about our progress and vision with trips to the Jersey shore. A truly tri-authored work is based on friendship, trust, and mutual respect, and we have sustained all three.

Abbreviations

ACORN	Association of Community Organizations for Reform Now
ACWU	Amalgamated Clothing Workers' Union
ADC	Aid to Dependent Children
AEA	American Economic Association
AFDC	Aid to Families with Dependent Children
AFL	American Federation of Labor
AFL-CIO	American Federation of Labor-Congress of Industrial Organizations
AFSCME	American Federation of State, County and Municipal Employees
AMA	American Management Association
ASPCA	American Society for the Prevention of Cruelty to Animals
BLS	Bureau of Labor Statistics
BNA	Bureau of National Affairs
BPW	National Federation of Business and Professional Women's Clubs
CIO	Congress of Industrial Organizations
CWA	Communications Workers of America
EEOC	Equal Employment Opportunity Commission
ERA	Equal Rights Amendment
FDR	Franklin Delano Roosevelt
FLSA	Fair Labor Standards Act
GNP	Gross National Product
IAF	Industrial Areas Foundation
IAM	International Association of Machinists
ICO	Interfaith Community Organization
ILGWU	International Ladies' Garment Workers' Union
ILO	International Labour Office
NAM	National Association of Manufacturers
NCL	National Consumers' League
NCPE	National Committee on Pay Equity
NEMA	National Electrical Manufacturers Association
NIRA	National Industrial Recovery Act

NMTA	National Metal Trades Association
NRA	National Recovery Administration
NWLB	National War Labor Board (World War II)
NWP	National Woman's Party
SEIU	Service Employees International Union
SSA	Social Structure of Accumulation
TANF	Temporary Assistance for Needy Families
UAW	United Automobile Workers
UE	United Electrical Workers of America

Part I

Laying the groundwork

Methodological frameworks and
theoretical perspectives

1 Introduction

Living wages, equal wages, and the value of women's work

Throughout history and across cultures, women have always worked, and their work has been essential in providing food, clothing, and shelter for their families. That work has taken many forms, from gathering wild food to churning butter, from selling handicrafts in the marketplace to working in a textile factory, from assisting executives to caring for the sick, from selling real estate to designing web pages and computer software. But women's work was not always work for a wage. In fact, at the beginning of the twentieth century, waged work was viewed as an essential part of men's, but not women's, identities.

Wage labor, in contrast to owning a farm or being an independent artisan, was once viewed as undesirable and analogous to slavery. In the nineteenth-century United States, the growth of industrialization and the influx of landless immigrants meant that an increasing proportion of people, especially men, came to rely on working for a wage as a means of provisioning. Bread-winning came to be viewed no longer as subjection to a master, but rather as a means to economic independence. By the turn of the twentieth century, working men joined unions and struggled with employers to achieve a family wage, defined as a wage sufficient to support a dependent wife and children.[1]

As masculinity was redefined to incorporate and legitimate wage labor, a family structure based upon a male breadwinner and female homemaker was idealized. The fact that some women also worked for wages became increasingly problematic. Women were largely excluded from wage labor unless their families had no other means of providing for their needs. This escape clause in the idealized vision of the male breadwinner family actually accounted for a substantial amount of economic activity in the formal and informal economy. Daughters in immigrant families, widows, and other poor women, including a higher proportion of African American than white women, participated in waged work. Other women continued their work in farming or handicrafts, took in boarders, did laundry at home, and performed a variety of other income-generating activities. This was market-oriented work, but it took place on the periphery of capitalist production.

Gradually over the twentieth century, women's productive work came to be incorporated into the industrialized economy. What was once made in the home – clothing and canned food, for example – was now produced in factories and purchased for use in the home. At the same time, women began to enter wage labor in rapidly expanding numbers.

From the moment women became an established presence in wage labor, questions were raised about what their labor should be worth. The struggle of male workers for a family wage implied the presence of a wife who did not financially support herself or children. Mothering was identified as women's primary life purpose. Should women, then, be paid as much as men, or should they be paid less, so as to maintain their dependent relation to men? Would paying women "too much" encourage them to abandon their roles as wives and mothers for lives of alleged waged comfort and ease? Would paying them "too little" injure their health (and therefore their futures as mothers) or drive them into prostitution? Was the relative value of mothering versus paid labor different for working-class and nonwhite women than their white, middle-class sisters? Debate over women's wages ranged over the entire twentieth century and continues today. And, as these questions make clear, it was not simply a debate over objective market values. What women should be doing and how women should live were questions that infused the debate from the beginning, with class and race-ethnicity playing central, although not always explicit, roles. Men, too, have gender, and debates over their wages were also inflected with gender, race-ethnicity, and class implications. As Nancy Fraser and Linda Gordon comment, "The family wage . . . was a vehicle for elaborating meanings of dependence and independence that were deeply inflected by gender, race, and class" (1994: 319).

Women's and men's wages therefore derived from a complex interaction of social and cultural assumptions, market forces, and government regulation. This book traces the debates leading to government regulations and policies regarding wages over the course of the twentieth century to illustrate this interaction. Public policy discussions offer a rare opportunity to examine the underlying assumptions about wage setting during a particular historical period. During debates over wage regulations and practices, economic actors often pause to articulate *implicit wage theories*, that is, what they see as the basis for setting wages. These implicit wage theories affect wage outcomes directly, as these same actors (employers, unions, etc.) interact in labor markets.

Wage theories also operate indirectly. Succinctly, implicit wage theories affect wage regulations which, in turn, affect wage-setting processes. Although, in the final analysis, wages may be set by firms interacting with employees or employee organizations, these market transactions are embedded in a social fabric constituted by such institutions as the state and families. Therefore, we view the process of wage setting as something that can be studied at the macro and meso (organizational, institutional) levels as well as the micro. Our research is meant to supplement microeconomic studies of wages, not supplant them. Wage setting, we argue, is a deeply political and cultural, as well as an economic, process. By recognizing that wages serve multiple functions and contain multiple meanings, we can better grasp the complexity of wage-setting processes.

We identify three implicit wage theories in twentieth-century debates over regulations in the United States: wages as a living, as a price, and as a social practice. By *wages as a living* we mean the argument that the purpose of the wage is to provide an adequate level of support for the worker (and, for some theorists, her dependents as well). Arguments for wages as a living were particularly prevalent among classical political economists of the eighteenth and nineteenth centuries, and continue to be espoused by political economists and political activists up to the present. *Wages as a price* focuses on the equality between remuneration and an employee's contribution to production. In addition, this intellectual construct treats the wage-setting process as analogous to that of any other commodity price, as an amount arrived at through the workings of supply and demand in the marketplace. While all schools of economic thought recognize the role of markets in wage setting, a narrow focus on wages as a price is primarily characteristic of mainstream, neoclassical economics.

To these two standard economic views we add *wages as a social practice*. The concept of wages as a social practice emphasizes the socially and historically specific process of wage setting. Wages are a means of reinforcing or changing cultural understandings of workers' appropriate "places." As a concrete social practice, wages shape as well as reflect gender, class, and race-ethnicity. Both mainstream and heterodox economic theories have tended to neglect this dimension of wages and therefore present incomplete analyses of wages. Rather than recounting alternative theories of discrimination and explanations of the wage gap between men and women, our detailed study of wage policies shows that the wage-setting process, itself, is gendered and racialized.

Working women: a turning point

To set the stage, we will begin by describing a contentious conference on women in industry held by the Women's Bureau of the U.S. Department of Labor in 1923. By this time, wage labor for women was causing social and political controversy. The January 1923 conference was attended by invited delegates from all over the country, some representing unions, but many more from women's colleges, women's clubs and religious associations, and social work organizations. They gathered for three days to hear and discuss testimony from employers, academics, activists, and representatives of the Women's and Children's Bureaus. The focus of the conference was on labor law, and the event was pervaded by underlying tension over the issue of protective legislation, the gender-specific labor laws that were passed in many states during the Progressive Era.[2] This tension was exacerbated by a very recent decision by the Federal Court of Appeals overturning Washington, DC's minimum wage law for women. The case was headed for the Supreme

Court where, contrary to a number of determinedly optimistic predictions by women present at the conference, the Appeals Court decision would be upheld, effectively closing the door on gender-specific protective legislation.

The Women's Bureau had, since its inception three years earlier, consistently supported protective legislation for women workers.[3] Although the roster of experts included a few, largely from management, who opposed such legislation, most of the speakers strongly supported it. Nevertheless, many also made clear that their ultimate goal was gender-neutral protective laws. This was clearly a politically strategic event, held at a politically delicate moment, staged to influence policy at the national level. The discourse among the delegates, as well as the roster selected by the Women's Bureau, illustrates the complex political-economic environment in which the regulation of wages takes place. Let's look more closely at this moment in 1923 to examine the forces that were at play.[4]

At the macroeconomic level, industrialization was firmly established, and the country was urbanizing rapidly. The 1920 Census was the first to record more of the population living in urban than in rural areas (with "urban" defined as towns of 2,500 or more). Mass-produced consumer goods, canned foods, and electric household appliances were becoming commonplace, and the first wave of suburbanization had begun. The period from 1915 to 1920 had seen a 100 percent rise in prices, largely but not entirely due to World War I. Politically, the country had entered a period of reaction. A vicious political purge had resulted in the jailing and deportation of immigrants accused of holding socialist or anarchist views. Highly restrictive immigration laws were looming on the horizon, soon to slam the door shut on a decades-long wave of immigration.

In 1923, social movements on behalf of working women were at a turning point. Class divisions were reflected in differing political and economic concerns. As thousands of young immigrant women had entered sweatshop industries, a growing number of affluent women had completed college, in some cases creating careers for themselves in the new field of social work. Women with high school educations, generally "native born," were entering the expanding and newly feminized clerical occupations. In the parlance of the time, they went into "business," with the status and respectability associated with white blouses and a clean, quiet working environment. For middle-class women who saw the possibility of increased opportunity, gender-specific protective legislation seemed an impediment. The National Woman's Party (NWP), headed by Alice Paul, represented this view. The NWP was increasingly adamant in its opposition to any gendered legislation, including minimum wages (which they had originally exempted from disapproval). As a result, the NWP was particularly at odds with the Women's Bureau. They had been invited to the 1923 conference, but agreed to come only if they were given a speaking slot. When this was refused, Alice Paul tendered an indignant refusal to participate that Women's Bureau Director Mary Anderson read to the assembled delegates with what we suspect was disingenuous regret. Anderson, a Swedish immigrant and former factory worker in the shoe trade, had previously organized women workers into unions with the Women's Trade Union League. Her strategic emphasis was on the problems of working-class women.[5]

In addition to class discord, racial differences were also being articulated. While no African American women were on the roster of "expert" speakers, three delegates were present from the National Association of Colored Women. All three spoke during the open discussion period, and each stressed the terrible conditions facing black women workers, reminded the organizations present that much of the protective legislation they had lobbied for excluded the industries in which black women predominated, and urged the white women to recognize the importance of solidarity across racial lines. Nannie H. Burroughs, an activist and educator who was listed as representing both Mississippi and Pennsylvania, challenged the audience most directly, noting that "57 percent of the colored women in this country who are wage earners work in the homes of the white women." The delegates at this conference, she pointed out, could engage in their public lives "because there are women back in their homes now who are caring for their children, who are laundering their clothes, who are looking after their work . . . ", while the delegates attended to the "interests of the white race of this country" (100–1).[6]

Women's recent acquisition of the vote, with passage of the Nineteenth Amendment in 1920, added both excitement and urgency to the gathering. It is probable that suffrage made the views of the women delegates of more interest to the politicians of Washington. Additionally, World War I created job opportunities for many new women workers. The conference delegates were addressed by the Secretary of Labor, received by President Warren G. Harding, and given a reception by the "ladies of the Cabinet" – that is, the wives of the Cabinet members. And the excitement of the group over the presence at the meeting of several women elected to the House of Representatives comes across clearly in the transcript. But the aftermath of suffrage left the feminist movement without a unifying cause. For feminists working to better the conditions of women in the economic arena, women's suffrage created concern that the nation would consider the problems of women solved. In fact, the subsequent Supreme Court decision invalidating Washington, DC's minimum wage would in part be based on the assertion that, having attained suffrage, women no longer needed special protection.

The rise of anticommunism and anti-immigrant sentiment, growing class divides among women, and the advent of suffrage were new themes permeating the conference. But they coexisted with an older theme that suffused much of the discussion. That young women worked for wages had become an established fact, but not one that sat easily with many of the presenters. More than one suggested that wage work for women was only desirable in the face of desperate economic circumstances. Too many women, speakers argued, worked for frivolous reasons, because they desired luxuries. This became symbolized as a quest for "silk underwear," to which Melinda Scott of the United Textile Workers retorted "Who has a better right to have them than those who work for them?" (118). Most notably, a number of delegates, particularly but not exclusively representing religious organizations, expressed their concerns that women were turning away from their true calling as mothers. Management representatives echoed this view, essentially "taking the pledge" in many cases not to hire women with children. While a few voices dissented and many speakers dodged the issue, the sacred duty of women to bear and raise children was a recurrent theme. Speaker after speaker warned that advocates for women in industry must not violate this primary role.

The opening presentation by Secretary of Labor James J. Davis is worth looking at, as he managed to merge traditional labor union concerns with political conservatism and a celebration of motherhood, in essence reflecting all of the forces converging to affect the regulation of women's wages. In the course of a rambling speech, he supported the limiting of immigration and the deportation of "Reds," restrictions on child labor, support for disabled workers and the unemployed, equal pay for equal work for women workers, and the elimination from industry of women with small children. Reflecting the emotional tone used by many speakers on the topic, Davis stated virtually at the beginning of his speech, "For I say to you that the spectacle of American mothers torn from their children while they strive in the toil and turmoil of industry to earn a livelihood for themselves and their little ones is an indictment of our modern civilization, . . . a menace to the whole structure of our national life." He charged the conference to make this their central goal: "If in this conference we can do this one thing, if we can each and every one of us, go hence filled with the determination to stamp out the need for the industrial exploitation of the mother whose babes need care, we shall have accomplished much" (4–5). Advocates for women, in Davis' view, should place less emphasis on women's wages and working conditions than on protecting women's traditional roles, presumably through the enforcement of family wages for men.

Although Secretary Davis endorsed equal pay for equal work, presumably to prevent employers from substituting cheaper women workers into male jobs, this principle was still controversial. A representative of the National Association of Manufacturers, Charles Cheney, expressed views that were fairly typical of employers at the time:

> The most controversial question in connection with the employment of women in industry is that of the compensation to be given as compared with that of men. Many claim that there should be actual equality, and many attempts have been made to express this thought as a formula. Perhaps the most successful attempt at such an expression is that "Women should have equal pay for work of equal value." This may

Plate 1.1 Secretary of Labor James Davis (standing) delivers the opening address at the national conference on women in industry, January 11, 1923. Seated third from the left is Grace Abbott, Director of the Children's Bureau. Women's Bureau Director Mary Anderson is seated to the right of Secretary Davis

Source: courtesy of National Archives (photo no. 86-G-9G-1)

> approximate the truth or be far from it, according to our understanding of what "equal value" means. How shall we measure value? (20)

The National Association of Manufacturers' spokesman argued that it was "natural" for women to be paid less than men. Employers, he asserted, must take a variety of factors into their calculations when determining how much to pay women and men. Value was not solely measured by length of time worked, nor by the quantity or quality of product alone. Worth was also determined, in part, by length of service, regularity of attendance, and capability of performing several duties. A deficit in any of these factors could lower the relative value of an employee's contribution and, therefore, Cheney claimed, the wage.

To the extent that these reductions "are arbitrarily attached to the employment of women, the greater will be the margin of difference between the pay of men and women. . . . It is folly to say that those differences can be set aside by any arbitrary dictum or law" (21–2). Cheney continued: "All of this argument is only an explanation of the world-wide fact that the market rates for women's work are less than men's rates. When there is found in operation a *universal law*, it is fairly safe to assume that there is sound foundation for it" (22, emphasis added).

These were precisely the kinds of ideas that the Women's Bureau and other advocates for working women were confronting for much of the twentieth century. Advocates of equal pay sought to fight the image that women worked for "silk underwear" or "pin money" and that they deserved less than men. They made three types of argument. First, advocates argued that women workers deserved more than they were earning because they were breadwinners and family providers. Wages were a *living* for them and their families. Second, women were productive and their labor was under-valued. The *price* of their labor was incorrect because pay systems were outdated and biased. Finally, wages were a product of established custom. Working women and their advocates came face-to-face with what we refer to as wages as a *social practice*. That is, wages were intertwined with issues of whether women should work, which women should work, and why women work for pay – not just the value of their work.

What this notable conference portrays is the contested nature of gender ideology and the indeterminacy of gender relations that would intensify over the remainder of the century. Although labor activists articulated that work-ers deserved a living wage, there were, in fact, a multiplicity of *living wages* and strategies for achieving them, reflecting multiple identities among mem-bers of the working class. A "living wage" for a woman was not necessarily equal to a "living wage" for a man; a "living wage" for a woman who was a racial-ethnic minority was even lower. The idea of *equal wages* by gender was a contradiction of prevailing norms, or, at best, a labor strategy to preserve men's jobs. However, out of the depression and war that the conference participants could not foresee would come a series of historical junctures that led to a shift in cultural norms. Living wages and equal wages, although not taking the form that many feminists wished, would become essential elements of the discussions of women's wages.

Feminist methodology and economic theory

When feminists who sparked the second wave of the women's movement in the late 1960s and early 1970s attempted to understand the economic pos-ition of women, they turned to the available economic methodologies for guidance. It quickly became apparent, however, that an analysis of economic outcomes in which gender took a central role required a level of complexity and an attention to components of economic and social life that were not generally incorporated into existing economic thought. Domestic labor, for example, was rarely addressed by economic theorists because it is unpaid. Many aspects of the sexual division of labor were naturalized, that is, seen as outcomes of women's and men's "natural" interests and talents.

Feminist economics since the 1990s has taken neoclassical economic theory as its subject, re-examining the gendered assumptions and principles underlying mainstream models of "economic man" (see, for example, Ferber and Nelson 1993; Woolley 1993; Kuiper and Sap 1995; Nelson 1996; Hewit-son 1999). Paula England, for example, asserts that economic models of market behavior incorrectly assume a "separative self," that is, individuals whose utility (happiness) is independently achieved. Economic actors supposedly "lack sufficient emotional connection to each other to make empathy possible" (England 1993: 37). Although posited as a universal scientific principle, this form of individualism is not hypothesized within the boundaries of the household. Economic theory postulates altruistic behavior among family members. England argues that the extreme bifurcation of two radically different modes of behavior obscures the presence of empathy and altruism within the economy at large as well as selfishness, power differentials, and distinct interests within families. The resultant theory systematically masks women's subordination. Correcting these biases would fundamentally alter the structure and "deductive certainty" of economic theory (50).

Myra Strober (1994), another pioneer in feminist economics, argues that the discipline of economics centers on the concepts of scarcity, selfishness, and competition. However, these three concepts present only half of a series of dichotomies: scarcity/abundance, selfishness/altruism, and competition/cooperation. By excluding abundance, altruism, and cooperation, economic well-being is narrowly conceived. Strober's identification of these dichotomies can be linked to feminist discussions of the definition of economics. Economics is frequently defined in contemporary texts as the application of rational choice by individuals under conditions of scarcity. This definition of economics focuses on methodology rather than subject-matter. Julie Nelson (1993, 1996) suggests that this definition renders economics a study of rationality under abstract conditions rather than a study of the actual material world. Instead, feminist economists have been drawn to institutionalist definitions of economics as the provisioning of human life, or, in Nelson's words, "the commodities and processes necessary to human survival" (1993: 32).

Neoclassical approaches to economics have dominated the economics discipline, especially since the late twentieth century. However, other theoretical approaches, often referred to as "heterodox" or "political economy," continue to influence many economists. Marxism (in its different guises), institutionalism (old and new), social economics, and post-Keynesianism, are among the schools referred to as "heterodox" or "political economy." The adjective "heterodox" indicates the diversity of economic thought rather than the hegemony of a particular theory or method. The term "political economy" was commonly used by such classical economists as Adam Smith, David Ricardo, and Karl Marx. Contemporary political economists generally embrace the label to signal the importance of power, politics, and public policy in the economic realm. It can also imply methodological pluralism or an engagement with interdisciplinary scholarship.

There has been a long history of feminists in dialogue with these other schools of economic thought (see Mutari 2000). Several feminist economists have taken strong positions regarding the affinity between feminism and particular schools of heterodoxy such as Marxism, radical institutionalism, or social economics.[7] Although acknowledging that women's experiences have been undertheorized within each heterodox theory, each of these writers believes that the methodological underpinnings of the theory is harmonious with the work of feminists. Unfortunately, these arguments tend to be clearer about the core principles of the more established schools than they are about feminism. The problem is not that of the individual authors but of the theoretical vagueness that still surrounds the idea of a feminist economic theory. Only through a clearer consensus on the core assumptions of feminist political economy can we address the issue of the relationship between feminism and other heterodox schools of political economy.

Feminists, therefore, have moved beyond critique and deconstruction of mainstream economic theories in order to reconstruct a unique theoretical perspective on economic life. One intention in writing this book is to contribute to the construction of an economic methodology that we term "feminist political economy." The term "feminist political economy" is used in lieu of the currently popular "feminist economics" to emphasize the critical approach to orthodox economic theory that feminists within the discipline share with other heterodox political economists. The term "political economy," rather than economics, also signifies the interdisciplinarity of this survey. Although work within the discipline of economics is the primary focus, this can only be understood as part of a feminist scholarship that crosses artificial disciplinary boundaries.

Our framework builds upon the bases provided by political economy and feminist (gender) theory to develop a methodology where gender relations, along with relations of class and race-ethnicity, are incorporated into the analysis from the very beginning. This approach is different than introducing gender and race-ethnicity specifically in the context of a theory of wage discrimination. Of course women and racial-ethnic minorities experience discrimination. However, associating gender and race-ethnicity solely with discriminatory processes assumes that basic wage-determination models remain unchanged. Discrimination becomes a special case of market failure. In contrast, the underpinning of our approach is the belief that gendered relations in society have fundamental effects on wages as well as other economic outcomes. Such a methodology must be sensitive to the dynamic interactions among all the institutions involved in the process of provisioning, unpaid as well as paid, domestic as well as market. It must recognize that culture matters, as does the relative power of employers and workers. Rather than a static, market-clearing analysis, the analysis developed must be dynamic, nondeterministic, and complex.

This methodological perspective, like that of institutional economics, is grounded in a view of theory that eschews economic naturalism. Economic naturalism treats economic systems as natural objects and economic science as the discovery of a series of natural laws.[8] In contrast, we view theory as necessarily a social construct.[9] Echoing the work of Gillian Hewitson, we contend that economic theory "does not describe an independent 'real world', but rather contributes to the production of the real" (1999: 4). Economic naturalism is consistent with the high status afforded mathematical modeling within the discipline. We agree with Julie Nelson that formal models can provide "misplaced concreteness." That is, they offer an unrealistic and misleading degree of precision (1996: 75). Neoclassical labor economics exemplifies this fallacy in that it develops models in order to deduce a definitive wage rate; thus it is referred to as a theory of *wage determination*. For this reason, we prefer to view our approach as a framework for understanding *wage setting*.

Overview

There have been major transformations in women's and men's economic lives and the meaning of economic activity in their lives. Static theories of wage setting cannot adequately account for such social and economic transitions. We need a dynamic theory of wages, including relative wages, that focuses on both rigidity and change. The remaining chapters in Part I of the book elaborate our methodological framework for understanding wage setting.

To provide a context, Chapter 2, "Waged Work in the Twentieth Century," summarizes the history of women's and men's work in the twentieth century. The central theme of the book, developed in the two subsequent chapters, is that wages are all at once a living, a price, and a social practice. The first two elements, wages as a living and a price, are posited through a survey of neoclassical and heterodox economic theories of wage determination in Chapter 3, "Two Faces of Wages within the Economics Tradition." As neoclassical economic models gained hegemony over other forms of theorizing, the concept of wages as a living has been shunted to the margins. In Chapter 4, "The Third Face: Wages as a Social Practice," we summarize the emergence of gender as an analytical construct and demonstrate the insights that are gained from attention to gender, class, and race-ethnicity as social processes and wage setting as a contended social practice. Social practices are a means of establishing and institutionalizing particular forms of gender, class, and racial-ethnic relations. Our treatment of social practice is derived from interdisciplinary gender and race theory (see Connell 1987, 1993, 1995; Omi and Winant 1994; Brewer 1999) as well as the methodological approaches of radical institutionalism and nondeterminist forms of Marxism (see Dugger 1989; Dugger and Waller 1992; Williams 1995).

The gendered and racialized nature of U.S. social welfare policy (especially aid to dependent children, old age assistance or social security, and unemployment insurance) has been extensively investigated by other scholars. However, labor market policies have been relatively unexamined. By influencing wage setting for particular groups of workers, wage regulations are important vehicles for institutionalizing particular social practices, and thus particular masculinities and femininities and specific definitions of whiteness and blackness. To assess the relationship between wage regulations and the three faces of wages, our methodology utilizes contemporaneous sources (such as Congressional testimony, U.S. Women's Bureau bulletins, wage manuals and textbooks, and publications by policy advocates) and interdisciplinary secondary research.

We examine key "moments" in the development of U.S. labor market policies in the twentieth century. The second part of the book, "Wage Regulations in the Twentieth Century," contains four chapters that examine specific wage regulations: state minimum wage laws, the federal minimum wage introduced under the Fair Labor Standards Act of 1938, the National War Labor Board's promotion of job evaluation and equal pay for equal work during World War II, and the Equal Pay Act of 1963. These four policies are landmarks in efforts to secure equal wages for women and living wages for all. They illustrate the dynamic interaction of the state, the market economy, and families and other social institutions in articulating how wages should be determined. As gender relations have changed and women's involvement in waged work has increased, social practices regarding wages have been transformed.

Chapter 5 focuses on one of the earliest attempts to legislate a living wage, gender-specific minimum wage laws instituted by a number of states during the Progressive Era. The chapter analyzes the arguments leading to their creation and the ensuing debate over what constituted an appropriate wage for a woman worker. The need for legislative protection signaled women's lack of equality. The debate over whether to establish minimum wages for women, and at what level, illustrates conflicting views over the nature and extent of women's paid employment, as well as the degree of economic autonomy they should be permitted. This "experiment" was brief, abruptly ending with a 1923 Supreme Court decision; while laws remained on the books in some states, they were no longer actually enforced.

The federal minimum wage is explored in Chapter 6, "A Living for Breadwinners." In this chapter, we examine the transition from minimum wages as a gender-specific form of protective legislation to an ostensibly gender-neutral federal minimum wage that exempted many occupations and industries in which women of all races and men of color were employed. The relationship between legislated wage floors and the more elusive concept of a living wage is analyzed. In debates over passage of the Fair Labor Standards Act (1938), advocates utilized alternative definitions of the term "living wage." In part, these alternative views reflected attempts to distinguish different forms of masculinity.

Chapter 7 looks at a key aspect of wage determination and its contribution to equal pay ideology. During the interwar period and after World War II, large employers adopted job evaluation plans as a means of stabilizing class relations. The practice of job evaluation rested on a theory of wage determination that set wages according to the principle of equal pay for equal work. That is, wages were based on the attributes of the job rather than the individual worker in the job. This approach to wage setting destabilized the prevailing practice of separate pay scales for men and women in the same job. The process of reconciling equal pay as an ideology and gender wage disparities was a political one. The National War Labor Board during World War II endorsed an equal pay principle and urged adoption of job evaluation by wartime industries. The job evaluation systems formalized after the war resulted in the institutionalization of unequal pay for men's and women's jobs, along with a narrow definition of equal work.

The legislation of equal wages is covered in Chapter 8. Here the relationship between an equal pay policy that focuses on women working in male-dominated and integrated jobs and policies to raise wages in female-dominated occupations is evaluated in depth. Following a brief summary of the legislative history of equal pay at the state and federal levels, the analysis focuses on passage of the Equal Pay Act of 1963. The struggle to define an appropriate public policy represented a negotiation over the definition of equal wages and which actors would take part in defining equality. Therefore, this chapter illuminates how wages also serve as a social practice that institutionalizes particular sets of gender relations.

The final section of the book is about "The Century Ahead." The struggle for equal wages and living wages continues. Due to the limited scope of the Equal Pay Act and the steadily eroding value of the federal minimum wage, activists have sought new policy approaches. Once again, decentralized policy experiments are creating models for public policy, as described in Chapter 9. In the 1980s, the comparable worth movement revived the effort for equal pay for work of equal value. Over the decade of the 1990s, a revived "living wage" movement became identified with a particular type of municipal ordinance placed before legislators and voters. Unlike the living wage movement of the late nineteenth century which privileged white male breadwinners, today's living wage and pay equity movements have a broader vision. Merging primary and secondary research, with a focus on one city-wide living wage campaign, this chapter examines the strengths and limitations of these strategies.

Chapter 10 revisits our feminist political economy of wage setting in light of the historical study in previous chapters. Using our discussion of the evidence from the twentieth century, we present a feminist model of wage setting that illustrates the contending forces at play. We conclude with the implications for labor market theory and policy in the twenty-first century.

2 Waged work in the twentieth century

Many of us take for granted the idea that most people, male or female, will hold down jobs for much of their lives. Waged work is so much a normal part of our lives that we lose sight of the fact that it was once a controversial activity. During the early days of U.S. nationhood, the Jeffersonian ideal was a relatively self-sufficient farmer who owned land, worked his farm with his family, and produced most necessities at home. In pursuit of this ideal, the territory of the U.S. was expanded westward, repeatedly displacing the Native American inhabitants, to carve out farms for European American settlers. Given access to land, who would choose to submit themselves to an employer or risk unemployment due to changed fortunes or mere whim? Wage labor was scarce. In its place, there was slavery or indentured servitude. In the South, those who could afford not to do their own labor often kept slaves. People who could not afford to pay the fare to come to the U.S. – debtors, and some criminals – were sold as indentured servants to work until their monetary or social debts were repaid, a temporary form of bondage. In the urban areas of the North, independent artisans (for example, silver-smiths, cobblers, and blacksmiths) took on apprentices and journeymen who lived with the family until they could set up their own business.

Industrialization, beginning around the 1820s, led employers to search out new sources of labor, in particular people who would work for wages. Some of the pioneers in waged work were young, white, single daughters of farm families. Sons were used in the fields or were migrating west, mothers ran the household, and fathers certainly would not submit to the indignity of employment. But time could be allocated in girls' lives between their training in household crafts and their future as farm wives for the earning of money to raise their families' standards of living, pay off farm debts, or build dow-ries.[1] In some of the first factories, they spun thread, just as they had done at home. Young women were also sent to work as domestic servants in the homes of wealthier families.

However, as the availability of land declined while industrialization expanded over the course of the nineteenth century, the nature and meaning of waged work began to change. "Heavy" industries developed, including railroads, iron and steel, and oil refining. Paid employment became defined as a man's world, and more specifically, as a white man's world. New definitions of whiteness and of masculinity went hand-in-hand with the growth of men's work. In his study *The Wages of Whiteness*, David Roediger (1991) contends that white working-class males came to accept wage labor by associating paid employment with whiteness, creating a contrast with slave labor. R.W. Connell, in research on masculinities, suggests that the expansion of capitalism coincided with the creation of a working-class masculinity based on "wage-earning capacity, skill and endurance in labor, domestic patriarchy, and combative solidarity among wage earners" (1993: 611). This was a "hegemonic" form of masculinity, that is, it was the cultural ideal of the moment, even though not every male was a married, heterosexual breadwinner.[2] Correspondingly, a "Cult of Domesticity" (or "Cult of True Womanhood") originating in the early-to-mid-nineteenth century insisted that women's virtue was found in submissiveness, purity, piety, and a unilateral focus on home and family.

Under this male breadwinner ideal, a young girl from a family of modest means might spend a few years contributing to her family's income before she got married. The jobs that she could respectably hold were few. Once married, the Cult of Domesticity dictated that she should concentrate on the private sphere of home and family. This cultural mandate was enforced by marriage bars, which were employer policies to fire women once they married. Unless, that is, they were the daughters of immigrants, immigrants themselves, or African Americans and other women of color. Public opinion countenanced the employment of married working-class immigrant women and women of color, as well as a few middle-class women that historian Lynn Weiner refers to as "women of rare talents" (1985: 104).

The dominant (or hegemonic) model of gender relations – based on a male breadwinner and a female, full-time homemaker – never became the norm for African American women. In a major study of black women's experiences since slavery, Jacqueline Jones (1986) establishes that African American women typically began self-sustaining work around age 15, stayed in the labor force when married and raising children, and worked through middle age. The necessity of paid labor by married African American women reflected, in part, the constraints imposed by racism against black men. For the first hundred years after slavery, relatively few African American men earned wages sufficient to support a family, a so-called breadwinner wage or family wage (Jones 1986; Amott and Matthaei 1996). In addition, employers, including the white women who hired black women as domestics, viewed African American women as workers first, to the detriment of their family life. Thus, black women were, by their circumstances, defined as "less than a moral, 'true' woman" (Giddings 1984: 47).

This definition was not passively accepted. There is evidence that African American women, both working class and middle class, forged an alternative set of gender norms. Two studies of the history of black women since the nineteenth century – one focusing primarily on working-class women (Jones

1986) and one focusing on middle-class women (Landry 2000) – agree that African American women defined their lives in terms of interrelated commitments to family, community, and paid employment. According to Landry, "just as a particular ideology of white womanhood influenced white wives' employment decisions, so too a particular ideology of black woman-hood, developed within the black community, shaped black wives' orientation to paid work" (2000: 30–1). Rather than embracing the male breadwinner model, African American women posited a "co-breadwinner" model.[3]

In this chapter, we examine the unraveling of the male breadwinner model and the ideal of women's domesticity, particularly as markers of whiteness. This overview is designed to situate the subsequent discussion of specific wage policies in the chapters that follow. We introduce a story about women's and men's economic lives in general and their employment status in particular over the course of the twentieth century, placed in the context of political economic transformations and shifts in gender norms.

Labor force participation: the twentieth century's gradual revolution

[Compared with a century ago, today, women of all racial-ethnic groups are more likely to be employed and spend many more years of their lives work-ing for wages.] Women's increased wage labor has been a gradual, but pivotal revolution. To demonstrate this trend, we present two important measures or indicators of economic status: labor force composition and labor force participation.

First a word on data. Since we begin our story in 1900, we follow the lead of other scholars and utilize published data from census sources to identify major trends. Despite pitfalls and inconsistencies in using the decennial Cen-sus to measure women's paid employment, it remains the key source used by historians and economists. One problem is that women's economic activity is undercounted in such official sources. Early in the twentieth century women often engaged in production for the market that was spatially located in the home. Women, principally married women, took in boarders, laundry, sewing, and needlework; worked in family businesses and agriculture; and engaged in piecework at home for manufacturers. This work is frequently overlooked by official government statistics. Economic historian Claudia Goldin (1990) explores this problem; however, she primarily identifies this undercount with the 1890 census, making adjustments to derive new esti-mates. The second problem is that the U.S. Census underwent a major revi-sion mid-century. Federal statistical agencies only adopted the concept of labor force participation in 1940. Prior to 1940, a more subjective concept called "gainful employment" was utilized. Again, Goldin asserts that the two measures will provide relatively consistent results for women's labor force participation in the sectors covered by the census. Recognizing its limita-tions, historian Lois Scharf argues that census data is the central source for quantitative measurement of women's employment (1980: 211; see also Weiner 1985: 8).[4]

The first indicator is *labor force composition*, or the percent of the total paid labor force in the U.S. that is made up of women. Imagine the total labor force as a pie. The total pie is divided into two parts, the portion of the labor force that is male and the portion that is female. Table 2.1 depicts the changing labor force composition, the percentage of the labor force that is male and female, from 1900 to 2000. At the beginning of the twentieth century, 81.7 percent of the total labor force was men and only 18.3 percent was women. In other words, eight out of ten labor force members in 1900 were men.[5] Change in these proportions was slow until the 1940s. Thus, paid work was largely a male domain, with pockets of employment for women.

The composition of the labor force began to change after World War II, with women representing a steadily growing proportion of the labor force. During the war, women, as new labor force entrants or as crossovers from female-dominated jobs, replaced the men who had entered the military and filled the growing need for wartime workers. As the wartime women in factories and defense plants, termed "Rosie the Riveters," gained experience and access to better wages, many sought to remain in the labor force following the war. At mid-century women were 27.8 percent of the labor force; by the end of the century, women were 46.6 percent of the labor force. The labor force today has almost as many women as men. The doubling of women's share since 1940 is referred to as a process of "feminization" of the labor force.

The other statistic that helps to express the growing involvement of women in the workforce is the *labor force participation rate*. For the labor force participation rate, the pie or denominator is all women (or all men) rather than the total labor force. The labor force participation rate is the number of women (or men) in the labor force divided by the number of

Table 2.1 Labor force composition, 1900–2000

Year	Percent female	Percent male	Year	Percent female	Percent male
1900	18.3	81.7	1960	32.1	67.9
1910	21.2	78.8	1970	37.2	62.8
1920	20.5	79.5	1980	42.6	57.4
1930	22.0	78.0	1990	45.2	54.8
1940	24.3	75.7	2000	46.6	53.4
1950	27.8	72.2			

Sources: U.S. Census Bureau (1975: Series D 11–25); U.S. Department of Labor, Bureau of Labor Statistics (2001: Table 2)

Notes
The labor force equals employed plus unemployed. The years 1980–2000 show the civilian labor force, otherwise total labor force.

women (or men) in the population who are over the age of 16, that is, "eligible" for work. This ratio is expressed as a percent. Sometimes the total population, including the armed forces and people in prisons and other institutions, is the denominator; more commonly today, the civilian, non-institutional population is used. To understand change over time, we look at different cohorts of women by mapping the labor force participation rate over different decades. This helps us picture women's labor market behavior over the life cycle, specifically whether married women or women of child-bearing years are more likely to drop out or work intermittently.

In 1900, only 18.8 percent of all women were in the labor force compared with 80.0 percent of men. Since then, men's and women's rates moved in different directions. As we can see from Figure 2.1, women's labor force participation rates rose steadily while the labor force participation rate of men gradually fell. The increases in women's labor force participation rates accelerated in the second half of the twentieth century, especially in the 1960s and 1970s. In 2000, the rate stood at 60.2 percent. This means that six out of ten women over the age of 16 were employed or were actively seeking work. In contrast, men's labor force participation rate peaked at 81.3 percent in 1910 and gradually declined, reaching 74.7 percent in 2000. Men in their prime earning years remained at work. Younger men pursued higher education while older men retired earlier, pulling down the overall rate.

Some secondary research culled from decennial U.S. Census data provides a telling story about the role of race-ethnicity and class. According to historian Julia Kirk Blackwelder, at the turn of the last century, the labor force participation rates for women whose parents immigrated to the U.S. and those who had immigrated themselves were higher than the rate for white women of native parentage (1997: 14–15). The labor force participation rate of single white women in 1900 was only 21.5 percent in contrast with 34.3 percent for those whose parents were born overseas and 60.9 percent for those who were themselves foreign born. Additionally, African American women consistently had higher labor force participation rates than white native-born women across all marital groups. For example, divorced black women had a labor force participation rate of 82.2 percent in 1900 compared with 26.0 percent of married and 47.4 percent of single black women. Bart Landry notes that in some urban labor markets, the percentage of married black women working for pay was as high as 65.0 percent (2000; see also Hunter 1997). High rates of immigration and the migration of Southern blacks to Northern cities brought new sources of waged labor to urban industries.

The movement of new groups of women into the paid labor force has been called a "subtle revolution" (Smith 1979: 2) or a "quiet revolution" (Blackwelder 1997: 3) because it is not traceable to any abrupt event. In fact, there were multiple factors leading to the rise in women's labor force participation and these factors interacted with each other in complex ways. Although some economists reduce this complex causation to a linear narra-

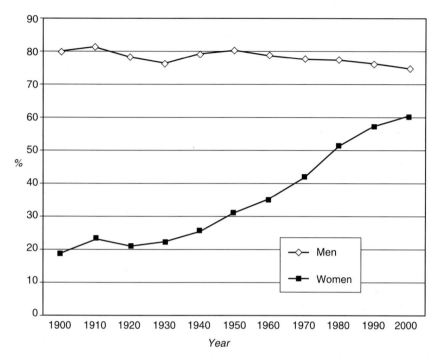

Figure 2.1 Total labor force participation by gender, 1900–2000

Sources: U.S. Census Bureau (1975: Series D 11–25); U.S. Census Bureau (1999: Table 651)

Note
1980–2000 includes civilian labor force only.

tive based on changes in either supply or demand,[6] we favor a more eclectic approach.

The expansion of the post-World War II economy clearly drew women into the labor force, especially in rapidly growing clerical and sales employment. Therefore, some economists and sociologists have looked to the types of jobs available to explain women's rising labor force participation (see, for example, Oppenheimer 1979). This approach, sometimes called the "suitable jobs theory," says it is the nature of the jobs that employers want to fill that generates a demand for women's employment. If the jobs involve tasks related to women's responsibilities in the home, employers hire women. Specifically, structural changes in the economy led to both increased employment in such traditionally female professions as teaching and nursing and also new opportunities in clerical and technical work, where shortages of qualified workers enabled women to gain entry (Goldin 1990; Blackwelder 1997).

However, women's movement into paid employment cannot be reduced to a primary explanatory variable such as increased demand in specific occupations. One reason is that the types of jobs considered women's work changes over time. Sociologists Barbara Reskin and Patricia Roos (1990) provide a more dynamic approach in their queuing theory. Employers rank the preferability of groups of workers in a symbolic queue depending upon their view of the characteristics of the job. Men are not always preferred; in some situations employers want to hire women so they can pay lower wages or induce higher turnover among employees (see Cohn 1985). Workers also have a queue, ranking jobs according to their preferences; jobs with higher wages tend to be ranked more highly by both men and women. The "best" jobs go to the most desired workers. Nevertheless, when an occupation is expanding or labor markets are tight, employers are forced to look further down the queue and take less-desirable groups of workers. Often, they redefine the necessary qualifications and characteristics of the job to explain or rationalize the presence of this new group.[7] The growth of occupations designated for women is therefore only a secondary factor in the growth of women's employment.

The steady commodification of more and more of the production that once occurred in the home is key to the story. People work in order to meet certain monetary needs that are socially defined and tend to escalate in capitalist economies. This was especially true during the postwar period (1945–73), when U.S. economic growth was predicated upon rising domestic consumption linked to gains in productivity (Hunnicutt 1988; Appelbaum and Batt 1994). A culture of consumerism influenced the social context in which economic decisions were made.[8] As the standard of living considered normal and desirable for working- and middle-class families increased and included more purchased commodities, additional income from family members was needed.[9] David Wells (1998) argues that attention to consumerism helps explain why the labor force participation rates of middle- and upper-class women increased during the 1960s, a decade of rising male real wages (see also Schor 1998).

Some scholars, such as Barbara Bergmann (1986), maintain that women were available for paid employment because the arduous household production performed by their mothers and/or their mothers' servants was being replaced by purchased commodities. Household appliances and other labor-saving devices in the home made cooking, washing, cleaning, and shopping easier. This argument assumes a fixed amount of housework that can be reduced through technological innovation. Far from being fixed, however, social standards regarding housework are quite fluid. In addition, the increase in household purchases itself raised the amount of time spent on household maintenance and record-keeping. Therefore, it is not clear that the total volume of housework has diminished over time, although the nature of the work has changed (Power 1983).

Finally, transformations in social attitudes and gender culture are crucial, especially in prompting the growing proportion of white, married mothers in the workforce in the second half of the twentieth century (see, for example, Kessler-Harris 1982; Weiner 1985; Blackwelder 1997). Declining birth rates, wrought in part by the availability of birth control, and rising divorce rates had tremendous implications for women's expectations regarding marriage and motherhood. The impact of the women's movement should not be underestimated. Gender ideology changed profoundly in concert with women's labor force participation. The idealization of the male breadwinner family lost its dominance, although it did not completely fade away.

Marriage, children, and women's work

Differences in the trends in labor force participation rates by marital status are indicative of shifting gender norms. According to Table 2.2, in 1900, the labor force participation rate of single women was more than double the rate for all women. This was the era of the "working girl," who contributed to her family's earnings while preparing for her future role as wife and mother. Even in 1940, on the eve of World War II, the participation rate of single women was 45.5 percent compared with 13.8 percent for married women with a husband present.[10] However, the era of the working girl would evolve into a world where working mothers became a cultural norm. This occurred in two stages, as first marital status and then the presence of children ceased to delimit women's paid employment.

A sweeping change in married women's work behavior took place following World War II. The civilian labor force participation rate of married women rose considerably (see Table 2.2), from 13.8 percent in 1940 to 61.2 percent in 1999. In contrast, the rate for widowed, divorced, and separated women remained relatively steady until the 1970s. Many women who reentered the labor force in these latter decades were "displaced homemakers" who had to work in the paid labor force to feed themselves and their families.

African American women have always had higher labor force participation rates than white women. But, as shown in Figure 2.2, the gap was wider in the first part of the century. The labor force participation rates of black and white married women began to converge after the Great Depression of the 1930s and narrowed significantly in the 1940s. This convergence was primarily due to white women's increased labor force attachment, that is, more continuous participation over the life cycle. While the rate for African American women more than doubled in the twentieth century, the labor force participation rate for white women increased more than 10 times, from 6 percent to 62 percent. Since 1970, white and African American women's labor force participation rates have increased at roughly the same pace.

The decade of the 1950s exposes a particularly important finding. It is often assumed or perceived as common knowledge that married women left the labor force after World War II to make room for returning veterans. The 1950s is sometimes termed the decade of the "nuclear family." However, Figure 2.2 reveals a steep increase in the labor force participation rate for

Table 2.2 Women's civilian labor force participation rates, by marital status (in percent), 1900–99

Year	Total	Single	Married, husband present	Widowed/divorced/separated
1900	20.6	43.5	—	32.5
1910	25.4	51.1	—	34.1
1920	23.7	46.4	—	—
1930	24.8	50.5	—	34.4
1940	25.8	45.5	13.8	30.2
1950	29.0	46.3	21.6	32.7
1960	34.5	42.9	30.6	36.1
1970	41.6	50.9	39.6	36.8
1980	51.5	64.4	49.9	43.6
1990	57.5	66.7	58.4	47.2
1999	60.0	68.7	61.2	49.1

Sources: U.S. Census Bureau (1975: Series D 49–62); U.S. Census Bureau (2000: Table 652)

Notes
1900–30 includes people aged 15 and over; 1940–60 includes people aged 14 and over; 1970–99 includes people aged 16 and over.

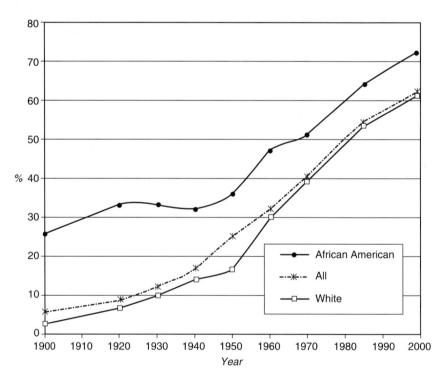

Figure 2.2 Labor force participation rates of married women, husband present, by race, 1900–2000

Sources: Weiner (1985: Table 6); U.S. Census Bureau (2000: Table 654)

married women; in fact the rates of increase (or slopes) for white and for black married women were steeper in the 1950s than in any other decade. Although women lost well-paid jobs in war industries, they fought to stay in the labor market, even if this meant lower-paid women's work (see Milkman 1987; Chafe 1991).

In the early decades of the century, as we have seen, white women's relationship to the labor force largely depended on whether or not they were married. By mid-century, the age of a woman's children was pivotal. Women with young children were less likely to work in paid employment than women with school-age children. As noted by historian William Chafe (1991), caring for children full time during the pre-school years was now seen as fulfilling women's responsibilities as mothers even if they returned to the labor force once their children began kindergarten. Employment, especially part-time employment that did not conflict with after-school care, was now deemed socially acceptable.

The gap between women with pre-school children and women with older children narrowed beginning in the 1970s. This trend is exhibited in Table 2.3. The labor force participation of women with children aged 6–17 years increased from 28.3 percent in 1950 to 77.1 percent in 1999, a relative increase of 172 percent. There was an even greater surge of labor force participation of married women with young children under the age of six. From 1950 through 1999, there was a more than fivefold increase (11.9 percent to 61.8 percent). The age of the working mother had arrived.

The data in the early decades in Table 2.3 reflect what economists have called an "intermittent labor force participation." Working women once had a bimodal distribution over their work lives, shaped like a letter "M," as in Figure 2.3. That is, young women began to work from age 16 through 19, then tended to drop out during the childbearing years of 20 to 34, then began to return to work when their children were grown or in school. Three

Table 2.3 Labor force participation rates of married women, husband present, by presence and age of children (in percent), 1950–99

Year	No children < 18 years	Children 6–17 years	Children < 6 years
1950	30.3	28.3	11.9
1955	32.7	34.7	16.2
1960	34.7	39.0	18.6
1965	38.3	42.7	23.3
1970	42.2	49.2	30.3
1980	46.0	61.7	45.1
1985	48.2	67.6	53.4
1999	54.4	77.1	61.8

Sources: U.S. Census Bureau (1975: Series D 63–74); U.S. Department of Labor, Bureau of Labor Statistics (1989: Table 57); U.S. Census Bureau (2000: Tables 653, 654)

clusters of women by age in the postwar U.S. illustrate this M-shaped distribution – women in 1950, 1960, and 1970. By 1980, women had a more
continuous labor force participation rate until near retirement; in 1990, the
distribution took on the shape of men's labor force behavior over the life
cycle. More and more women with children sought to balance work and
family, boosting their labor force attachment.

One impressive statistic that signifies the shift in men's and women's labor
force participation is a comparison of the number of male versus female
workers in the household. The number is nearly equal today, and was vastly
different a century ago. Table 2.4 shows the contrast from 1900 to 1990. Like
the male labor force participation rate, the number of male workers per
household has declined steadily. Early in the century, more than one male
contributed to family earnings as sons (as well as daughters) went to work.
As sons have gone to college and as female-headed families have increased,
the average number of male workers per household diminished. The number

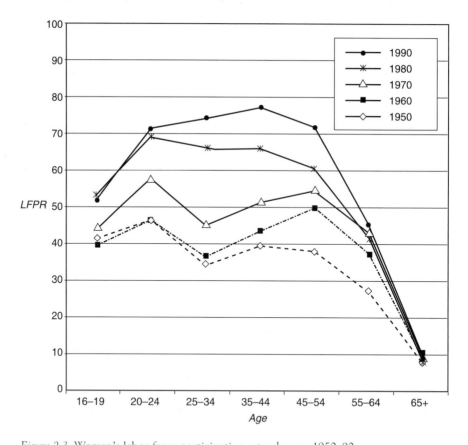

Figure 2.3 Women's labor force participation rates, by age, 1950–90

Sources: U.S. Department of Labor, Bureau of Labor Statistics (1980: Table 4); U.S. Census
Bureau (1999: Table 650)

Table 2.4 U.S. wage earners by gender, 1900–90

Year	No. male workers per household	No. female workers per household
1900	1.69	0.38
1910	n.a.	n.a.
1920	1.51	0.39
1930	1.41	0.40
1940	1.18	0.38
1950	1.14	0.43
1960	0.99	0.46
1970	0.92	0.54
1980	0.78	0.58
1990	0.73	0.61

Source: Blackwelder (1997: Table 9.1)

Notes
1900–50 includes workers aged 10 and over; 1960 includes workers aged 14 and over; thereafter aged 16 and over

of female workers per household has risen from 0.38 in 1900 to 0.61 in 1990, an increase of 60 percent. The table also belies the existence of the male breadwinner family (relying upon one male wage). The "average" household always relied upon more than one income.

The increase in women's labor force participation and attachment has indeed been a social revolution, perhaps subtle, perhaps not. This revolution has redefined what it means to be a worker, a breadwinner, and even a wife and mother. Yet the sexual division of labor within the home remained intact. As feminist economists Teresa Amott and Julie Matthaei have argued, "Although the relationship between productive and reproductive labor was changing in this way, the sexual division of labor between the two did not change – if anything, it became more extreme" (1996: 297). Acknowledging that women still do the majority of the unpaid housework and child care, we focus our attention on the jobs in their labor market.

Women's work now and then: the ongoing problem of occupational segregation

Technological and industrial change have played a role in the kinds of jobs available to both men and women over the last century. The shift from an agriculturally based economy to manufacturing, and then to the service sector can also be seen as the extension of the market into more and more forms of production that once occurred in the home. From goods to services, from clothes and cars to fast food and child care, such increased commodification has reshaped the labor market. Further, beginning at the end of the nineteenth century, the growth in the size of enterprises also led to an expanded clerical workforce to keep records and increased layers of management and supervision to maintain control. Nevertheless, women remained in a small subset of occupations and industries for most of the century. Compared with the impressive change in women's labor force participation, the kinds of occupations in which women have been employed has changed relatively little.

Tables 2.5 and 2.6 contrast the trends in occupational distribution of black and white women respectively. We focus on the distinction between African American and white women since these were the dominant racial categories in U.S. national data during much of this period. In 1910, for example, nine out of ten black women were employed in either farming (52 percent) or private household service (38.5 percent). These two fields were the major occupations for white women as well, but only employed 29.3 percent of white women workers. White women had more occupations open to them, working in clerical and sales positions as well as low paid blue-collar operator and laborer positions. Clerical and sales positions required more education, an expensive wardrobe, and provided a cleaner work environment. Therefore, such jobs were financially inaccessible to poorer women and reinforced a class distinction between "respectable" women's jobs and lower-status occupations. Even when African American women had access to education and financial resources, cultural biases excluded them from occupations involving face-to-face contact with customers and clients. In other words, African American women were screened out of occupations where they were "visible" in serving the public or working in proximity to a white male boss (Jones 1986; Chafe 1991). A small group of white women found employment in professional-technical fields, but this was less than 12 percent. Women managers, white or black, were rare. Women who worked did so largely from necessity and for the most part toiled in relatively low-status and low-paid occupations.

By 1940, technological improvements in agricultural production meant that labor requirements were reduced. The percentage of black women in agriculture diminished from 52 percent in 1910 to 15.9 percent thirty years later. Over the same period, the percentage of white women in agriculture fell from 12.1 percent to 2.3 percent. The use of servants and other private household workers also declined as electric appliances made housework less physically demanding and as former domestics found increased access to other, "better" jobs. For white women, their share in private household employment began falling in the 1940s; for black women, it was a decade later. Black women began to shift out of private household work and into clerical, sales, and service work in the 1950s, but even more rapidly in the 1960s and 1970s (see also Power and Rosenberg 1995). White women also moved into these same job categories at a swift pace with the growth of bureaucracies and paperwork in the 1940s and 1950s. As Randy Albelda (1985) and Mary King (1992) also find, occupations of white and black women converged during the immediate postwar period. By century's end, the single largest broad occupational category employing both black and white women was clerical/sales work. The second most predominant job

Table 2.5 Occupational distribution of black women (in percent), 1910–2000

Occupation	1910	1940	1950	1960	1970	1980	1990	2000
Professional-technical	1.5	4.3	5.3	7.7	10.0	13.2	14.8	17.8
Managers	0.2	0.7	1.3	1.1	1.4	2.9	7.5	10.7
Clerical and sales	0.3	1.3	5.4	9.8	21.4	33.1	39.1	34.9
Craft	2.0	0.2	0.7	0.7	0.8	1.2	2.3	2.1
Operators and laborers	2.3	7.0	16.8	15.5	17.7	14.1	12.2	9.1
Private household	38.5	59.9	42.0	38.1	19.5	7.5	3.1	1.4
Other service	3.2	11.1	19.1	23.0	28.5	26.8	24.2	23.7
Farming	52.0	15.9	9.4	4.1	0.5	0.3	0.3	0.2

Sources: Based on Aldridge (1999: Table 11.1); U.S. Department of Labor, Bureau of Labor Statistics (2001: Table 10)

Notes
After 1970 "Professional-technical" is professional specialty plus technicians and related support; "Managers" is executive, administrative, and managerial; "Clerical and sales" is administrative support, including clerical plus sales occupations; "Craft" is precision production, craft, and repair; "Operators and laborers" is operators, fabricators, and laborers; "Farming" is farming, forestry, and fishing. Totals may not equal 100 percent due to rounding.

Table 2.6 Occupational distribution of white women (in percent), 1910–2000

Occupation	1910	1940	1950	1960	1970	1980	1990	2000
Professional-technical	11.6	14.7	13.3	14.1	15.5	16.9	19.1	22.1
Managers	1.5	4.3	4.7	4.2	4.7	7.6	11.6	14.8
Clerical and sales	17.5	32.8	39.3	43.2	43.4	42.3	45.3	36.9
Craft	8.2	1.1	1.7	1.4	1.1	1.8	2.1	2.1
Operators and laborers	22.7	21.2	22.2	18.1	14.9	11.8	7.8	6.4
Private household	17.2	10.9	4.3	4.4	3.7	1.7	1.2	1.2
Other service	9.2	12.7	11.6	13.1	15.1	16.7	15.2	15.2
Farming	12.1	2.3	2.9	1.5	1.6	1.1	1.1	1.3

Sources: Based on Aldridge (1999: Table 11.1); U.S. Department of Labor, Bureau of Labor Statistics (2001: Table 10)

Notes
After 1970 "Professional-technical" is professional specialty plus technicians and related support; "Managers" is executive, administrative, and managerial; "Clerical and sales" is administrative support, including clerical plus sales occupations; "Craft" is precision production, craft, and repair; "Operators and laborers" is operators, fabricators, and laborers; "Farming" is farming, forestry, and fishing. Totals may not equal 100 percent due to rounding.

category for black women was service work, while white women moved into professional and technical work.

Neither black nor white women have been able to break down the entry barriers into skilled blue-collar craft occupations. No more than 2 percent of all working women, white and black, were employed as craft workers throughout most of the twentieth century (see Tables 2.5 and 2.6). When women did obtain jobs in manufacturing, they were relegated to lower-paid and less-unionized operator and laborer positions. These jobs typically involved repetitive assembly in textiles, apparel, food processing, and small electrical appliances. When on the factory floor, the dirtier, more hazardous jobs were likely to be filled by women of color. Few African American women were machine operators before the 1950s (see also Women's Bureau 1938). During the postwar period, African American women began to gain access to machine operator jobs. With the flight of manufacturing jobs overseas in the 1970s, even these inroads were undermined as women of color lost their jobs along with other factory workers.

While occupational distribution indicates the influence of sectoral change on the types of jobs women hold, percent female in an occupation evaluates women's parity with men.[11] A job is generally considered to be feminized or "female dominated" if 70 percent of the incumbents are female and "male dominated" if less than 30 percent of the incumbents are female. This is demonstrated by looking at the percentage female by occupation in Table 2.7. The feminization of clerical work is dramatically illustrated. Clerical workers were 24.2 percent female (male dominated) in 1900 and 73.6 percent female (female dominated) by 1970. More than nine out of ten private household service jobs were and still are held by women, with imperceptible changes over time. In contrast, skilled blue-collar craft work remained the preserve of men, primarily white men. Even less-skilled blue-collar occupations, operators and laborers, remained male dominated from 1900 through 2000.

What we consider to be typically female professions such as teaching, nursing, social work, and librarianship were feminized early in the twentieth century. As white-collar work grew over the course of the century, women made more inroads into professional and managerial jobs. Over time, the broad category of professional and technical workers has been relatively

Table 2.7 Percent female by major occupation, 1900–2000

Occupation	1900	1910	1920	1930	1940	1950	1960	1970	1983	2000
Professional-technical	35.2	41.3	44.2	44.8	41.5	39.5	38.1	40.2	48.1	53.5
Managers	4.4	6.1	6.8	8.1	11.0	13.6	14.5	16.7	32.4	45.3
Clerical	24.2	34.6	47.7	51.8	54.2	62.3	67.6	73.6	79.9	79.0
Sales	17.4	21.6	26.3	24.1	26.8	34.3	36.4	39.9	47.5	49.6
Craft	2.5	2.5	1.9	1.7	2.2	3.0	2.9	5.0	8.1	9.1
Operators and laborers	19.1	18.2	16.9	15.6	18.0	21.6	22.8	26.9	26.6	23.6
Private household	96.6	96.4	96.4	95.6	94.4	94.8	96.4	96.8	96.1	95.6
Other service	34.3	36.8	37.0	37.7	38.9	44.7	52.4	55.7	57.4	58.8
Farming	9.3	10.2	10.3	8.8	5.6	8.6	9.5	10.0	n.a.	20.6

Sources: U.S. Census Bureau (1975: Series D 182–232); U.S. Census Bureau (1999: Table 675); U.S. Department of Labor, Bureau of Labor Statistics (2001: Table 9)

Notes
After 1970 "Professional-technical" is professional specialty plus technicians and related support; "Managers" is executive, administrative, and managerial; "Clerical" is administrative support, including clerical; "Craft" is precision production, craft, and repair; "Operators and laborers" is operators, fabricators, and laborers; "Farming" is farming, forestry, and fishing.

gender-integrated (neither male dominated nor female dominated), although the kinds of professional and technical jobs held by women and men are quite different. In the 1970s, women, especially white women, entered professional fields that were formerly male bastions, including law and medicine. This occurred, however, as some of the autonomy in these professions began to diminish. Large law firms, medical and legal clinics, and health maintenance organizations pushed out the sole practitioners (Carter and Carter 1981). Independent pharmacies were replaced by chains (Reskin and Roos 1990). Even more dramatic than the change in the professions is the increase in the percentage of managers who are women. What was an overwhelmingly male-dominated profession, 4.4 percent female in 1900, became an integrated occupation, 45.3 percent female in 2000. However, once again women are overrepresented in fields that have been redefined as requiring "feminine" skills: marketing, human resources, and public relations. Men, on the other hand, predominate in production, financial management, and other areas providing a fast track up the corporate hierarchy. Women managers, especially women of color, have experienced obstacles to advancement within firms (Weber and Higginbotham 1997), a problem evoked by the image of a "glass ceiling."

As working women's advocates have consistently declared and documented, women's waged work contributes to their family's income and well-being. In 1997, the share of family earnings contributed by wives was over one-third. The percentage of total family earnings contributed by African American women was nearly 44 percent (see Figure 2.4). Latina women accounted for 37.5 percent of earnings in the family pot, followed by white women at 35.8 percent. Women are breadwinners. Nevertheless, the wages they earn, especially in female-dominated occupations, continue to be influenced by institutionalized job hierarchies and outdated social norms.

These constraints are reflected in the gender-based wage gap. The wage gap is an overall measure of the difference between men's and women's earnings. To determine the wage gap, first calculate the female-to-male wage ratio by dividing the median (or average) earnings of women by the same gauge for men. If men's and women's earnings were the same, the ratio would equal 1.00 or 100 percent. But women earn less than men on average, so the gender-based wage ratio is less than 100 percent. The gap is equal to the difference between the wage ratio and 100 percent. For example, in 1955, the wage ratio, based on median annual earnings, was 63.9 percent and the wage gap was 36.1 percent. Figure 2.5 traces the gender-based wage gap from 1955 to 2000. Notice that the gap widened from 1955 to 1965 and was stable in the late 1960s. The gap gradually narrowed in the late 1970s. The most marked narrowing of the gap occurred in the 1980s. Policy analysts such as the Institute for Women's Policy Research in Washington, DC, report that over half of this "improvement" in the 1980s was due to an erosion of men's real wages. At century's end there was still a substantial, relatively stable gap between what men and women earn.

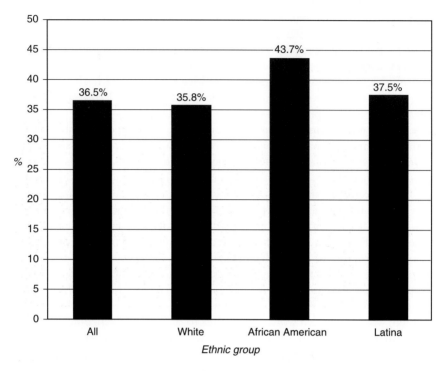

Figure 2.4 Percentage of family earnings contributed by wives, by ethnic group, 1997
Source: U.S. Department of Labor, Women's Bureau (1998: Appendix B, Table 6)

Conclusion

The patterns of women's employment by race reflect broad economic transformations and shifting boundaries of gender and race-ethnicity. Waged work, once a mark of degradation, became an important means of provisioning for family needs. A century ago the preferred mode of gender relations relied upon a male breadwinner, temporary employment spells for young, single women, and married women's domestic labor. Immigrant women and women of color had continuous labor force participation. Over the course of the twentieth century, white married women, especially those with young children, redefined their relationship to paid work. The growth of the service sector, rising consumption standards, and shifting gender ideology all contributed to legitimating women's paid employment.

Men and women, white and nonwhite, work, but not in the same places. Occupational segregation by gender and race-ethnicity have maintained hierarchies. Hierarchies are also reinforced by relative wages for different groups. Wage practices, for example, either extend the concept of a male breadwinner family to working-class and/or African American families or keep it

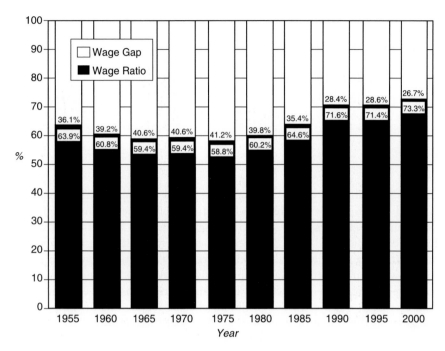

Figure 2.5 Gender-based wage ratio and wage gap (median annual earnings of full-time workers in current dollars), 1955–2000

Sources: U.S. Department of Labor, Women's Bureau (1998: Appendix B); U.S. Census Bureau (2001a: Figure 3)

as a white, middle-class prerogative. Wages encourage or discourage particular groups of women's labor force participation, occupational segregation by gender and/or race-ethnicity, and/or class divisions among members of the same gender or racial-ethnic group.

3 Two faces of wages within the economics tradition

Wages as a living, wages as a price

In our examination of the regulation of wages in the twentieth century United States, we pay a great deal of attention to the arguments among academics, regulators, and social reformers about the definition of a fair wage for women and men. These arguments reflect differing assumptions about the process of wage setting in general and the setting of women's and men's wages in particular. Rather than assigning priority to one narrow view of wage setting, we have discerned three simultaneous aspects of wages that can be woven together to help build a richer understanding of the politics, process, and meaning of wage setting. We label these (1) *wages as a living*, (2) *wages as a price*, and (3) *wages as a social practice*.

These three concepts articulate three economic and social functions that wages perform within market economies. They also depict alternative wage-setting processes. We do not claim that these three aspects exhaust the possible understandings of wages from different standpoints. Rather, we recognize that our framework is bounded by our historical and cultural position, by our focus on U.S. experience and labor market policy, and by the initial questions that we chose to ask. Despite these caveats, we propose that a framework that examines the dynamics of living, price, and social practice provides a more nuanced and complex interpretation of gendered labor markets than traditional economic theory. Further, we maintain that wages are set through the interaction among the dynamics we label as living, price, and social practice.

In this chapter and the next, we introduce our theoretical framework for the analysis of wage regulations in Part II of the book. We explain the concepts of wages as a living and a price, and illustrate their development in the writings of economists. This will not be an exhaustive history of theorizing on wages, but an illustrative discussion of the major currents informing these differing views. This survey is followed in Chapter 4 by an examination of the contributions of contemporary feminist writers to an understanding of gendered economic outcomes, highlighting recent developments in practice theory.

While theorizing wages as a price is most associated with neoclassical economics, and wages as a living with Marxism and social economics, it would be oversimplified to create rigid theoretical boundaries. All schools of economic thought acknowledge the presence of market forces in wage setting, although only neoclassicals privilege market analysis over other factors. In fact, it was not until the post-World War II period that neoclassical economics abandoned institutional and normative analysis to produce purely market-based analyses of wage determination. Further, although we draw upon feminism in defining wages as a social practice, institutionalism and other heterodox theories also recognize the roles played by historical, cultural, and ideological factors in creating economic outcomes.[1]

The different wage policies over the twentieth century, discussed in the chapters to come, can be viewed as reflecting the relative emphasis given to each of these themes. The implicit wage theories articulated by economic and political actors and the policies associated with them are shaped in part by prevailing academic economic discourse. Participants in specific policy debates (about, for example, minimum wages for women or equal pay for equal work) often viewed wages complexly, from more than one of these perspectives. And the policy outcomes tended to reflect the relative strengths of one or more of these facets of wages.

Wages as a living

Economic theories emphasizing wages as a living begin with the premise that the wage paid to labor must be sufficient to guarantee the continuing health and productivity of the worker. More than this, the wage must enable the working class to raise a healthy and productive next generation, to "reproduce" itself over time. Arguments for wages as a living are often expressed normatively, in terms of considerations of fairness. But the concept of wages as a living has also been employed analytically, as a precondition for the efficient and effective functioning of a market-based economic system. Classical economists of the eighteenth and nineteenth centuries in particular tended to argue that the economy could not flourish without an adequate supply of laborers. And an adequate supply of laborers could not be guaranteed over time unless wages allowed for the reproduction of the working class.

Even analytic arguments for a living wage, however, have to address the question of what, exactly, constitutes a "living." Unless it is viewed as a biological minimum below which survival is unlikely, the living wage is a social construct, based on the historically specific, accepted standard of living for the working class. Further, the notion of a living is gendered and racialized, as social understandings of an appropriate wage have varied historically according to the sex and race of the worker. Both its social nature and its gendered and racialized content make the concept of the living wage a potent subject of contention, as we will document in the chapters that follow.

Classical economists and subsistence wages

Adam Smith's *The Wealth of Nations*, published in 1776, is widely viewed as providing a foundation for subsequent analysis of the newly emerging industrial capitalist economic system. In his chapter "On Wages," Smith built on the tradition of political economy of his time in asserting that wages have a base in subsistence – defined as "the lowest which is consistent with common humanity": "A man must always live by his work, and his wages must at least be sufficient to maintain him" (Smith 1937: 67). The use of the male pronoun was intentional on Smith's part because he recognized that wages reflected the gendered division of labor that he viewed as natural. Thus, men needed to earn not just enough to support themselves, but "on most occasions . . . somewhat more," in order to support children. A wife, Smith supposed, could earn only enough to support herself "on account of her necessary attendance on the children" (1937: 68). But he did not view wives as requiring support from their husbands.

Smith's richly complex chapter on wages in fact incorporated all three threads of the discourse on wages. Forces of demand and supply, he argued, could cause wages to deviate from the subsistence level. Indeed, his hope was for a sufficient level of economic growth that demand for labor outran supply, allowing wages to rise to a level of comfort. Smith also recognized wages as reflecting power differentials between employers (who in his day were allowed to combine with each other) and laborers (who were not allowed to form unions), and thus reinforcing class positions. In a famous passage early in the chapter, Smith claimed that "Masters are always and everywhere in a sort of tacit, but constant and uniform combination, not to raise the wages of labor above their actual rate" or, worse, to "sink the wages of labor even below this rate" (1937: 66–7).

But he was consistent in viewing wages as a living as the central force in wage setting, "otherwise," Smith argued, "it would be impossible for (the worker) to bring up a family, and the race of such workmen could not last beyond the first generation" (1937: 68). Note that Smith's understanding of a living wage was a family wage. Reflecting common social practice in Britain in the pre-Industrial Revolution period (Pinchbeck 1969), he argued that both men and women contributed to family support, at the same time that he took it for granted that men needed to earn a family wage while women would earn less.

In Volume I of his major three-volume economic analysis, *Capital*, first published in 1867, Karl Marx developed a theory of wages that built upon Smith's classical conception of wages as a living. However, Marx placed his analysis more firmly within the historically specific and contentious relationship between capitalist employers and workers. Throughout human history, people have needed to combine their labor with natural materials in order to create use-values, products on which they can subsist. Marx described this labor process as the "everlasting Nature-imposed condition of human existence" (1967: v. I, 184). The organization of production, and the resulting relationships among people, are historically specific human constructions. Wage labor as a widespread and systematic practice, Marx argued, was unique to capitalist production. It could only occur when substantial numbers of workers appeared, willing to offer to sell their labor power (ability to labor); and this could only occur under two concrete historical circumstances. First, workers had to be in possession of their own labor power. They could not be either slaves or serfs, neither of whom could freely offer their labor power for sale. And second, they had to have nothing to sell except for their labor, nor could they be in a position to use their own labor power to produce commodities for sale (1967: v. I, 168–9). Both of these conditions came together with the development of capitalism, as industrialization drove independent craft producers out of business and the transformation of agriculture moved former serfs off the land. Marx emphasized that this process, unlike the labor process in general, was human-constructed: "Nature does not produce on the one side owners of money or commodities, and on the other men possessing nothing but their own labor-power" (1967: v. I, 169).

Once labor power became a commodity, commonly offered for sale in the market, it commanded a systematic price, arrived at by the same principle as other commodities. Where Marx differs from neoclassical theories of wages as a price, however, is in the nature of how commodity prices are set. For Marx as for many other classical economists, the inherent value of commodities was proportional to the labor time required to produce them. (This was termed the *labor theory of value*.) A wage, then, had to reflect the labor embedded in the commodities and services required to produce the worker's labor power – in other words, the *necessary living expenses* of the worker. In a passage very reminiscent of Smith, Marx noted that this living wage had to be sufficient not only to support the worker, but to support his children as well "in order that this race of peculiar commodity-owners may perpetuate its appearance in the market" (1967: v. I, 172).[2] The exact amount considered sufficient to reproduce the worker's labor power over time would depend on the historically specific standard of living for members of the working class. This standard, of course, could be a point of contention between workers and capitalists. Marx had little illusion about the tendency of employers to drive down living standards whenever possible.

In his initial discussion of wages, Marx, unlike Smith, made no mention of women workers. In subsequent chapters of *Capital*, he documented the tendency of employers to substitute the labor of children and women for that of men, with a resulting decrease in wages, and often appalling working conditions. Like most analysts of his period, Marx naturalized the gendered division of labor in the family, seeing it as based on "a purely physiological foundation" (1967: v. I, 351). In the workplace, however, he viewed this division of labor as largely driven by capitalists' attempts to cheapen labor. Mechanization lightened tasks and therefore allowed the employment of women and children.[3] But more importantly, in Marx's view, employing all members of the family lowered wage costs for the employer, since the cost of reproducing the working class was spread over, perhaps, four people rather than only one.

Incorporating women into wage labor was very costly to working-class families, Marx argued, because women were then unable to provide much of the unpaid domestic labor families needed to survive. While total family income was likely to rise when women and children entered wage labor, the family was nevertheless likely to find itself in fact worse off, as ready-made products had to be purchased to replace the mother's labor (1967: v. I, 395 n. 2). The employment of female children compounded the problem since girls missed the opportunity to learn domestic skills from their mothers.

This discussion is interesting because it shows Marx's awareness of the importance of domestic labor for the support of working-class families and because it demonstrates his assumption that the gendered division of labor in the home was a natural, rather than a social construct. Marx's analysis has been criticized by feminist writers for naturalizing the subordination of women (Hartmann 1981 [1979]; Folbre 1993). His tendency to conflate women and children, and implicit assumption that women should appropriately remain at home, to avoid "moral degradation" (1967: v. I, 399) reflected the prominent gender ideology of his day.[4] Perhaps more to the point, this view limited his analysis of wages. While Marx, as we saw, developed a living wage analysis, and while he was clear that this wage was contended between workers and employers, he offered no explanation for the lower wages received by women and children other than their "more pliant and docile character" (1967: v. I, 403). Nevertheless, both his identification of the connection between domestic labor and wages, and his systematic examination of the social construction of wages through market forces and conflict between workers and capitalists, constituted substantial further developments of living wage analysis.

The inefficiency of parasitic industries

In the late nineteenth century, Sidney and Beatrice Webb took living wage analysis in a different and very influential direction, arguing that the payment of living wages to the working class was in the interest not only of workers but also of the middle class and, ultimately, even of most employers. The Webbs were members of the Fabian socialist movement. They supported socialism on the grounds that it was more efficient than capitalism, which they saw as wasteful and corrupt. Socialism, by being more efficient, had the potential of making everyone better off.

In their book *Industrial Democracy* and other writings, the Webbs used living wage analysis as part of their critique of capitalism: capitalism was inefficient, in part, because it fostered employers who paid less than living wages. Echoing Smith and Marx, they defined a living wage as one that would

support workers "unimpaired in numbers and vigor, with a sufficient number of children to fill all vacancies caused by death or superannuation"
(1920: 751). A far-sighted employer would want to pay this wage, recognizing
that living wages would "increase the activities and improve the character of
both brain and manual workers" so as "to heighten the faculties and enlarge
the enjoyments of the community as a whole" (1920: 703).

However, even far-sighted employers could not always set wages as they
wished. Wages were set through "higgling of the market" between frequently
unorganized workers and employers who were very inclined to combine with
each other. In these bargains, workers were doubly disadvantaged. They
lacked knowledge of the employer's economic condition with which to judge
how much to ask for in wages. And second, workers were too poor and too
desperate to hold out for a higher wage. The employer, by contrast, knew
both the state of the market and the "essential economic weakness" of the
worker (1920: 655–7). Shortsighted and greedy employers would be motivated to drive wages down as far as possible, and the far-sighted employers
would be forced to follow suit in order to remain competitive.

The result was a widespread problem of wages below the necessary level
that would allow workers to work to capacity and raise a healthy and productive next generation. In some cases, in so-called "sweated" industries,[5] the
pay would be so low that workers could not survive without a subsidy either
from the income of other family members in better-paid industries, from
private charities, or from public poor relief. Such employers the Webbs
termed "parasitic," because they reaped profit by paying their workers less
than the total social costs of reproducing their labor. Women and children,
they argued, were particularly likely to be paid less than a living wage (1920:
749, 750).

The existence of parasitic industries was a problem not only for the workers they employed, but for the society as a whole. Society would have to pay
the difference between the wage and a living for the workers. Additionally,
low wages provided no incentive for employers to improve their production
techniques or use their workers efficiently. Because of their lower costs, these
sweated trades could expand at the expense of self-supporting trades, with
negative effects on national productivity. The Webbs advocated a nationally
mandated minimum wage at a level that provided an adequate living. By
forcing parasitic trades to pay the true social cost of the labor they employed,
national efficiency would be improved through innovation and through
improvements in workers' health and productivity. Some sweated trades
might go under or leave the country, but this would allow the capital and
labor they had employed to be redistributed to more profitable uses (1920:
779).

The Webbs' concept of "parasitic industries" was very influential among
social reformers, who employed it in their campaigns to improve pay and
conditions for workers (see Chapter 5). While the notion of a living wage was
for the Webbs, as for Smith and Marx, an analytic concept, many reformers

also used it in a moral sense: society owed a living to those who worked hard. This normative use of a living wage also occurred in the writings of early neoclassical writers, whose theories of wage setting are more usually associated with wages as a price (to be addressed below). While, as we will see, the theorizing of neoclassical economists generally presumes that markets work well and wage bargains are freely arrived at, the early neoclassicals qualified their market analysis with acknowledgments that markets in practice may involve coercion, and with assertions about society's responsibility to provide a living for its citizens.

A. C. Pigou in Great Britain and John Bates Clark in the United States were two early and rigorous developers of market-based analyses that presumed that workers would be paid according to the marginal value added by their labor, a wage that Pigou labeled "fair." Interference with this fair wage was unwarranted since, assuming markets operated well, if a worker was paid less than a living wage, it was because that worker's labor was worth less. This low wage, therefore, did not waste community resources, he believed, and did not constitute parasitism (Pigou 1960 [1932]: 601). However, while Pigou opposed minimum wages on this ground (with some small and grudging exceptions), he did in fact believe that workers should be guaranteed a living. In an article in the periodical *Nineteenth Century* in 1913, Pigou called for a guaranteed minimum income, paid by the state and adjusted for family size.[6] His justification was moral: "Though the sky should fall, there are some conditions below which we, as a civilized people, can never allow any fellow-citizen to fall" (1913: 646).

John Bates Clark, an important early developer of the theory of wages as a price, also expressed moral support for a living wage, and in fact reluctantly endorsed a minimum wage to achieve this goal. While he based his work almost exclusively on market-based analysis, an article in *Atlantic* in 1913 indicated his awareness of market imperfection. He began his article with the following assertion: "If in every large city thousands of persons must continue to work hard and get less than a living, the fact is an indictment of civilization" (1913: 289). Workers might be earning less than a living because they lacked skills or because their employers were unproductive. But they might also earn less than a living, Clark conceded (echoing Smith, Marx, and the Webbs), because workers without unions to bargain for them could find themselves easily coerced into accepting too low a wage. Bluntly put, "Hunger-discipline disqualified the worker for making a successful bargain" (1913: 292). Whether low wages were a result of low skill or coercion, the state had a responsibility to ensure the workers a living. If establishing a minimum wage at a living level caused workers to lose their jobs, the government should provide emergency employment for them.

The ethical obligation of employers

During the early part of twentieth century, many economists related their work to religious as well as political movements to raise wages and reduce poverty; they held that the "doctrine of *laissez-faire* is unsafe in politics and unsound in morals" (Gearty 1953: 86–93; see also McLoughlin 1978). Richard T. Ely, one of the founders of the American Economic Association, was himself devoutly Christian and based his support of movements to improve the wages and working conditions of labor on his theological as well as economic beliefs. In his autobiography *Ground Under Our Feet*, Ely defended the idea that economics should be "first and foremost a science of human relationships" (1938: 121). He decried the *laissez-faire* orthodoxy that dominated the discipline, arguing that a "crust" had formed over political economy.[7] By reducing economics to the study of natural laws and principles that were supposed to hold in all times and places, abstract economics had devalued human beings as mere instruments of the free market mechanism. In protest, Ely and his fellow "rebels" founded the American Economic Association as an organization committed to freedom of discussion.[8] The original platform of the organization began with the assertion that "We regard the state as an agency whose positive assistance is one of the indispensable conditions of human progress" (Ely 1938: 140).

Ely wrote the introduction to one of the major U.S. works in defense of a living wage. *A Living Wage: Its Ethical and Economic Aspects* was written by ethicist, teacher, and scholar-activist Monsignor John A. Ryan (1906). In his introduction, Ely, a Protestant, avows that Ryan's *A Living Wage* is "the first attempt in the English language to elaborate what may be called a Roman Catholic system of political economy" (Ryan 1906: xii). Ryan was the first director of the Social Action Department of the National Catholic Welfare Conference (predecessor of the National Conference of Catholic Bishops–United States Catholic Conference). He became a high-profile activist during the New Deal. Closely connected to economic policy makers in the Roosevelt administration, Ryan was a key supporter of a federal minimum (living) wage and passage of the Fair Labor Standards Act of 1938 (see Chapter 6).

Ryan's work was a landmark in the development of social economics, a movement with theological roots in Roman Catholic doctrine. Activity by Catholic social movements to remedy economic injustice within industry in Europe prompted the encyclical *Rerum Novarum* or *On the Condition of Labor* in 1891. In this encyclical, Pope Leo XIII "converted the Living Wage doctrine from an implicit to an explicit principle of Catholic ethics" (Ryan 1906: 34). In the section titled "Just Wages," Pope Leo wrote:

> that the remuneration must be enough to support the wage-earner in reasonable and frugal comfort. If through necessity or fear of a worse

evil, the workman accepts harder conditions because an employer or contractor will give him no better, he is the victim of force and injustice.

(Leo XIII 1891: 27–8)

Rerum Novarum drew upon the scholastic idea of a just price in the works of Thomas Aquinas to advocate a specific economic practice, a just wage.[9] Elaborating upon the role of the state in a later encyclical, *Quadragesimo Anno*, Pope Pius XI (1931) wrote that if an employer cannot pay a living wage, the state is obliged to change the situation so that workers can receive a living wage. What was implied in *Rerum Novarum*, but directly alluded to in the later encyclical, was more precisely a *family* living wage for a male head of household and his dependents: "In the first place, the wage paid to the workingman must be sufficient for the support of himself and of his family" (1931: 20). In general, Catholic teaching promoted the view that a family wage enabled women to concentrate on their work, and their duty, in the home (Fogarty 1957: 91).

Ryan, an avid student of economics, was deeply impressed with and heavily influenced by *Rerum Novarum* (Beckley 1996). Combining ethical and economic arguments, Ryan offers that human dignity is possible only if workers have the material conditions necessary for survival. Material well-being is based not on subsistence, but a reasonable and decent living. Further, material support is necessary so that the family can serve as a locus of spiritual education and formation. A living wage, according to Ryan, is a "decent livelihood," the ability to live in "a reasonable degree of comfort" (1906: 73).

Ryan's program for social justice was solidified with the publication of his Distributive Justice in 1916. In *Distributive Justice*, Ryan specifies the elements of a living wage as access to:

> food, clothing, housing sufficient in quantity and quality to maintain the worker in normal health, in elementary comfort, and in an environment suitable to the protection of morality and religion; sufficient provision for the future to bring elementary contentment, and security against sickness, accident, and invalidity; and sufficient opportunities of recreation, social intercourse, education, and church membership to conserve health and strength and to render possible the exercise of higher faculties.

(Ryan, in Beckley 1996: 115)

Any employer who does not pay a living wage is declared unreasonable: "the ethical value of labor is always equivalent to at least a living wage, and the employer is morally bound to give this much remuneration" (Ryan, in Beckley 1996: 119). The only exception is when an employer has an inability to pay; in this case, the state must supplement the worker through public allowances or public policy.

The history of economics is replete with theorists who espoused *need* as one of the cornerstones for wage setting. The concept of a living wage represented not only a normative stance but also an analytical necessity for social reproduction. From this perspective, society has an interest in assuring adequate wages, although the precise definition of adequacy may be politically contested. Nevertheless, many of these writers implicitly or explicitly focus on men's wages as the basis for family support. These economic theories are thus a product of the period in which the male breadwinner family was the hegemonic ideal. Therefore, they reflect gendered assumptions about men's and women's economic contributions.

Wages as a price

Theorists who view wages as a price emphasize the workings of supply and demand in the market. As we have seen, the role of markets in setting wages was acknowledged by proponents of wages as a living as well. Yet they viewed a socially determined acceptable living as a base toward which, however they might fluctuate, wages would (or should) return. For the price theorists surveyed in this section, wages did not reflect socially designated living standards, but rather the value of the work performed. Neoclassical economists came increasingly to view markets as smoothly functioning entities in which all participants would receive a share reflecting their true value. Institutional economists, in contrast, viewed markets as imperfect institutions in which differentials in power and access to information would critically affect distribution. Labor markets were augmented by administrative practices within firms as well as by custom. Both neoclassical and institutional schools, however, shifted the focus of wage theory to the level of the firm.

Markets and the workings of "natural laws"

The emerging school of neoclassical economics in the late nineteenth and early twentieth centuries relied upon highly abstract models that viewed the workings of capitalist markets as the outcome of natural laws. In this context, power differentials were not considered. Markets were theorized as smoothly functioning interactions among freely choosing and fully informed individuals. Workers, in this view, entered the market with full awareness of the value of their labor, and the ability to continue to bargain until this value (Pigou's "fair" wage) was achieved. In the words of John Bates Clark's 1899 text *The Distribution of Wealth*,

> the distribution of the income of society is controlled by a natural law, and . . . this law, if it worked without friction, would give to every agent of production the amount of wealth which that agent creates. However wages may be adjusted by bargains freely made between individual men,

the rates of pay that result from such transactions tend . . . to equal that part of the products of industry which is traceable to labor itself.

(Clark 1965: v)

In this analysis, employers continued to purchase units of labor as long as adding additional units continued to be profitable; workers continued to sell labor units as long as the price received – the wage – seemed to them adequate to compensate for the loss of leisure time. Since workers and employers were theorized as equally possessing solid information about the value of additional units of labor, and since both were assumed to be motivated to maximize their own interests, wages would exactly reflect the marginal value of the final labor unit (which economists termed the marginal revenue product). Employers wouldn't pay more, and workers wouldn't accept less.[10]

Neoclassical economists after Clark formalized and expanded upon his model, but the conclusion that market forces resulted in wages equal to the marginal revenue product of labor remained unquestioned, and in fact strengthened. British economist John Hicks, for example, began his 1932 book *The Theory of Wages,*

The theory of the determination of wages in a free market is simply a special case of the general theory of value. Wages are the price of labor; and thus, in the absence of control, they are determined, like all prices, by supply and demand.

(Hicks 1963 [1932]: 1)

One of Hicks' purposes was to argue that collective bargaining by trade unions could not result in a violation of this principle of market wages. If unionized workers managed to raise wages above the going level, employers would respond by decreasing employment (the quantity of labor) to the point where the marginal revenue product of labor equaled the new, higher wage. Thus, nothing workers could do collectively would serve to raise the standard of living of the working class as a whole.[11] This conclusion stood in contrast to Clark, who at times argued that collective bargaining was necessary to insure that workers had adequate power vis-à-vis employers to demand their "fair," productivity-based wage (for example, 1913: 292, discussed above).

Neither Clark nor Hicks raised the possibility that different workers might receive different levels of pay for the same or similar work.[12] Both economists wrote at a high level of abstraction, without references to actual economic conditions, but their theoretical examples refer almost always to working *men*. Neither developed a theory of discrimination. Discrimination would, in fact, violate their understanding of the natural law of markets, since it would imply paying less for some labor (and possibly more for other) than its marginal product, on a systematic rather than accidental basis.

Institutional economics and the era of methodological pluralism

Despite their theoretical orthodoxy, such early neoclassical economists as Pigou and John Bates Clark combined their abstract, market-based models with a willingness to make ethical judgments about the responsibilities of the economy to social well-being. In the period of economic theorizing between the world wars sometimes referred to as "Interwar Pluralism" (Morgan and Rutherford 1998), neoclassical economics, Marxian economics, and the emerging field of institutional economics coexisted and at times collaborated with each other. Morgan and Rutherford comment: "Pluralism meant variety, and that variety was evident in beliefs, in ideology, in methods, and in policy advice. . . . Economists felt at liberty to pursue their own individual combinations of ideas" (1998: 4). This period of pluralism is indicated by the belief in engaged tolerance that was one of the touchstones of the founding of the American Economic Association in 1885 by Ely and others.

Institutional economists tried to "infuse economic theory with a greater realism than is (or was held to be) afforded by reasoning in purely market terms" (McNulty 1984: 153). The original framers of institutionalism included Thorstein Veblen and John R. Commons. The work in this tradition, now called "old" or "original" institutionalism, had much in common with classical political economy. Veblen, for example, rejected the individualism within neoclassical theory, arguing that the economy and economic relationships could not be analyzed as an aggregation of individuals. Economics was regarded as a process of provisioning to meet social as well as individual needs. The original institutionalists were not enamored with abstract, deductive theories, preferring concrete, inductive analyses that referred to real historical conditions (see Commons 1923).

A second generation of institutional scholars who contributed to wage theory in the 1940s and 1950s are sometimes called "neo-institutionalists" because their theories combined marginal analysis and supply and demand with cultural factors to explain wages.[13] One distinction between neo-institutionalist labor economists and neoclassical labor economists was the former's emphasis on a multiplicity of labor markets and wage rates, defined in relation to each other. Within these wage clusters or bands, relative wages were subject to institutional rigidities and habits linked to custom. Their research on wage setting was accomplished through extensive case studies, such as John T. Dunlop's *Wage Determination Under Trade Unions* (1966 [1944]) and Lloyd Reynolds' *The Structure of Labor Markets* (1971 [1951]). Other labor economists within this research tradition include, for example, Clark Kerr, Richard Lester, and Sumner Slichter.

John Dunlop may well be considered "the premier theorist of all the structuralists" (Gimble 1991: 630). He used the analytical tools of neoclassical theory, including supply and demand functions, to model the economic objectives of trade unions, and indifference curves to evaluate union bargaining power. In an edited volume on *The Theory of Wage Determination*, Dunlop accepted that "All wage theory is in a sense demand and supply analysis. A wage is a price, and the wage structure is a sub-system of prices" (Dunlop 1964: 14). However, like Clark and Pigou, he also understood that unions were both political and economic institutions and that the government can set minimum wage laws and other wage policies: "In the contemporary period there is need for the formulation of a body of wage analysis suitable to the labor market developments and to the wage-setting institutions of the day, drawing upon the central body of economic analysis" (1964: 13). He acknowledged that nonmarket factors, politics and society, could influence wage policies and wage setting. Firms were also institutions. Their wage-setting decisions were affected by other firms, unions, and the government. In describing his volume on wages, Dunlop warned:

> One of the more dangerous habits of mind that economic theory may create is an imperialism that insists that all aspects of behavior, particularly any activity related to markets, can be explained by models with the usual economic variables. . . . A fundamental tenet of the following pages is that modes of behavior that are broader than economic theory contribute materially to the understanding of wage behavior.
>
> (Dunlop 1966: 5)

Dunlop's emphasis was not on a single equilibrium but a cluster of related product and factor markets. To Dunlop (1966), all wage structures – intra-plant, interplant, and inter-industry – contained a number of "key" or "benchmark" rates. Wages of other jobs in a job cluster (a group of occupations, job classes, or work assignments linked together inside a firm by managerial organization and social custom) were pegged to these rates. Key or benchmark pay rates were shaped by the external labor market (outside the firm), and pay of other jobs within the cluster were linked to this rate to help form an internal wage structure (inside the firm). Dunlop's characterization of these processes reflects the prevalence of the job evaluation procedures described in Chapter 7. Furthermore, Dunlop noted, the wages set in the external labor market were, in part, explained by wage contours that were interfirm by industry. Key firms in an industry, linked by similar product markets, similar sources of labor, or custom, would have an array of key wage rates that established a wage contour. The wage contours were then a base, and wages could be further affected by collective bargaining or public policy. Firms within the contour might follow along loosely or closely.

Lloyd Reynolds' major study of a New England factory city, based on thousands of interviews, was clearly influenced by Dunlop's job clusters and wage contours. A "going wage" is actually a band of wage rates, according to Reynolds (1971 [1951]). Once the wage structure was established, Reynolds found there was strong inertia to preserve relativities. Thus, one of the primary contributions of this school of institutionalism was the analysis of wages as *prices*, rather than simply wages as *a price*. By rejecting the neoclassical convention of one, uniform equilibrium wage rate, neo-institutionalist economists tried to introduce a more realistic portrayal of wage-setting practices.

In Richard Lester's words: "Actual wage facts seem contrary to what one might expect according to conventional wage theory. Demand and supply do not eliminate gross 'inequities' or gross irrationality. Perfect competition seems to be the exception rather than the rule" (1946b: 152; see also Lester 1946a). Sumner Slichter (1950) compared the structure of wages in the labor market to ordered chaos. Mapping out a structure for labor markets "may lack the elegance of marginal analysis, but it substitutes therefore for the virtue of some approximation to the facts of life" (Phelps 1957: 403). Specifically, customs, norms, internal relativities, inertia, and other economic factors such as technological change and productivity were crucial in explaining the actual practice of wage setting inside firms and the functioning of labor markets. Their scholarship was interdisciplinary and "they perceived labor economics to be inextricably linked to practice, that is, identifying actual labor problems and implementing various remedial policy measures to mitigate them" (Gimble 1991: 628). Institutionalists' attention to the influence of historical practice and the limits of markets foreshadows the feminist analysis of practice theory presented in the next chapter.

Wages and the macro economy

All of the theorists of wages as a price discussed to this point focused on the level of wages for individuals or groups in the economy. This survey would not be complete without a brief mention of John Maynard Keynes' discussion of the relation of wages to the overall (macroeconomic) level of employment. Keynes, one of the most influential economists of the twentieth century, presented his analysis of the causes of unemployment and his case for government intervention in the economy in *The General Theory of Employment, Interest, and Money* (1964 [1936]). Written in a period of worldwide economic depression, this work was instrumental in establishing the theoretical framework of macroeconomics, the study of the economy as a whole. Keynes deviated from neoclassical theory by arguing that capitalist economies could not be counted upon to be self-regulating. Governments had to be actively involved in order to achieve economic stability at full employment.

Neoclassical economics explained entrenched unemployment as the result of real wages (that is, wages measured in actual purchasing power) that were set too high. Market forces, they argued, could correct this problem without government interference. Workers who wanted jobs would respond by offering their services in the market at lower wages; the overall level of wages would be decreased as a result. Employers would respond by hiring more labor, and full employment would be achieved. Keynes challenged this analysis on a number of points. Workers attempted to secure an acceptable wage through bargaining, a process that was haphazard, uneven, and unequal, with "those in the weakest bargaining position suffer[ing] relatively to the rest" (Keynes 1964 [1936]: 267). Further, they bargained over the money wage (the wage in monetary value), not the real wage. Real wages were determined by the price level and were therefore not within their control. Workers could not influence the level of employment through their wage bargains because they could not affect real wages.

Even if the overall level of money wages could somehow be lowered through "wasteful and disastrous struggle" (Keynes 1964 [1936]: 267), the likely outcome would be a partial lowering of prices because of lower labor costs. There would also be a redistribution of income toward owners of capital and raw materials, and particularly toward the "rentier" class who existed through speculation (in the stock market, for example) rather than entrepreneurship or labor. Keynes labeled this outcome "unjust" (268). Most significantly, Keynes argued that the level of employment was the outcome of the willingness to invest in plant and equipment since more capital necessitated more labor. Willingness to invest was the outcome of the state of investor confidence, which, in turn, was affected by the cost of borrowing (the interest rate), the expected level of future demand for goods and services, and expectations of future profit.

While a fall in money wages, with resulting declines in prices, could cause a decrease in interest rates, in most other respects it was bad for investor confidence. The fall in prices made paying off current debt difficult. The fall in wages increased the likelihood of worker unrest. In addition, if employers expected that wages would continue to fall, they would postpone investment and thus decrease current employment. Finally, the redistribution of income toward rentiers would likely lower consumer demand, since Keynes assumed that rentiers as a class would have a lower "marginal propensity to consume" (or tendency to consume out of additions to their income) than workers. In other words, workers spent their wages while the wealthy saved their income or speculated with it. Advocates for living wages since Keynes' time have frequently stressed this connection among wages, consumption, and employment (see, for example, Chapters 6 and 8).

In sum, Keynes argued that the positive effects of a fall in interest rates could be better achieved through government monetary policy by a central bank. Government policy should stabilize money wages in the short run, and allow them to rise slowly with improvements in productivity over time. Equity as well as effectiveness played a role in Keynes' advocacy of government intervention. He viewed the increased emphasis on speculation and short-term profit in capitalist economies as leading to increased instability and inequality: "The outstanding faults of the economic society in which we live are its failures to provide for full employment and its arbitrary and inequitable distribution of wealth and incomes" (Keynes 1964 [1936]: 372). Full employment could be achieved, he believed, through government regulation of the economy, not through the painful, unjust, and ultimately ineffective strategy of cutting wages.

Neoclassical hegemony emerges

As a number of authors have documented, this period of pluralism – during which neoclassical and heterodox economists freely debated both theoretical and policy issues – came to an end after World War II (see Rutherford 1997; Backhouse 1998; Goodwin 1998; Boyer and Smith 2001). A growing orthodoxy among neoclassical economists endorsed economic models premised on the primacy of the unregulated market. Neoclassical analyses of wages came to be increasingly reliant on market explanations, providing models of wages as a price unmodified by examination of wages as a living or as a social practice. As noted by Stephen Woodbury, "Too often the tradeoff between the clutter of institutional complexity and the limited applicability of abstraction has been resolved in favor of greater abstraction" (1987: 1782).

The emergent hegemony of simplified models of wages as a price determined by market forces can be seen by examining the textbooks currently used to inculcate and socialize budding economics scholars. The first edition of a top-selling introductory economics textbook by N. Gregory Mankiw, for example, discusses wage determination in a chapter entitled "The Markets for Factors of Production," reflecting the neoclassical approach of theorizing wages as a price determined in the same manner as prices of other inputs into the production process. Mankiw establishes two "facts" about wages in this chapter: "The wage adjusts to balance the supply and demand for labor," and "The wage equals the value of the marginal product of labor" (1997: 389). Subsequent chapters raise issues such as discrimination by race and gender, the efficacy of minimum wages, the effects of collective bargaining, and comparable worth; but all are treated with extreme brevity, and the conclusion in all cases is that free, unregulated markets are the best strategy to correct any temporary inequities.

Most contemporary labor economics textbooks share this preoccupation with neoclassical labor market analysis.[14] Two of the top-selling labor textbooks in the United States are *Modern Labor Economics* by Ronald Ehrenberg and Robert Smith (2000) and *Contemporary Labor Economics* by Campbell McConnell, Stanley Brue, and David Macpherson (1999). The opening pages of the McConnell, Brue, and Macpherson text do acknowledge that labor markets are more complex than product markets because of institutional considerations. However, these institutional departures from market mechanisms are portrayed as regrettable. For example, the authors refer to the "restrictions on [labor] mobility *imposed* by such institutions as government and unions" (1999: 271, emphasis added). Ehrenberg and Smith use comparable worth as an opportunity to assert the virtues of supply and demand analysis:

When asked to answer why it is, then, that mechanics are paid more than child-care workers, economists tend to answer in terms of market forces: for some reasons, the supply of mechanics must be smaller relative to the demand for them than the supply of child-care workers. Perhaps this reason has to do with working conditions, or perhaps it is more difficult to learn and keep abreast of the skills required of a mechanic, or perhaps occupational crowding increases the supply of child-care workers. *Whatever* the reason, it is argued, wages are the price of labor – and prices play such a critical *practical* role in the allocation of resources that they are best left unregulated.

(Ehrenberg and Smith 2000: 454–5)

Skill differentials as an explanation for relative wages have their roots in human capital theory. Unlike neo-institutional economists who viewed wage differentials as embedded in job characteristics and historical practice, neo-classical economists focused on the individual characteristics of the workers themselves. Individual characteristics that affect productivity were defined as "human capital." These include years of education, experience and job tenure, training in job-related skills, etc. Different levels of human capital investment and attainment would garner different wages. In the context of the civil rights movement of the late 1950s and early 1960s, human capital acquisition became economists' rationale for improving education, training, and job access for racial-ethnic minorities and others in poverty (see, for example, Schultz 1961; Becker 1964). Rather than societal discrimination, the problem was perceived as one belonging to individuals.

Later applied to justifying the wage gap between women and men, human capital theory emphasized differences in women's educational choices, commitment to their careers, and family responsibilities (see, for example, Mincer and Polachek 1974; O'Neill 1985). Because women supposedly made different life choices than men, it was argued that much of their lower pay was for legitimate reasons. However, empirical research has only been able to trace a portion of the wage gap to these factors (England 1982, 1992; Sorensen 1990). As women's labor force experience becomes closer to men's, supply-side theories lose even more explanatory power.

Some neoclassical economists are returning to more complex theorizing about wages, with models that allow for the effects of cultural notions of fairness on worker behavior; but these models still rely on market-clearing methodologies. George Akerlof and Janet Yellen (1986), for example, have developed the theory of "efficiency wages," advancing that employers who pay more than the going wage (or more than the marginal revenue product of labor) are seen as engaging in a gift exchange with their workers, who respond with the gift of increased effort and efficiency. This model, however, still views wages as the market-clearing outcome of individual bargaining between highly informed and equally empowered workers and employers. As such, it is an elaboration of the neoclassical view of wages as a price. The causality is simply reversed: productivity is, in part, a function of the wage rate rather than the other way around.

Conclusion

Since the late nineteenth century, there has been tension between the two explicit visions of the process of wage determination in capitalist economies. One perspective, embedded in market theory, views wages as impersonal and linked to the characteristics of the work to be done. Contemporary neoclassical economic theory concludes that competitive labor markets produce wage rates linked to productivity. In the absence of meaningful differences between workers' skills and other characteristics, wages reflect the job that is being performed. However, public policy discussions have frequently invoked an alternative view of wages, more in keeping with the ideas of classical economists. In this view, wages are based upon workers' needs, that is, a socially defined level of subsistence. These needs are determined in concrete historical circumstances, and therefore reflect power differences between employers and workers as well as macroeconomic conditions. Wages are not only a price, but a living.

Although they are posed as alternative theories, viewing wages as a price need not be inconsistent with viewing wages as a living. As indicated in concrete studies of wage setting by neo-institutionalists, the process of setting wages is complex and historically specific, with both market forces and cultural views about what is owed to workers playing central roles. Further, wages are a social practice. How much one earns is central in determining one's place in society, and societal norms about behavior and place are historically strongly affected by cultural notions of gender, race-ethnicity, and class. Wages have been used to signify and to enforce accepted places for different social groups; and groups in their struggles to free themselves from social oppression have demanded that their wages be established on a different basis. Feminist theorizing, to which we turn in the next chapter, has been central in understanding such social practices.

4 The third face

Wages as a social practice

Historically, debates over wage theory have largely concentrated on the tension between wages as a living and wages as a price. Feminist thought contributes to this conversation about wages and wage setting through the central concept of gender. While most contemporary feminist thought is grounded in gender as an analytical construct, there are different understandings of what gender is and how it is constituted. Therefore, in this chapter we trace alternative understandings of gender, beginning with an examination of the classic work of Simone de Beauvoir. De Beauvoir's influence on the so-called second wave of feminist theorizing and activism in the 1960s and 1970s is summarized. Next we examine the polarization between structural theories of women's oppression (i.e., patriarchy) and ideologically based theories of the social construction of gender.

We introduce feminist interpretations of "practice theory," an important development in contemporary gender theory since the 1990s. Practice theory is an attempt to reconcile structure and agency as influences on gendered outcomes. We utilize this perspective and explain how its innovative approach to gender can help us better understand wage setting by illuminating a third dimension to wages, wages as a social practice. The interdisciplinary gender theory, methodological approaches, and literature we discuss are aimed at generating our feminist theory of wage setting.

The Second Sex and the second wave

In writing *The Second Sex*, Simone de Beauvoir (1974 [1952]) crystalized many of the ideas that have continued to guide the development of feminist thought. She astutely noted the limits of biological categories, beginning her opus with a denial of the universality of a simple duality between male and female. She also denied the existence of a universal female nature. In fact, de Beauvoir contended that "it must be repeated once more that in human society nothing is natural and that woman, like much else, is a product elaborated by civilization" (1974 [1952]: 806). Although she did not use the term "gender," de Beauvoir articulated the idea that femininity was separable from biological sex. In perhaps her most famous assertion: "One is not born, but rather becomes, a woman" (301). Further, she offered that to be a "man" was a compliment and a signifier of power and status in the world, whereas to be a "woman" was to be not fully human – in her words, to be *Other*.

The process of defining what it meant to be a woman was neither fixed nor deterministic. Elaborating upon the Marxist existentialism within her circle of intellectual peers, de Beauvoir emphasized human agency within the context of strong social forces and social norms. She applied this idea of praxis – or practice – to women's condition: "the body of woman is one of the essential elements in her situation in the world. But that body is not enough to define her as woman; there is no true living reality except as manifested by the conscious individual through activities and in the bosom of society" (1974 [1952]: 41). While de Beauvoir's distinction between biology and identity became the cornerstone of late-twentieth-century gender theory, her methodological insights were not preserved. It is only in recent years that some feminists have returned to the idea of practice as a means of reconciling tensions between different theoretical schools.

The wave of feminist activism and scholarship that resurfaced in the 1970s used the work of de Beauvoir and earlier feminists in elaborating a distinction between sex as biological and gender as a social construct. Anthropologist Gayle Rubin (1975) argued that society attaches meanings and interpretations to a biological category, "sex," formulating designations of masculinity and femininity, "gender." These social constructions became embodied in a *sex/gender system*, "a set of arrangements by which the biological raw material of human sex and procreation is shaped by human, social intervention and satisfied in a conventional manner, no matter how bizarre some of the conventions may be" (Rubin 1975: 165). Rubin viewed patriarchy as one form of sex/gender system, just as capitalism was one mode of production. However, she argued that a sex/gender system was more than a mode of *re*production; it involved production as well, including the production of gender identity.

Much of the feminist theoretical scholarship of the late 1970s and early 1980s explored the systemic aspects of gender relations. Marxist structuralism and historical materialism influenced these accounts. In particular, scholars and activists utilized the concept of patriarchy as a gender system. In her essay on "The Unhappy Marriage of Marxism and Feminism," Heidi Hartmann (1981 [1979]) argued that men's control over women's labor power constituted a material base for patriarchy. Hartmann's work marked a contrast with radical feminist theory during the same period, which often grounded patriarchy in biological differences. Sylvia Walby defined patriarchy as "a system of interrelated social structures through which men exploit women" (1986: 51). Walby depicted a series of relatively autonomous structures within the overall system labeled "patriarchy", including a patriarchal mode of production within the household; patriarchal relations at paid work; male violence; a patriarchal state; and sexuality. Each might take primacy at different periods, she posited: "However, when patriarchy is in articulation with the capitalist rather than other modes of production, then patriarchal relations in paid work are of central importance" (1986: 50). Patriarchy became identified with the male breadwinner family and a division of labor in which women were primarily responsible for unpaid domestic labor.

The image of two materially based systems, capitalism and patriarchy, was the basis for what was called "dual systems theory." In her early writing, Zillah Eisenstein (1979) portrayed the process of mutual accommodation as leading to a fusion into one system that she termed "capitalist patriarchy."[1] However, dual systems theory came under increasing criticism by the mid-1980s. Patriarchy was variously viewed as ahistorical, economistic, or functionalist (see Sargent 1981; Burris 1982; Folbre 1987; Barrett 1988; Vogel 1995). Patriarchy theory was seen as ahistorical for failing to account for changes in gender relations and their periodization within different modes of production. It was said to be economistic for emphasizing materialism and underplaying ideological forces. And it was charged with functionalism for simplifying how patriarchy serves capitalism. Empirically, critics charged that the theory generalized from the experiences of middle-class and upper-class white women in industrialized countries, the only women who were full-time homemakers. By focusing on the interaction of capitalism and patriarchy, dual systems theory tended to slight the theoretical importance of racial-ethnic domination.

R. W. Connell has referred to patriarchy as a form of categorical theory in which "Theoretical attention is focused on the social place or category into which the individual is inserted" (1987: 56). One problem, he argued, is that the construction of these categories frequently relies upon a representative individual. In this case, full-time homemakers and care givers were often taken as representative of women in general and women were defined solely in terms of their roles in a domestic division of labor. While sex role theory treated gender as the product of individual actions to socialize boys and girls, categorical theories tended to dissolve the individual into the requirements of one or more systems. Lise Vogel has also observed that "questions of subjectivity and agency fall outside theory of this sort" (2000: 165). However, she was less troubled by this limitation than was Connell, sharply distinguishing theory from concrete historical studies.

Theory does not move in lockstep. Several theorists have continued to develop the concept of patriarchy in conjunction with gender theory rather than abandon the concept altogether (see, for example, Cockburn 1991; Walby 1997). Although Walby now focuses on transformations in what is termed gender relations, she has asserted that "[this] should not be interpreted as suggesting that systematic gender inequality of patriarchy is over" (1997: 6). She has continued to delineate private patriarchy (men's control in the household) and public patriarchy (government policies and programs that subordinate women) as contemporary gender regimes. Cynthia Cockburn has suggested that the contemporary system might be better labeled "fratriarchy" since it is no longer grounded in father-right (1991: 7). However, Cockburn also persisted in referring to the current sex/gender system as patriarchy. Despite the critiques of dual systems theory, she opined that "In practice, women continue to use the terms patriarchy, capitalism, sex, class and race, to describe our lives. We know it is the articulation of these sets of relations, the way they are lived and reproduced, we have to study and specify" (1991: 8). In contrast, Judith Lorber (1994) chose not to use the term "patriarchy" as an explanatory concept because it lacks clarity. Yet Lorber's assertion that gender can be "conceptualized as a social institution often rooted in conflict over scarce resources and in social relationships of power" (1994: 6) clearly rests on ground shared with patriarchy theorists.

The construction and deconstruction of gender

Partly in response to the limitations of patriarchy as an analytical construct, gender as the production of identities, and thus as ideology, moved to center stage in the late 1980s. As indicated in the previous discussion of patriarchy, this is not meant to suggest unanimity among feminist theorists during any particular period. Feminist theory in general and gender theory in particular continued to be marked by diversity. However, most formulations of gender theory during this period were grounded in the distinction between biological sex and gender identity. Gender was a social construction. Although the focus was on the ideological processes that created gender rather than material conditions, gender was construed to be more than the collective bias, prejudice, or stereotypes of individuals. According to Barbara Laslett and Johanna Brenner:

> Gender refers to socially constructed and historically variable relationships, cultural meanings, and identities through which biological sex differences become socially significant. . . . More than an individual characteristic, gender refers to the social relationships between women and men that shape personal identity.
>
> (Laslett and Brenner 1989: 382)

Feminists thus used the term "gender" to signify society's ideas about differences between men and women embodied in definitions of masculinity and femininity. In a highly influential book of essays, historian Joan Scott (1988) suggested that the definition of gender rested on two propositions: "gender is a constitutive element of social relationships based on perceived differences between the sexes, and gender is a primary way of signifying relationships of power" (1988: 42). Therefore, male and female were socially constructed as opposites, and a hierarchy was established between them.

This new wave of gender theory built on the second wave literature with a more aggressive challenge to the historical materialism and primacy of production in orthodox Marxism. Gender shaped political and economic institutions rather than simply reflecting the organization of power and resources (Benhabib and Cornell 1987; Laslett and Brenner 1989). Such scholars were skeptical of Marxism, which they saw as a "grand theory" or "meta-theory" that projected a teleological direction to historical development based upon a particular human essence or nature. Socially constructed definitions of masculinity and femininity varied historically, cross-culturally, or even within a given society. Because gender interacted with class, race-ethnicity, and sexuality – constructs that were also socially, not biologically, determined – more than one mode of gender relations might coexist. For example, the hegemonic ideal of the full-time homemaker/mother for white, middle-class, married women in the early twentieth century was distinct from married black women's expected labor force participation (Brewer 1999). This diversity of gender relations enabled gender theorists to respond to some of the criticisms leveled at descriptions of patriarchy (Mutari 2000).

In the late 1980s and early 1990s, one school of feminist theorists, grounded in the humanities rather than the social sciences, analyzed gender ideology as a form of social discourse (see, for example, Benhabib and Cornell 1987; Weedon 1987; Butler and Scott 1992; Landry and MacLean 1993). Discourse analysis, pioneered by French theorists such as Jacques Derrida and Michel Foucault, focused on how subjectivity (or consciousness) is shaped by language. From this focus on language and ideology, feminist scholars turned to a critique of the process of knowledge production itself. The dominant strain of academic feminism thus concerned itself with articulating the gendered assumptions embedded in the major "scientific" theories (see, for example, Harding 1986, 1987; Cancian 1992).

Linda Nicholson (1990), writing on the relationship between knowledge production (epistemology), science, and theory, argued that there is an overlap between feminist and postmodernist critiques of the alleged objectivity of academic knowledge. The Enlightenment (or modernist) perspective was accused by both groups of privileging reason and rationality as foundations for epistemology.[2] The Enlightenment view of science (still the foundation for much of economic theory) posits an objective reality that can be understood through rational analysis. Instead, Nicholson claimed that all human knowledge is situated, that is, filtered through the experience of the observer (1990: 3).[3] De Beauvoir's concept of women as "other" played a key role in this theoretical approach. Not only women, but other subordinated groups were argued to have distinct standpoints that were not incorporated into existing knowledge systems.

With this shift towards ideology and away from materialist analyses of sex/gender systems came a critique of social constructionism itself (Lorber 1994; Hewitson 1999; Squires 1999). The distinction between sex and gender made by social constructionists in some early feminist writings was based on the idea that sex itself was biological, thus natural. Social constructionism had become associated with a dichotomy between biological sex as a fixed category and gender as fluid. However, newer work by feminists argued that biology itself is shaped and interpreted by its historical context. Science and medicine have enforced a biological dualism between men and women surgically, while Western culture naturalized the duality between male and female through designations of deviance.[4] Similarly, the naturalization of biological sex contributed to the conceptualization of (hetero)sexuality as defined by nature. The advent of queer theory and other scholarship on sexuality therefore posed challenges to the understanding of men and women as an ahistorical and fixed dualism. If categorization into two sexes was both socially constructed and enforced, the next step was to question the usefulness of thinking in terms of only two genders. Perhaps there are multiple genders, with different sets of appropriate appearance and behavior.[5]

If biological sex itself has no constant meaning across time, between cultures, and among individuals, this poses problems for theory and practice in which "men" and "women" are central categories. As articulated by political scientist Judith Squires, "Feminist theory, which created the category of gender in order to answer the question 'what is a woman?' in a non-deterministic manner now finds itself unable to speak of 'woman,' or even 'women,' without major discomfort" (1999: 61). What commonality is there among women whose views of reality are developed in different places, different times, and different life situations? This trajectory is troubling for those of us who view feminism as a theory that can promote and advance social change. According to Connell (1987), the way the theory was constructed precluded discussion of common political goals and strategy. In response, gender theory fragmented into increasingly divergent camps.[6]

The feminist critique of orthodox economic theories has utilized the critiques of science, objectivity, and rationality that were born of postmodern-influenced gender theory (Ferber and Nelson 1993; Strober 1994; Nelson 1996; Benería 1999). In the introduction to one of the first books presenting feminist economics as a unique theoretical perspective, *Beyond Economic Man: Feminist Theory and Economics*, Marianne Ferber and Julie Nelson asserted:

> If we instead recognize that the discipline we call economics has been developed by particular human actors, it is hard to see how it could fail to be critically influenced by ... the social, cultural, economic, and political milieu in which it has been created.
>
> (Ferber and Nelson 1993: 1)

The emphasis of much of this recent scholarship in feminist economics is deconstructing androcentric bias within the discipline's theories, conceptual categories, and methodologies. Gillian Hewitson (1999), however, has suggested that most feminist economists have rejected the more radical deconstruction of gender by postmodernism (see also Nelson 1996). They have continued to utilize biological categories of men and women in empirical research on the labor market, development policies, and the division of household labor (Macdonald 1995). Many have also continued to advocate political agendas based on a commonality of interests among women and sometimes other constituencies.

Practice theory

The postmodern challenge to the concept of "women" as a unified category has generated a quandary: How can the legitimate insights of contemporary feminist theory be attended to by those of us in the social sciences without losing sight of the emancipatory project that sparked feminism? This quandary has led to the search for "a form of social theory that gives some grip on the interweaving of personal life and social structure without collapsing towards voluntarism and pluralism on one side, or categoricalism and biological determinism on the other" (Connell 1987: 61). For some, practice theory meets this challenge. Practice theory has its roots in the existentialist thought of de Beauvoir, Jean-Paul Sartre, and in recent work by Pierre Bourdieu, Anthony Giddens, and others. It has been elucidated by gender theorists such as Connell in his books *Gender and Power* (1987) and *Masculinities* (1995), and Sherry Ortner, in her book *Making Gender* (1996). We propose that their interpretation of the relationship between gender and practice can be a fruitful basis for a feminist political economy of wages.

The concept of practice focuses on human agency in constituting the social relations in which we live. However, social practice is not comprised of random or purely individual acts. Connell, for example, conveys that "Social practice is creative and inventive, but not inchoate. It responds to particular situations and is generated within definite structures of social relations" (1995: 72). Methodologically, Sherry Ortner (1996) proposes that practice theory therefore walks the tightrope between determinism and relativism. She claims that attention to practice can recover the role of power and agency lacking in much of poststructural gender theory. Human agency is constrained by the prevailing social order but is also capable of remaking these structures, although not according to an underlying narrative or historical trajectory. Similarly, Evelyn Nakano Glenn argues for an interpretation of gender that considers both material relations and cultural meanings, a "middle ground between essentialism and antiessentialism" (1998: 32).

In practice theory, gender is treated as an "organizing principle" of social structures rather than simply a characteristic of individuals (Glenn 1998: 33). Family and kinship are not the only locus of gender. Indeed, confining gender analysis to a single locus (e.g. the family) is itself a form of masculine bias. All social structures and institutions, including the labor market and the state, are structured by gender. As development theorist Naila Kabeer suggests: "Gender is seen to be an aspect of *all* organizational relations and behavior, more distinct and explicit in some institutional locations than others, but always interacting to shape the identities, practices and life-chances of different groups of women and men in quite specific ways" (1994:

61). Gender relations are continually reproduced or transformed through a series of social practices; this is an ongoing historical process. There may be more or less harmony about prevailing gender structures, depending on the level of discord and resistance (Connell 1987: 63). For example, the waves of feminist activism were periods in which gender structures were intensely questioned and, to some extent, modified.

Although gender as a structure of social practice has been the primary subject of this literature, gender is not the only way of organizing social practices. Race-ethnicity, class, and nationality are other means of structuring social practice (see Williams 1995; Brewer 1999). In fact, there are multiple masculinities and femininities as gender intersects with these other structures. How gender is structured in a particular time and place thus reflects the relative dominance of different social interests. Connell (1995) uses these insights to develop the concept of hegemonic and subordinate masculinities. Hegemonic masculinity is the cultural ideal of the moment – such as being a married, heterosexual breadwinner – even though diverse forms of masculinity may be practiced.

Feminist practice theory has important implications for wage setting. We are introducing an application of this theory in asserting wages as form of social practice. A working definition of this aspect of wage setting is that *wages are a socially embedded activity that can either reproduce or transform social relations and institutionalized norms.* In fact, economic actors involved in debates over wage regulations clearly and overtly acknowledged that wages reflected *and* influenced gender relations. First, cultural and ideological understandings of workers' appropriate places, centrally affected by notions of gender, class, and race-ethnicity, affect actual wage outcomes. Further, wages were seen as a means of establishing particular forms of gender, class, and race-ethnic relations. Wage practices, for example, could extend the concept of a male breadwinner family to working-class families or keep it as a middle-class prerogative. Wage practices could encourage or discourage women's labor force participation, occupational segregation by gender and/or race-ethnicity, and/or class divisions among members of the same gender or racial-ethnic group.

Gender relations are not the only structures or institutions constituted by wage practices. There is a parallel literature examining the social practices that constitute race. Michael Omi and Howard Winant (1994 [1986]) present an analysis of racial formation since the 1960s, examining the various contexts in which racialized meanings and identities are created and contested. Focusing on "the social practices that reproduce [labor market] discrimination," Rhonda Williams argues for a contingent historical approach (1995: 304). She critiques neo-Marxist theories that reduce discrimination theory to a "divide and conquer" strategy by employers (see, for example, Reich 1981). Cross-class alliances between capitalists and white male workers were not inevitable, but rather the result of complex and contradictory forces. One of these was the agency of white workers themselves.

Our treatment of social practice stresses the similarity of these inter-disciplinary gender and race theories and the methodological approaches of radical institutionalism and nondeterminist forms of Marxism. The founders of institutional economics emphasized the importance of cultural norms and values in the development of economic institutions. Methodologically, the economy was treated as a process in which causality is both contingent and cumulative; the neoclassical quest for equilibrium conditions was rejected. More directly related to our discussion of wages as a form of social practice is the "Veblenian dichotomy" between two forms of valuation. Inspired by Thorstein Veblen's work, institutional economist Clarence Ayres distinguished between instrumental value, based on the degree of enhancement of the quality of social life, and ceremonial value, based on status (Waller 1999b). Wage setting as a social practice can be used to confer status and permit "invidious distinctions" between different groups. Contemporary radical institutionalists draw upon and expand this tradition (Dugger 1989; Dugger and Waller 1992; Peterson and Brown 1994). There is tremendous overlap between this work and non-determinist schools of Marxism (Brown 1989; O'Hara 1995; DeMartino 1999).

Social practice and public policy: an application

In applying practice theory to wage setting and, more specifically, to wage regulations, we also draw inspiration from extensive, interdisciplinary feminist research on gender and social welfare policy. This research suggests that the state is a site for the generation of social practices that can either reproduce or transform existing gender relations. Feminist analyses of the state have focused on the emergence of "welfare state capitalism." Welfare, in this context, refers to a range of government policies aimed at modifying market forces in order to achieve a public purpose. Welfare state programs can include direct provision or subsidization of social goods such as health care, education, or child care. However, prior feminist research has largely focused on income replacement programs such as social security, unemployment compensation, and the more narrowly conceived definition of "welfare" as transfer payments to poor mothers. These income replacement programs partially compensate for lost wages (due to retirement, disability, job loss, or the absence of a primary breadwinner).

In this feminist literature on the welfare state, labor market policies, specifically wage regulations, have been relatively unexamined. In Part II of the book, we draw attention to wage regulations because they are also important vehicles for institutionalizing particular social practices and thus particular masculinities and femininities or specific definitions of whiteness and blackness. In this section, we highlight the insights of feminist writings on the welfare state as an illustration of policy as a gendered social practice.

In the 1980s, feminists took a harsh view of many of the social policies that constitute a major component of the welfare state, building on the landmark study *Regulating the Poor* by Frances Fox Piven and Richard Cloward (1971). These studies took a functionalist approach to understanding the welfare system – narrowly focusing on poor relief. Mimi Abramovitz (1988), for example, argued that welfare state policies had to negotiate competing purposes. On the one hand, borrowing from a version of Marxian analysis, the welfare state was designed to ensure the reproduction of the labor force. On the other hand, providing women and children with an alternative means of support threatened patriarchal control. By constructing welfare as a system of "public patriarchy," the first function could be met without threatening the latter. Abramovitz's work was characteristic of socialist-feminist (or dual-systems) theory.

The unilateral pessimism of such functionalist approaches was challenged in the 1990s, as feminists responded to the attempted dismantling of the welfare state. The next wave of feminist research emphasized the historical contingency of particular policy outcomes as well as the role of women social reformers in the development of the welfare state. The methodological significance of this new work was the shift away from categorical analysis with its emphasis on structures such as capitalism and patriarchy. Methodologically, these studies give central importance to women's own agency in political processes.[7] Further, feminist scholars argued that the role of culture – specifically a maternalist ethos – in shaping state policy had been neglected by previous scholars.[8] That is, social reformers advocating government programs, many of them middle-class women, positioned their work as designed to promote maternal and child welfare. As we will see in Chapter 5 on state minimum wage laws, maternalism provided an ideological basis for state intervention in the market to promote a larger public purpose. Gender was thus integral to the political processes that created social welfare policy.

Linda Gordon, for example, examined the policy debates that led to passage of the Social Security Act of 1935 in the United States, particularly Aid to Dependent Children (ADC), the program for single (including widowed and abandoned) mothers that was one of seven programs incorporated by the Act.[9] Women activists, both white and black, actively lobbied for a federal program of mothers' pensions. By giving women an alternative to dependence on men, ADC improved women's bargaining power and gave them a measure of autonomy (Gordon 1994: 289–90). The policy also valued women's unpaid caring labor by offering income support for the work of raising children. These positive attributes had been ignored by scholars who simply viewed welfare policy as reflecting the needs of capitalist patriarchy.

However, Gordon does concur with welfare's critics that the policy that emerged reinforced the idealized male breadwinner family. Welfare was modeled as "mothers' pensions." It was intended to facilitate full-time homemaking in the absence of a male breadwinner, especially for war widows. In effect, social welfare programs replaced an absent husband/father with government agencies/social workers. Nevertheless, several contending visions of ADC were debated prior to passage. The resulting policy was an historically contingent outcome, subject to the relative strength of political actors. It was not inevitable that welfare would take a particular form. Gordon's careful case study of passage of the Social Security Act is echoed by others in research on social welfare policies in various industrialized countries. Comparative studies demonstrate the diversity of social welfare policies among countries with different gender norms and culture and with dissimilar opportunities for effective political mobilization by women (Lewis 1992; Koven and Michel 1993; Orloff 1996).

Additional studies of U.S. welfare policy have analyzed the strengths and limitations of maternalism as a basis for public policy. Sonya Michel (1993) argues that maternalist ideologies circumscribed the types of polices created to provide income support for unmarried women with family responsibilities. Because maternalism accepted mothering as women's essential role, mothers' pensions were deemed preferable to programs such as state-sponsored child care that would have enabled women to combine paid and unpaid work. Thus, the hegemonic model of full-time homemaking supported by a male breadwinner fostered and was reinforced by the development of social welfare policies. Gwendolyn Mink (1995) argues that social welfare policies posited a singular model of mothering, that is mothering as a full-time activity that precluded paid employment. Immigrant and African American women, who often viewed their paid labor as equally important contributions to their families, were supposed to be assimilated into this model. Other researchers have also noted the exclusion of African Americans from New Deal social welfare policy prior to the 1960s (Quadagno 1994; Boris 1995; Davies and Derthick 1997; Lieberman 1998).

Gordon also argues that the policy that was institutionalized linked welfare, narrowly defined as a program for lone mothers with children, to the concept of charity. In contrast, deserving groups such as the elderly, the disabled, and unemployed workers received "entitlements" to social security pensions and unemployment insurance. The Social Security Act instituted a two-track system of public aid, with more generous benefits to the "deserving" rather than the "undeserving" groups. Gordon further suggests that deserving or being entitled to something from the state is a mark of true citizenship. The elderly, for example, deserved their social security pensions because, as former workers and their spouses, they had contributed to society. Women who cared for children without the support of a male breadwinner, in contrast, were to be "pitied, but not entitled." In essence, mothers, confined to the private rather than the public sphere, were not treated as full citizens. Gordon's work, along with other research on social welfare policies, thus challenges the gender neutrality of citizenship as an analytical concept (see Orloff 1996). Further, if income replacement programs can shape how women and men are perceived as citizens and members of society, so too can wage policies and practices. We extend this framework for analyzing public policy to wage regulations in the twentieth century.

Looking ahead

Feminist political economy contributes to the discussion of wage setting in two ways. First, feminist critiques of existing theory assert that market wages and concepts of a living wage are gendered, that is, influenced by prevailing gender norms. As we have seen, gender does not actively figure into these theoretical constructs developed by classical and neoclassical economists. Gender is a complication to models in which the basic process of setting wages is thought to be gender neutral. At best, gender is treated as a bias that distorts "pure" outcomes. Gender is empirically treated as a "dummy variable," something to be controlled; this implies that it is marginal to the analysis (Figart 1997).[10] As noted by sociologist Joan Acker, "Variables interacting with other variables are only constructs with no agency to do anything" (1991: 391). Thus, if we limit our understanding of wages to these two dimensions, living and price, we lose sight of the centrality of gender, not as a variable but as an active feature, in labor market processes.

Second, and more specifically, we argue that wages are a means of establishing and reinforcing what men and women should be doing and how they should live. The assertion that wages constitute a gendered social practice is based on a series of premises: (1) The concept of gender is the foundation of feminist theory; (2) although there are alternative formulations of gender theory, recent work in practice theory seems most useful, especially for political economy; and (3) applied to labor markets, we suggest that wages are themselves a social practice, and that the institutional arrangements and public policies that influence wages are also important social practices. Feminist research on the welfare state provides a model for analyzing gendered and racialized public policy as a social practice. Therefore, three theoretical threads – wages as a living (the basis for classical political economy), wages as a price (the core of neoclassical and neo-institutional economics), and wages as a social practice (our feminist contribution) – are the basis upon which economic actors make claims about what wages, men's as well as women's, should be.

In the succeeding chapters in Part II of the book, we scrutinize specific periods in the regulation of women's wages. Our discussion provides concrete illustrations of the interaction among wages as a living, a price, and a social practice. We use these concepts to argue that wages earned in a concrete historical moment are the nondeterministic outcome of contending forces involving markets, political structures and other institutions, and cultural and ideological underpinnings. For each policy initiative, we investigate how public policy, economic trends, managerial strategies, institutional arrangements, and the activities of different constituencies in labor markets and the political arena have shaped wage practices. We find that prevailing wage practices have shifted in response to changes in all of these factors. Our historical investigation will provide the basis for a further elaboration of the three dimensions of wages within a feminist political economy theoretical framework in Chapter 10.

Part II

Wage regulations in the twentieth century

5 An experiment in wage regulation
Minimum wages for women

Two principles have laid the foundation for efforts to regulate wages during the twentieth century. First, relying upon the wage theories described in Chapter 3, social reformers have contended that employers and the state are obligated to ensure some minimal standard of living to all citizens who participate in waged labor. Not surprisingly, the definition of what constitutes a living, especially whether it incorporates self-sufficiency and/or the ability to support dependents, has varied according to time, location, and the gender, class, and race-ethnicity of the citizen-worker. Second, these activists have disputed gender and racial-ethnic hierarchies by asserting a principle of equal wages. Drawing upon both living and price constructs, equal wages have been interpreted to mean that appropriate living standards should not reflect gender and racial bias and that equally productive workers should receive comparable compensation. Social movements, dating to the earliest days of the century, have attempted to institutionalize the two broad principles of living wages and equal wages in wage-setting practices.

The period from roughly 1900 to 1920 in the United States is commonly referred to as the Progressive Era. It was a time of sharp change, with rapid growth and concentration of industry, mass immigration, particularly from southern and eastern Europe, and increased urbanization. These factors, along with the misery wrought by a nationwide economic depression in 1893, led to the development of a political reform movement focused on curbing the power of large corporations and improving the conditions of workers. Progressive reformers advocated factory safety and inspection laws and protective legislation such as maximum hours and minimum wages. This legislation was frequently gender-specific, that is, applied to women (and children) but not adult men. Therefore, the debate surrounding it often reflected explicit beliefs about the appropriate economic roles of men and women.

This chapter will focus on one particular aspect of legislation to protect women workers: the creation and demise of gender-specific minimum wages in a number of states during the Progressive Era. Efforts to pass state-level minimum wage laws and discussions about the appropriate level for a minimum once legislation was passed provide clear examples of how wages are simultaneously a living, a price, and a social practice. Debates over women's living standards also factored into the implementation of minimum wages by state wage commissions. Were women's wages an important contribution to family earnings or simply a means of attaining luxuries? Should women earn enough to live independently?

Social reform in the Progressive Era

The Progressive Era was highly politicized and characterized by the creation of interest-based organizations. Predominately white male industrial workers organized under the auspices of the American Federation of Labor. Heads of large corporations coalesced with political leaders and some labor leaders in the National Civic Federation, while smaller capitalists organized the National Association of Manufacturers. Women of the expanding middle class formed both settlement houses to provide direct assistance to the poor and social reform organizations such as the National Consumers' League. They forged somewhat uneasy alliances with working-class women in the formation of Working Girls Clubs and the Women's Trade Union League. The anarcho-socialist International Workers of the World, an active Socialist Party, and widespread populist sentiments provided continuous reminders of the ongoing tensions between workers and capitalists, and between corporations and communities (see, for example, Foner 1982; Frankel and Dye 1991; Sklar 1995).

The new reform movements in the Progressive Era fostered growing awareness of the conditions of women and children in sweatshop industries. Sweatshops were small manufacturing operations, sometimes located within the home, that were characterized by crowded conditions, health and safety hazards, and minimal pay (Tax 1980; Boris 1994). Largely associated with the garment industry, sweatshops also existed in other industries such as cigar manufacturing and the production of luxury goods. The crowding of recent immigrants into urban areas in the northeast created a population vulnerable to such exploitation. Economists of the period frequently described the immigrants working in sweatshops and in other low-paid jobs as unskilled workers. But whether they possessed marketable skills or not, the immigrants were rarely in a position to bargain effectively with employers, hampered as they were by language barriers, lack of organization, and dire economic necessity.

Generally pressed into wage work by desperate economic conditions, immigrant women were forced by lack of mobility and by social custom into a limited set of jobs, at wages far below those of their male counterparts and in factories with loathsome working conditions. Young immigrant women found work in retail stores and as domestics in private homes, as well as in factories. After marriage, they were most likely to leave employment for wages (in the formal sector), but frequently continued to earn income in the informal economy through taking in boarders, doing laundry, or home assembly work (Amott and Matthaei 1996). Native-born white women of the working class followed patterns similar to immigrant women, although with access to slightly more desirable and better-paid manufacturing jobs (Murolo 1997). The attention of social reformers, however, was particularly drawn to women's factory work in sweatshops.

The reformers' focus was primarily on white women, native born and immigrant. African American women in the Northeast, often new arrivals from the South, were clustered in the lowest-paid sectors, including laundry work. African American women in the South remained primarily in agriculture. Throughout the country, African American women were hired as domestics, replacing white women who found better jobs. They were also considerably more likely to continue formal employment after marriage.

Concerns providing the impetus for protective legislation ranged from fear of contagion from purchase of clothing made in unsanitary conditions to opposition to the use of the labor of women and children to force down men's wages. Low wages, it was argued, endangered future generations through their effects on women's health. They stood in the way of efficiency and progress by giving unscrupulous and incompetent employers an advantage over their reform- and innovation-minded competitors. There was widespread conviction among reformers and economists that employers who paid below a living wage were "parasitic," a net cost to the community as a whole, since that community was called upon to fill the gap between sweated wages and a living (Power 1999). There was substantial support for legislation limiting the degree of exploitation of women workers because this legislation was seen as in the interest of the community as a whole.

State minimum wage legislation

Writing in 1927, the Women's Bureau of the U.S. Department of Labor issued a report that began, "For the past 15 years an experiment in wage regulation has been carried on in widely varying sections of the United States" (Women's Bureau 1928: 1). The experiment was the implementation of minimum wages for women workers, and its stated intention was the assurance of a living wage for women at the bottom of the wage scale. This attempt to regulate wages was bracketed between Supreme Court decisions which initially suggested that protective legislation could pass muster for women but not for men (*Lochner* v. *New York* in 1905, *Muller* v. *Oregon* in 1908), and a later decision rejecting minimum wages even for women (*Adkins* v. *Children's Hospital* in 1923).[1]

From 1912 to 1923, minimum wage legislation was passed in fifteen states, the District of Columbia, and Puerto Rico. However, many state policies were delayed by court challenges until the Supreme Court in 1917 ruled in favor of Oregon's minimum wage law. Three states repealed or never implemented their laws, and four others set inflexible flat rate minimums that quickly became irrelevant due to the high inflation between 1915 and 1920.

In all, by the Women's Bureau's calculations, ten states had active minimum wage laws for women.[2] The Women's Bureau (1928) estimated that the actual period of implementation in the ten states varied from a high of thirteen years (Washington State) to a low of under four years (District of Columbia). In 1923, in *Adkins v. Children's Hospital*, the Supreme Court struck down Washington DC's minimum wage law, effectively ending this "experiment" in gender-specific legislation. While laws remained on the books in some states, they were no longer actively enforced. It is clear from this brief summary that the experiment in wage regulation was brief, and even within that short period, it was continually contested.

Since the legislation was aimed at establishing industry-specific minimums, it required a laborious process of hearings to establish minimums on an industry-by-industry basis. This meant that even in those states with active implementation, coverage had been extended to relatively few women by 1923. In Washington, for example, the first state to actually set and implement a minimum (in April 1914), the rate was for women in mercantile establishments. Massachusetts followed two months later by assigning a minimum for the brush-making industry, in order to implement its 1912 law (Women's Bureau 1928: 11).

The reach of minimum wage laws was limited in a number of other ways as well. As the Women's Bureau noted, of the most industrialized states, only Massachusetts enacted minimum wages (Women's Bureau 1928: 7). Elsewhere, minimum wage efforts were defeated. New York, for example, had an active reformist movement that had initiated some of the earliest calls for improvements in conditions and wages for women workers. Yet it repeatedly failed to pass wage laws during the Progressive Era. This was due in part to opposition from the American Federation of Labor, concerned about a weakening of collective bargaining, and in part to division among feminist reformers who were increasingly focused on suffrage as a priority (Hart 1994: 80–3). The Women's Bureau estimated that there were only about two-thirds as many gainfully employed women in the seventeen minimum wage states and territories as there were in the eight most industrialized states without minimum wage laws (Women's Bureau 1928: 7).[3]

Even within the states covered by laws, some important low-wage women's occupations were excluded, either explicitly or by the structure of the laws. The most notable exclusions were agriculture and domestic work. While only North Dakota, Texas, and the District of Columbia explicitly excluded domestic work by law, and only North Dakota, Texas, and Arkansas explicitly excluded agriculture, in practice no state commissions actually established minimum wages for these occupations. This exclusion seemed unproblematic to the Women's Bureau, which saw it as natural for occupations in which "The character of the relationship between employer and employee would seem to make enforcement of a minimum-wage decree by a State commission difficult, if not impossible" (Women's Bureau 1928: 15). The Women's Bureau was presumably referring to the likelihood that women in these occupations lived in the households or on the farms where they worked. Yet the exclusion of these occupations severely limited the benefits of the laws for African American women, for whom the most common occupations at the time were domestic work and farm labor (see Chapter 2). A rough estimate by the U.S. Women's Bureau indicated that one-fourth of all black women lived in states with minimum wage laws but only one in ten was actually covered by the legislation (Women's Bureau 1938: 14). In effect, the implicit exclusion of African American women could be seen as an example of wages as a social practice; their segregation in exceedingly low-paid work was seen as "natural" and unproblematic, thus not requiring legislative correction.

In sum, the minimum wage legislation of the Progressive Era was extremely limited both in length of enforcement and scope of coverage. Nevertheless, the laborious and contentious process of establishing legislation and estimating living wages for the various industries covered generated a vigorous and ongoing debate that provides a wealth of insight into the role of gender, race-ethnicity, and class politics in the construction of the concept of a fair wage. Policy makers, reformers, and academic economists debated the role of markets versus societal values in the determination of wages, the responsibility of industry to the community, and the relation of a "fair" wage for women to a "fair" wage for men. They spoke of women's appropriate place in wage labor and in the family, and the use of wages to manipulate, coerce, or encourage women to assume these socially accepted roles.

The minimum wage discussions of this period resonate with the classical and Marxian economic theories of distribution, which maintained that wages have an exogenous base in societally determined levels of subsistence. These discussions further suggest that this notion of accepted living standards varied by gender, as well as class and race-ethnicity. As such, they provide insight into the origins and persistence of wage differences. The debates of the time are also deserving of attention because of the example they provide of a period in which community interests were given an articulate and relatively powerful voice. Finally, the minimum wage legislation raises provocative questions for the "equality versus difference" public policy debate.

Protective legislation for whom?

Protective legislation for women did not originate in the Progressive Era, however, this period marked the culmination of earlier campaigns both in the U.S. and overseas (see Wikander, Kessler-Harris, and Lewis 1995). The impetus for this particular wave of legislation began in the late nineteenth century, with the formation of the New York Consumers' League.[4] In 1889–90, working-class women involved in the Working Women's Society undertook a study of the conditions of women retail clerks in New York department stores. Their documentation of low wages, long hours, and poor conditions became a catalyst for reform-minded middle-class women to form an organization to press for improvements. The Consumers' League declared its purpose to be:

> to ameliorate the conditions of the women and children employed in the retail mercantile houses of New York City, by patronizing, so far as practicable, only such houses as approach in their conditions to the "Standard of a Fair House" as adopted by the League.
>
> (quoted from the constitution of the Consumers' League as adopted in 1891, in Nathan 1926: 25)

The Consumers' League constitution (quoted in Nathan 1926) began the process of defining a "fair house" by stating as its first principle that "the interest of the community demands that all workers should receive, not the lowest wage, but a fair living wage." Responsibility for assuring fair wages and conditions lay largely with the public, in the League's view, since neither workers (particularly women workers) nor employers were able unilaterally to improve conditions. The League's constitution placed responsibility firmly on consumers to discover whether the products they purchased were produced under conditions that were "at least decent, and consistent with a respectable existence on the part of the workers;" and argued that this "duty" was particularly pressing in the case of women's work "since there is no limit beyond which the wages of women may not be pressed down." Employers, they believed, were "virtually helpless" to improve conditions alone, even if they believed they should, since they would be undercut by less scrupulous firms. Progressive employers needed to be "sustained by public opinion, by law, and by the action of consumers."

The Consumers' League adopted a Standard of a Fair House (modified from a draft by the Working Women's Society) that specified hours and conditions, as well as a more rigorous definition of a fair wage. A fair house, in the League's view, gave equal pay for work of equal value, irrespective of sex. In addition, no experienced adult should receive less than six dollars a week, with only a "few instances" of earnings below eight dollars (Nathan 1926: 26–7; see also Sklar 1995).

A number of themes articulated in this early document were repeated consistently in the discussions of the minimum wage for women in the early twentieth century. First, the minimum wage was defined as a living wage, and tied to notions of decency and respectability. Second, the women workers were seen as incapable of improving their condition without outside help; they were viewed as helpless and exploited, with "no limit" to the degree of their exploitation. Third, public pressure had to be brought to bear, because competition among capitalists would prevent unilateral improvements in the conditions of their work forces even if progressive capitalists viewed those improvements favorably. Finally, the public was seen as having a compelling interest in the improvement of the condition of women workers. Establishing minimum wages, maximum hours, and acceptable conditions of work for women was not solely a charitable act, but an act of public self-preservation, since the difference between a wage and a living would be made up at the public expense through such state-level programs as mothers' pensions. This last theme, only implicit in the League's constitution, became a major component of the debate in subsequent decades.

The requirement that a fair house provide equal pay for work of equal value is also worthy of note. This principle, paying the rate for the job, may be seen as an argument for wages as a price rather than wages as a living. At the beginning of this period, this principle was not perceived as being in conflict with the notion of a gender-specific minimum wage, since women were rarely employed in the same job categories as men, and the possibility of comparing value across job categories was rarely raised. Additionally, the proposed level of the minimum wage for women was so much lower than usual wages in male occupations that a female minimum wage was not considered to affect the wages of the few women lucky enough to find a niche in a male occupation. However, these two definitions of a fair wage, the rate for the job and a living wage for the (specifically female) worker, came into conflict early in the twentieth century, as feminists began to disagree among themselves over the use of protective legislation for women workers.

As states began to legislate minimum wages for women, the process resulted in considerable discussion and debate. Although there was popular support for the legislation, there was also opposition – often from employers, but not infrequently from unions as well. Even among those in support of a minimum wage, there was ample room for debate about its specific level and the purposes it was to serve. In what follows, we will examine the discussion surrounding the establishment of minimum wages for women, focusing on the themes introduced by the newly created National Consumers' League under the leadership of Florence Kelley.[5] First, why were women, in particular, seen as requiring this protective legislation? Second, why was protecting working women seen as a compelling public interest? And third, what, precisely, constituted a living wage for a woman worker?

Why a minimum wage for women?

The National Consumers' League leadership first became acquainted with the use of minimum wages to combat sweating by looking to Great Britain, which had established industry-specific minimums in 1909. The British law, however, applied to both women and men in the sweated trades. In the translation to the United States, the legislation became gendered. Given their familiarity with the British law, social reformers' choice of a gendered strategy had to be conscious and explicit. Proponents of minimum wages for women made arguments that could be divided into three basic, not mutually exclusive, categories: (1) essentialist, (2) pragmatic, and (3) strategic. Each of these discourses provided rationales for targeting women workers under minimum wage laws.

Essentialist arguments

Arguments supporting a minimum wage for women in the Progressive Era nearly always made reference to their essentially different natures from men. Reformers often referred to working-class women as naturally timid and unable to defend their interests. In addition, some reformers believed that the inability of young women workers to bargain for adequate wages, combined with their desires for adornment and amusement, could lead them to immoral behavior. Popular literature in the late nineteenth and early twentieth centuries offered cautionary tales of poor working girls led into prostitution. These accounts became increasingly racialized in the early twentieth century in response to the wave of immigration from southern and eastern Europe and African American migration from the South to eastern cities. Native-born middle-class club women often viewed the new arrivals as morally weak. Historian Priscilla Murolo notes:

> Polite society's aspersions on working women's character were now aimed for the most part at race-specific targets. . . . Genteel reformers involved in protective work on behalf of new immigrants or African American migrants from the South regularly broadcast warnings that women from these groups were apt to wind up in houses of sin if left to their own devices.
>
> (Murolo 1997: 130–1)

Perhaps because of this racialized content, many more progressive reformers chose to skirt the issue of prostitution, and spoke more generally about the problem of living "decently" on low wages. In addition, reformers were worried about moral pitfalls short of prostitution, stemming from the need of the impoverished inhabitant of a one-room tenement apartment to entertain male guests in the presence of her bed or to depend on a male friend for her supper.

Essentialist arguments about women's wages offer a clear example of wages as a social practice. Women's wages needed to be neither so high nor so low that they jeopardized hierarchical gender roles. Most reformers were in agreement that women's natures were such that they were uniquely in need of familial and public defense. But more importantly, most reformers believed that women's appropriate role was in the home, not in the workplace (see, for example, Kelley 1912: 1003). Waged work was to occupy a relatively brief interlude between an early-ending childhood and the life of marriage and motherhood that was to be every woman's true vocation.[6] As such, women earned wages on a different basis than men, as temporary and presumably casual workers. It seemed inevitable then that their wages should diverge markedly from those of men. Economist C. E. Persons, in an analysis of data documenting women's role as young, unskilled temporary workers, argued, "In the total labor force they form a separate non-competing group lower than any male group" (1915: 233). Further, according to this view, their wages needed only to support themselves, while men's wages needed to support a family.

Despite this "natural" divergence of wages, however, there was need for public vigilance to ensure that women's wages did not fall below the level necessary for decency and morality because working women were the future "mothers of the race." Taking their cue from the *Muller* ruling validating protective legislation, reformers argued that women who were weakened by long hours and poor diets jeopardized their all-important future role (see, for example, Hutchinson 1919: 82). The combination of weaker natures and the overriding importance of fulfilling their destinies as mothers made societal protection seem appropriate for them in a way it was not for men. This assumption about women's proper role was deeply held and rarely questioned. Those arguing for a more generous minimum tended to point out that a young woman needed to be able to afford a good outfit so that she could attend church socials and other respectable events where she might find a proper husband.

In addition, establishing a minimum wage specifically for women seemed logical because women and men were seen by most participants in the public discourse as differing in fundamental ways in their consumption needs. Much of the difference can be explained by the assumption that men needed to support families on their wages. But beyond this, men and women were viewed as different in their habits and customs and in their biological requirements to such a great degree that establishing a living wage specifically for women seemed quite unproblematic. It was commonplace in setting up subsistence budgets to calculate expenses separately for men and for women. Women's budgets differed from men's in, among other factors, the presumption that they required less food. Benjamin Rowntree, a British social reformer of the period, for example, calculated that an adult man might require eight ounces of bread and one-and-one-half pints of porridge for breakfast, while a woman would require only four ounces of bread and one pint of porridge (cited in Armstrong 1932: 669).

Indeed, the Women's Bureau, in its review of state minimum wage laws, complained about the prevalence of men on the wage boards that established minimum budgets, arguing, "When it is realized that these boards were engaged in determining how much it cost working women to live, it is amazing that a task whose problems were those of most women should have been given so largely to men" (Women's Bureau 1928: 87). Men, the Women's Bureau and other authors suggested, didn't have a clue; women's lives, needs, and lifestyles were too fundamentally different from theirs.

Pragmatic arguments

The second and third categories of arguments for gender-specific legislation – pragmatic and strategic – were frequently permeated with essentialist language as well, but represent separate strands of thought. Pragmatic arguments pointed out that women were the lowest-paid workers and that their wages frequently left them in desperate circumstances. Government studies published from 1905 on, combined with reports by economists and social reformers, consistently documented that women's wages were in many cases below what was considered the minimally accepted level of subsistence, and consistently well below the wages earned by men (Persons 1915: 208–19; Hutchinson 1919: 15–27; Brandeis 1935: 503; Tentler 1979: 17f.; Meyerowitz 1988: 34). The Triangle Shirtwaist fire in New York City in 1911 focused public attention and indignation on the condition of working women and provided an impetus for legislation.[7]

Legislation was seen as the appropriate means to raise wages for women because they were almost entirely nonunionized.[8] Economists of the period frequently argued that workers would be able to earn a wage reflecting their worth only when they were organized to bargain collectively with employers.[9] Singly, they were too ill-informed and desperate to make a good bargain (Seager 1913: 82; Webb and Webb 1920: 655–6; Seligman 1926: 429). Economist John Bates Clark, one of the founders of neoclassical wage theory, for example, reluctantly endorsed the principle of a minimum wage for this reason: "Hunger-discipline disqualifies the worker for making a successful bargain, and if the employer were everywhere at liberty to take men for what, under such pressure, they might individually offer to work for, he might get them for very little" (1913: 292).

While unorganized male workers were disadvantaged in bargaining with employers, economists and reformers argued, this disadvantage was compounded for women workers. The typical woman worker was young, unmarried, and relatively unskilled, and had been raised to show deference toward older men. How was such a woman, reformers asked, to be expected to defend her interests in the workplace (see, for example, Hutchinson 1919)? Often recent arrivals from the countryside or from Europe, the women lacked information about local wage rates. They were under family pressure to work and, in many cases, turned their pay envelopes over unopened to their mothers at the end of the week (Persons 1915).

In fact, Persons argued, the presence of young wage-earning women was a symptom of the "bankrupt condition of the working families" (Persons 1915: 227). Women were working to provide badly needed support to their families, in situations where every penny counted. This dire necessity, compounded by their inexperience and lack of mobility, forced women workers to accept far below a living wage. To this analysis, Barnard College economist Emilie Hutchinson added the role played by institutionalized discrimination: "Custom and tradition in themselves dictate the offering of lower wages to women than to men and put definite limits on their occupations and opportunities" (1919: 66).

Strategic arguments

There were strategic reasons as well for advocating minimum wages and other protective legislation specifically for women. In the face of growing industrialization and conflict between workers and employers, court rulings beginning in the late nineteenth century increasingly defined male workers' rights in terms of the individual's "right" to compete freely in the market-place (Holcombe 1912; Kessler-Harris 1990; Hart 1994). In what was seen as a definitive ruling in 1905, *Lochner v. New York*, the Supreme Court over-turned a law limiting working hours of male bakers, asserting that bakers' freedom of contract was unduly curtailed. The hours "in which grown and intelligent men may labor to earn their living" was to be determined between those men and their employers.

As a result of this ruling, many reformers believed it was pointless to advocate gender-neutral policies. Since the decision in *Muller v. Oregon* in 1908, however, the Court seemed willing to allow protection for women workers, specifically because they were in a weaker bargaining position in the labor force and because the government could be said to have an abiding interest in their health and morals as future mothers (Vogel 1993: 21–5; Hart 1994: 91–2). Passing protective legislation for women, then, not only pro-vided some protection to these most exploited of workers, but also was a legislative strategy that could at times improve conditions for men as well. For example, if an eight-hour day was established for women in a factory, the men who worked in the factory might also achieve an eight-hour day if it was impracticable to operate the factory without the women. Setting a minimum wage for women would provide a floor for male wages as well, keeping wom-en's low wages from becoming a "menace to the wage standards men (had) struggled to establish and maintain" (Hutchinson 1919: 13). Gender-based protective legislation was potentially an opening wedge for class-based protection.

Minimum wages as a compelling public interest

Clearly, one reason the public was seen as benefiting from higher wages for women stemmed from its abiding interest in a healthy and well-brought-up next generation. Women as "mothers of the race" (a phrase used repeatedly in the discussion of the time) were a social asset; and weak, sickly, or immoral women who brought forth unhealthy or disruptive children were a liability. This was the logic of *Muller v. Oregon* and the impetus behind much of the support for state legislation protecting women workers. For example, the slogan of clubwomen who were the force behind the minimum wage in California was "Employed womanhood must be protected in order to foster

THE WOMAN WORKER

WAGES MAKE THE DIFFERENCE

Shall we build our national life on the underpaid work of tired women or on a foundation of strength, vitality and eager effort?

Plate 5.1 "The Woman Worker." Poster advocating higher wages for women, from a general photographic file of the Women's Bureau

Source: courtesy of National Archives (photo no. 86-G-9K-4)

the motherhood of the race" (Women's Bureau 1928: 130). A rationale for regulating wages was to sustain social practices that preserved pre-existing gender relations in which women were defined as mothers.

The phrase "mothers of the race" is illuminating. Protective legislation during the Progressive Era was rationalized in part on the basis of society's interest in women's reproductive responsibilities. The exclusion of occupations held by African American women was indicative of the *absence* of a perceived social interest in their mothering role. As noted by historian Eileen Boris, the exclusion of jobs held by women of color from protective legislation "suggests how the term 'mother' in the judge-made discourse [of the *Muller* decision] referred to white women" (1993: 234). It was the white race whose social reproduction was at stake in these early attempts at labor legislation.

Many participants in the discussion of minimum wages in the early decades of the twentieth century expressed a suspicion of industry and its tendency to take advantage. There was a sense of community or public values at war with the amorality and unabashed greed of capitalism. Following Fabian socialists Beatrice and Sidney Webbs' influential parasitic industries argument, economists and reformers argued that employers who paid less than a living wage to women workers were parasitic on the community, because they were being, in effect, subsidized by the wages of other family members or by public charity. Industries not paying a living wage were a liability, not an asset, to the community. If they could not improve, it was preferable that they leave or even go out of business (see also Holcombe 1912: 34; Seager 1913: 90; Hutchinson 1919: 82–3). Maud Swartz of the Women's Trade Union League expressed this sense of the priority of community over industrial interests very strongly at a Women's Bureau conference:

> Will a living wage . . . tend to close down certain industries in the United States? Yes and no. We will not deny that it will tend to close down the industries that prosper purely on low standards. . . . They are nothing but people who are living on the bounty of the Nation. . . . It is not only other industries and other workers who are supplementing these people, but the vast aggregate of charitable organizations that are maintained throughout this country, and into which millions of public and private funds are poured yearly. Therefore we say that, yes, it will force out the inefficient businesses; it will force out the inefficient employers. And I say God speed the day!
>
> (Swartz in Women's Bureau 1923b: 80–1)

This concern about parasitic industries causing a net loss to the community was powerful and pervasive in discussions of both the need for a minimum wage for women and the requisite level for that wage. Academics, reformers, and public opinion frequently asserted that employers had a social obligation to pay a living wage. But calculations of how much it cost a woman to live depended on the lifestyle considered appropriate for women, reflecting the dynamics of wages as a social practice.

Defining a minimum wage for women

Assumptions about lifestyle patterns played a crucial role in the calculations of minimum wages for women. Women were assumed to spend most of their lives as economically dependent members of families. Wage earning was to be a relatively brief interlude in a woman's life, while for men earning (and supporting dependents) was seen as extending over their life cycle. Nevertheless, within these generally held assumptions about women's natures and appropriate roles, there was room for considerable disagreement about what constituted the minimum wage necessary for health and decency. These disagreements, moreover, reflected fundamental political differences.

Writing in the *Quarterly Journal of Economics* in 1920, economist Dorothy Douglas of the University of Washington categorized the debate over what constituted a living wage for women workers into five basic views or "theories" (Douglas 1920: 225). First, was the "pin-money theory," suggesting that women's wages need cover only part of their expenses. This theory Douglas termed "ultra-reactionary," although she noted that in practice it described a reality of meager earnings for many working-class women. Second, "joint-cost theory" presumed the worker lived with her family, and "that her wage, in order not to be parasitic, must cover simply her individual expenses in the family group." Third, "temporary independence theory," argued that the wage must be sufficient for the daily support of a woman living away from her family (in the parlance of the day, a woman "adrift"). Fourth, "permanent independence theory" argued that a living wage must not only support the daily needs of a woman adrift, but also provide sufficient income for insurance and savings for periods of illness and for old age. Finally, "family support theory" argued that a woman, like a man, should earn a family wage, enough to support dependents. This theory Douglas termed "ultra-radical."

As states set up wage boards and held hearings to determine the appropriate minimum wage for women, most of the discussion clearly fell into the middle three categories. Employers most often argued for a joint-cost (or, at times, pin money) notion of a living wage, pointing out that most working women lived with their families, particularly among low-wage earners (see Women's Bureau 1928). Sears, Roebuck and Company and Lord and Taylor department stores, in fact, testified to state commissions that they made it their policy in low-wage positions *only* to hire women who lived at home (cited in Weiner 1985: 75).

The economy of family life

This argument for establishing a minimum wage based on women's presumably lower costs of living within a family group was defended by Harvard economist Frank W. Taussig, writing in the *Quarterly Journal of Economics* in 1916. Taussig disagreed with the finding of the Massachusetts wage commission that a living wage for a woman worker should be $8.00 a week. He pointed out that the majority of women workers lived with their families, and argued for the existence of an "economy of family life," asking rhetorically: "Suppose that into the budget of a family whose head earns $12.00 or $15.00 a week, a girl brings an additional $6.00. . . . Is the girl . . . a parasite? Is she a drag or a prop?" (Taussig 1916: 417–19). Taussig apparently misread reformers' arguments that it was the *employer* who paid less than a living wage who was viewed as a parasite, not the *worker*.

Advocates for a wage based on the costs of a woman adrift offered three justifications. First, they attempted to refute the notion of economies of family life, arguing that calculations such as Taussig's failed to take into consideration all the costs of support for a woman worker, in particular her share of the value of her mother's domestic labor. Second, they questioned whether families of low-wage women workers in fact lived at the standard of decency implied in the minimum wage statutes. And third, they argued that employers who benefited from women's labor had responsibility to pay the full support of that labor, without subsidy from other family members, private charities, or public funds.

Dorothy Douglas set out to specifically challenge Taussig's argument for economies of family life. She argued that he treated the "expenses of the woman at home as supplementary to, rather than an integral part of, the family budget" (1920: 235). Douglas estimated the living costs of a working woman living at home, including not only her share of the expenses of rent, fuel, food, and so on, but also her share of support of the housewife/mother whose services she employed. At a time when Douglas' study of women adrift in Philadelphia suggested minimum necessary expenses of $9.05 a week, her estimate of the expenses of a woman at home (including her mother's services) was $7.80, only $1.25 less (1920: 245–6).

Further, Douglas noted, this estimate assumed that the father was earning an adequate wage himself. Wages of unskilled male workers, however, had not risen as fast as prices in the inflationary climate of World War I, making this assumption increasingly unrealistic. She concluded:

> In the face of such facts, how dare we assume that the lower-class working woman at home is necessarily the member of a "standard" family? And if she is not – if her family is substandard – how dare we assume that it will cost her less than the girl who boards to secure the food and shelter she needs?
>
> (Douglas 1920: 249–50)

Similarly, Barnard economist Emilie Hutchinson (1919) cited studies in both Massachusetts and New York that found that when the value of the mother's labor was included as an expense, very little savings were to be had by living at home. Echoing Douglas, she added:

> Families in which a normal standard of living obtains and where the daughters are at work in manufacturing establishments are probably very exceptional. If, then, the family plane of living is below the minimum requirements of a normal standard, it is apparent that the fact that a wage-earning girl lives at home does not assure her the necessities of a decent and reasonable existence. . . . Living at home under these circumstances simply means sharing the common adversity.
>
> (Hutchinson 1919: 47)

Douglas herself advocated a temporary independence minimum – which she argued was roughly the equivalent of a properly calculated joint-cost minimum – as the standard. Her reasoning was that, in fact, most working women live outside their families for only a short period of their lives. Most become wives and mothers, and "of those who remain celibate or become widowed, a large proportion naturally fit before long into some family circle" (Douglas 1920: 256). Widows and other women supporting dependents were a rare occurrence, in her view, and should in any event be supported by pensions or institutional care rather than wage labor. Finally, the needs of single women in old age could be provided from within the temporary independence budget, by thrift in middle age that would come, depressingly, from "savings naturally incident upon the decreased expenditure of the older woman for clothing and amusements" (Douglas 1920: 256).

Ultra-radicals and a family wage for women

Douglas' arguments reflected the widespread concern among reformers who wished to improve the living standard of wage-earning women without challenging the priority given to their roles as wives, mothers, and dependents on male breadwinners. Given this concern, it is possible to see why Douglas could view those reformers calling for a family wage for women as "ultra-radicals." Douglas particularly targeted Mary Van Kleeck as an advocate of a minimum wage enabling family support. Van Kleeck had been an investigator with the Russell Sage Foundation, researching the conditions of women workers in New York sweatshops and producing books and testimony that were influential in the establishment of protective legislation for women. During World War I, she began working for the Labor Department. She was appointed head of the Women in Industry Service when it was formed in July 1918 to oversee conditions of women involved in war work. The office was the precursor to the Women's Bureau, and Van Kleeck was an active and influential head. She acted quickly to enforce laws limiting work hours and protecting women in hazardous industries (Lieberman 1971).

In October 1918, Van Kleeck convened what the *Monthly Labor Review* described as the first conference of trade union women ever called by the U.S. government to develop a platform of principles to govern the employment of women in industry. This conference strongly endorsed the principle of equal pay for equal work by women and men, "which, according to the delegates, is not now the case," and called for "the fixation, by wage boards, of a minimum wage for women, not on the basis of a living for a woman alone, but for the support of a woman with dependents, just as for a man with dependents" ("Conference of Trade-Union Women" 1918: 1341). These wage principles, however, did not become part of the contractual obligations issued by governmental agencies for their wartime contracts (Van Kleeck 1919: 90), and the Women's Trade Union League complained repeatedly about employers paying women less than men for the same work (Lieberman 1971: 366).

After the signing of the armistice at the conclusion of World War I, the Women in Industry Service drafted a statement of standards for employment of women in industry, recognizing that the federal government would need a new method of enforcing labor standards, "since the power of enforcement resting on its contracts with industry was decreased with the curtailment of contracts" (Van Kleeck 1919: 90). Along with provisions on hours, working conditions, and supervision, Van Kleeck reiterated the principles of equal pay for equal work and the provision of a minimum wage that would "cover the cost of living for dependents and not merely for the individual" (1919: 91). Van Kleeck offered two justifications for paying women a family wage, drawing on the ideas that wages provided a living as well as constituting a social practice with the power to affect gender relations. First, paying single-support wages to women could undercut the wages of male workers since "women have entered a wider range of occupations it will be possible for them to become unwilling competitors of men in lowering standards of wages." Second, Van Kleeck asserted that "women are working to earn a living and the facts show that many are also supporting dependents" (1919: 93).

It was this last assertion that Dorothy Douglas focused upon in critiquing the family support theory of the minimum wage, which she asserted was "bristling . . . with inconsistencies and hasty generalizations" and more in keeping with the statements of trade unionists and feminists than "the published statements of a federal agency" (Douglas 1920: 236). Douglas and other opponents of the family wage argument denied that women in any numbers supported dependents in the same sense that men did. Since the typical wage-earning woman was single and living with her parents, her paycheck could be seen as *supplementing family income*, but "it would be absurd to compare the amount of their per capita obligation to that of the typical workingman" (Douglas 1920: 238).

While Douglas' arguments are logical, the intensity of her opposition to family support arguments is intriguing. Perhaps she feared that such ultra-radical demands would jeopardize the passage of more minimum wage laws for women. Or perhaps these arguments, redolent with trade unionism and feminism, seemed a dangerous challenge to the male breadwinner model that underlay Douglas' analysis. Van Kleeck had not made a clear argument, however, about why women's support of dependents should be seen as comparable with men's. In correspondence with Douglas in November 1918, she simply stated that "in general the typical unmarried wage-earning woman is a member of a family in which there are dependents, sometimes the father, sometimes the mother, sometimes young brothers or sisters, or a combination of all three" (quoted in Douglas 1920: 238).

Van Kleeck's influence, however, can be seen in subsequent work by the Women's Bureau, the successor to the Women in Industry Service. Beginning with its founding in 1920, the Women's Bureau began a series of studies documenting that a substantial minority of wage-earning women were supporting dependents, either partially or as sole breadwinners in their families (see Women's Bureau 1923a). With titles such as *What the Wage-Earning Woman Contributes to Family Support* (Peterson 1929), *The Employed Woman Homemaker in the United States: Her Responsibility for Family Support* (Pidgeon 1936), and *Employed Women and Family Support* (Pidgeon and Mettert 1939), the Bureau sought to substantiate the number of employed women, their earnings and working conditions, and the value of their labor toward "the economic life of the nation" (Peterson 1929: 3). According to the Women's Bureau, their research offered "conclusive evidence of the fact that women's contribution to family support is considerable. In fact, the data suggest that in many homes in the United States women form the last line of economic defense" (Peterson 1929: 1). This was true for both single and married women (Pidgeon and Mettert 1939). Marriage failed to give women economic security, in part because many homes relied upon two incomes. These studies were part of an attempt to redefine the notion of a family wage to apply to women as well as to men.

Wage commission policies

Despite the evidence that many women did support dependents on their wages, the argument for a family wage for women played little role in the policy debates as states established their minimum wage guidelines. Virtually all advocates for the minimum wage argued for a wage based on the expenses of a woman living independently from her family, but without dependents. It is striking that this is the standard that was adopted in all the states which passed minimum wages for women, despite lobbying by employers. Wage commissions accepted reformers' arguments, based on parasitic industries analysis, that employers of women had to pay the full cost of their support, without a subsidy from the earnings of other, higher wage earners (generally male) in the family (Women's Bureau 1928: 75).

But having adopted this general principle, state commissions still faced considerable disagreement about what, exactly, comprised a "decent and acceptable" standard of living. Wage boards generally included representatives of labor, of employers, and of the "public."[10] In their search for an objective basis for a minimum decent cost of living for working women, wage boards commissioned detailed budget studies. Not surprisingly, these budgets, and the arguments within the boards about them, reflected the fundamental subjectivity of the figures debated. In Elizabeth Brandeis' words, employers

> usually questioned the inclusion of many items such as laundry or vacation or 'party dress' or 'best hat'. . . . How much is necessary to spend on a dress or a coat which is to last two years? Which is the least for which a healthful lunch can be bought?
>
> (Brandeis 1935: 525)

In one case, an employer alienated the public members of the Board by apparently questioning the need for lunch at all, declaring that he had convinced the American Society for the Prevention of Cruelty to Animals (ASPCA) that his horses were better off with only two meals a day (Brandeis 1935: 527f.).

Douglas' useful distinction between temporary and permanent independence does not appear to have explicitly entered discussions in front of the wage boards, but it was certainly implicit in the struggles over budgets. Formally, most states adopted criteria for a fair minimum wage that seemed to fit Douglas' description of permanent independence, a wage that would permit a lifetime of living outside a family (but not supporting dependents). Massachusetts, for example, adopted guidelines for its wage boards that instructed them to include in their budgets medical expenses, vacation, a reserve for emergencies, mutual association dues, and insurance (Women's Bureau 1928: 127). However, despite these formal guidelines, according to Brandeis, in Massachusetts and other states "in the end the rate arrived at was almost always a compromise" (1935: 527), and rates were frequently set below the estimated cost of living. The Women's Bureau echoed Brandeis' observation, commenting wryly, "It seems probable that constant repetition of the phrase 'economies of family life' has influenced these determinations, even when official statements maintain that all workers should be self-supporting" (Women's Bureau 1928: 75).

Race also factored into calculations of the appropriate minimum wage, as illustrated in the process of wage setting for laundry workers in Washington, DC. Laundry work was hot, strenuous, and very poorly paid. In Washington, DC, at the time minimum wages were instituted, 90 percent of laundry workers were black women (Giddings 1984: 146). The Washington, DC,

Wage Board estimated an across-the-board minimum adequate weekly wage of $16.00 in 1918 (Women's Bureau 1928: 134). However, actual minimum wages were to be set by industry conferences involving representatives of employers, labor, and the public. Despite the recommendation of the Wage Board, the laundry conference initially proposed a $14.50 minimum. The Wage Board objected, and raised explicit concerns about racial bias: "Since women employed in laundries are predominantly colored it was alleged that the lower rate was due to a crystallization by the conference of the popular belief that it cost colored people less to live than white" (quoted in Hart 1992: 13). A compromise rate of only $15.00 was narrowly approved by the laundry conference, and put in place in 1921.[11] This rate was not only below the minimum adequate rate estimated by the Wage Board, but was also below the rates for other industries. Table 5.1 indicates that higher minimum wages had already been established in the printing and publishing, mercantile, and hotel and restaurant industries. Wage setting for laundry workers did not follow these precedents.

The end of an era: the defeat of minimum wages for women

Just as the Supreme Court decisions in the *Lochner* and *Muller* cases could be seen as influential in focusing reformers' efforts on gender-specific minimum wage legislation, the 1923 *Adkins* v. *Children's Hospital* decision effectively ended the experiment. Momentum, though, had been lost earlier. No new legislation was passed after 1919, and the movement was shaken by legislative losses in Ohio in 1921 and, devastatingly, in New York, the birthplace of the National Consumers' League, in 1920. A number of forces converged to effectively end the Progressive Era and, with it, this phase of the minimum wage movement. The socialist revolution in Russia in 1917 and anti-immigrant sentiment in the United States were used by employers to lobby against labor reform legislation. An organization called the Associated Manufacturers of New York, for example, organized a "League for Americanism" in 1920, which accused Progressive reformers of "Bolshevik propaganda" (Lieberman 1971: 399–400).

In addition, the surge in demand for women's labor during World War I had resulted in increased pay. Although the 100 percent inflation during the

Table 5.1 Minimum wage rates established in Washington, DC (by sector), 1919–21

Industry	Weekly rate ($)	Year
Printing and publishing	15.50	1919
Mercantile	16.50	1919
Hotel and restaurant	16.50	1920
Laundry	15.00	1921

Source: U.S. Department of Labor, Women's Bureau (1928: 134–6)

period from 1915 to 1920 meant that real wages had risen little or not at all, public support weakened in the face of higher money wages. Historian Jacob Lieberman comments, "the average person remembered pre-war prices and wages and found it hard to feel sorry for the 'poor working girl' who was earning $12 or $13 a week" (1971: 404).

The victory of the suffrage movement with the Nineteenth Amendment in 1920 also diluted support, and, in fact, would be cited by the Supreme Court as part of the justification for rejecting Washington, DC's minimum wage law. Post-suffrage public opinion was less inclined to view women as needing special treatment. In addition, the middle-class feminist movement that had finally won suffrage was beginning to focus its attention on new employment opportunities for young, unmarried middle- and upper-class women. These women were entering jobs in clerical work, teaching, and social work, and even, in a small number of cases, traditionally male professions. Some feminists, most particularly Alice Paul of the National Woman's Party, came to see protective legislation, including minimum wages, as an impediment to their goal of equality. Not only could some of the legislation – largely limits on hours and night work – exclude women from desirable male occupations, but also, in their view, the protection, and the usual justifications for it, suggested that women were childlike and less competent than men to make decisions for themselves. Praising the Supreme Court's decision in the *Adkins* case, the National Woman's Party's journal *Equal Rights* concluded, "one can feel that at last the world is beginning to realize that women are adult human beings" (April 1923, cited in Lieberman 1971: 423).

In *Adkins v. Children's Hospital*, the Supreme Court ruled that Washington, DC's minimum wage law violated women's freedom of contract as guaranteed by the Fifth Amendment's due process provisions. The opinion, written by Justice George Sutherland, argued that the *Muller* decision could not be applied to the minimum wage in the District of Columbia because mandating wages interfered with the conducting of business to a degree that hours limits did not. According to *Adkins*, wages represented "the heart of the contract." A minimum set above the "fair value of the services rendered" would be in effect "a compulsory exaction from the employer for the support of a partially indigent person." The Justice thus asserted that price ("fair value") should triumph over subsistence needs or living standards as a rationale for wage setting. However, Justice Sutherland also invoked the familiar "economies of the family group," arguing that the minimum amount necessary to a woman's support depended on her individual situation (including her intelligence and habits of thrift, as well as her living situation) and could not be standardized. Further, he suggested that the justification for any protective legislation might be past, since the Nineteenth Amendment (women's suffrage) and other, unspecified, changes in the "political and civil status of women" had brought their differences from men "almost, if not quite, to the vanishing point" (*Adkins v. Children's Hospital* 1923).

The argument against special treatment in the Sutherland decision echoed the arguments made by Alice Paul as head of the National Woman's Party as it attempted to have Congress pass an Equal Rights Amendment (ERA) that would broadly prohibit unequal treatment.[12] Indeed, some historians suspect Paul of active participation in the defeat of Washington, DC's minimum wage (see, for example, Zimmerman 1991; Storrs 2000). In any event, the *Adkins* decision effectively ended the era of gender-specific minimum wages. Although some laws remained on states' books, there was little hope for rigorous enforcement.

Feminist reformers who had supported protective legislation, such as Florence Kelley, began to formulate new directions, even before the *Adkins* decision was rendered. For many, gender-specific minimum wage legislation had been a strategy fostered at least as much by necessity as by conviction, and they began to build arguments for a universal minimum wage law. Others believed that women workers' weak bargaining position still made protection necessary and that the proposed ERA would leave women in the sweatshops vulnerable to exploitation. Alice Paul had initially agreed to include a clause permitting protective legislation in the wording of her equal rights amendment. But over time she became convinced that gender-specific protection was not compatible with equality (Zimmerman 1991: 217). A tactical and ideological split thus emerged between feminists who placed their hopes on passage of an Equal Rights Amendment and the fundamental equality between men and women and those at the National Consumers' League and elsewhere who continued to focus on the specific problems of working-class women. This division has been termed the "equality-versus-difference" debate, juxtaposing two approaches to improving women's status (Kessler-Harris 1987). Yet some historians note that even the social feminists in the National Consumers' League were shifting their rhetoric from protection to rights during this period, prior as well as subsequent to the *Adkins* decision (Lipschultz 1996).

University of Chicago professor and consumer economist Sophonisba Breckinridge's remarks to the 1923 Conference on Women in Industry, later expanded into an article in the *Journal of Political Economy*, illustrate both the objections of social reformers to an Equal Rights Amendment and their arguments for a gender-neutral minimum wage. Her critique of the reasoning behind the women's rights slogan "equal pay to men and women for equal work" (1923: 521) noted that women rarely had opportunities to perform work "equal" to men's. Further, Breckinridge argued, wages were determined neither by the value of the work nor by the needs of the worker, but rather by the bargaining position of the worker. Women's disadvantaged bargaining position meant that "the bargain becomes rather an instrument in exploitation than a free contract" (1923: 523).

Women needed wage protection, in Breckinridge's view. But as long as their minimum wages were lower than men's normal rates there would be a temptation to replace men with cheaper women workers, with the risk that women be viewed as "the perpetual scab(s) in industry" (1923: 523). Building on research done by reformers in England and by the Women's Bureau in the United States, Breckinridge repeated Van Kleeck's argument for a family wage for women, reinterpreting the concept of a "breadwinner" as a worker who was partially or wholly responsible for the support of other family members rather than the sole or primary provider for the family. Presenting data that showed that many women workers had dependents (and that some male workers did not), Breckinridge argued that "no safe line can be drawn between the sexes on the basis of the support of dependents" (1923: 535). Although Breckinridge and other reformers were aware that minimum wages for men were not politically possible in the United States in the 1920s, they were clearly beginning to build a case for a uniform wage, for both men and women, at a level that would recognize the need to support a family. Chapter 6, therefore, continues the story of the fight for legislated minimum wages, examining the enactment of an ostensibly gender-neutral, federally mandated wage floor.

Conclusion

The debate surrounding the rise and ultimate defeat of minimum wages for women clearly included arguments for wages as a living, as a social practice, and as a price. Wages as a living, and the belief that women workers were entitled to a living wage, were at the heart of the initiative. Employers who hired their labor had a moral obligation to the women and to the community to provide for their support; to fail to do so meant the employer was parasitic, a net cost to the community. As we have seen, this view that wages constituted a living was widely held. Even employers arguing against the minimum tended to emphasize that women's needs were low – because of the economies of family life – rather than denying their obligation to pay a living.

While wages as a living can be seen as the impetus behind the legislation, wages as a social practice informed the debate over its implementation in two ways. First, many supporters of minimum wages for women raised the argument that poorly paid women workers might be substituted for male workers, undermining the male breadwinner wage, and with it the male breadwinner family. Moreover, the debate over the level at which women's minimum wages should be set reveals deeper questions about how women should live. Should they be living as dependent members of male-headed families, earning a supplementary income? Should they earn enough to live "adrift," supporting themselves independently over their lifetimes? Should they earn enough to themselves support dependents? As we have seen, toward the end of this period and continuing into the 1930s, the Women's Bureau and some of its supporters began an intriguing campaign to appropriate and reinterpret the concept of breadwinner in a way that could include women workers.

Many participants in the debate made reference to wages as a price as well. Reformers used market-based arguments when they claimed that women workers lacked the bargaining strength to command their fair wage from employers. Employers at times raised the notion of wages as a price, arguing that women were paid low wages because they were inexperienced and unproductive; their labor was not worth more than the current wage. Raising wages would simply force them out of work. Interestingly, economists who supported minimum wages often agreed that some workers would be unemployed as a result, but argued that this would be a desirable outcome. Forcing employers to pay a living wage, these economists argued, would bring to the attention of the community those members who were "unemployable," defined as unable to command a market wage sufficient for their support. The state could then take responsibility to offer training and education to those who would benefit from it and poor relief to those who could not (Holcombe 1912; Seager 1913). Ultimately, the argument for wages as a price was employed by the Supreme Court in the *Adkins* case to defeat the minimum wage initiative. As was clear from Justice Sutherland's language, pride of place was to be given to "fair value of the services rendered," as determined by market forces.

The defeat of state-level minimum wages for women can be seen as at least a temporary victory of the understanding of wages as a price over wages as a living. Further, the apparent involvement of Alice Paul in the defeat of the minimum wage and Sutherland's references to women's newly won right to vote suggest that shifting understandings of wages as a social practice, at least for women of the growing middle class, were also important. In these new views, protection was becoming an impediment to access to traditionally male jobs. Working-class women and their allies, faced with harsher working conditions and less sense of expanding opportunity, continued to view protection as desirable. The legal rulings validating wages as a price thus reflect a new sense of the social location of some, mainly middle-class, women during the period, at the expense of those with fewer social privileges. Wages as a price arguments, in this sense, were not socially neutral in terms of whose living or social norms they favored.

6 A living for breadwinners
The federal minimum wage

The devastating onslaught of the Great Depression, rising political pressure against *laissez-faire* economic doctrines, and the experimental policy approach of newly elected Democratic President Franklin Delano Roosevelt changed the climate and context for wage regulations. Wage and hour laws, the hallmarks of protective legislation for women and children during the Progressive Era, became national, gender-neutral regulations in the Fair Labor Standards Act (FLSA) of 1938. In fact, during Congressional testimony on the proposed legislation, William Green, President of the American Federation of Labor (AFL) asserted

> The act is not a minimum wage law for women and minors. It is designed to establish minimum wage standards under very limited and special circumstances for workers engaged in the private industries covered by the act – men as well as women.
>
> (U.S. Congress 1937: 219)

The enactment of federal wage and hour legislation during the New Deal was significant on many levels. It was an accomplishment for networks of social reformers who succeeded in institutionalizing their policy program. The New Deal welfare state was a direct outgrowth of female-led organizations, such as settlement houses and the National Consumers' League, created to ameliorate the sweatshop conditions of factory labor in urban areas. The first drafts of the U.S. welfare state were written at the state level early in the twentieth century, as reformers moved from providing social services for the poor to demanding state intervention in economic affairs. The drafts became text during the Depression, as the Supreme Court legitimated the welfare state and Congress passed legislation that reshaped the political economy.

For fifteen years following its 1923 decision in *Adkins* v. *Children's Hospital* nullifying the District of Columbia's minimum wage law, the Supreme Court remained a primary obstacle to passage of wage regulations. A minimum wage, especially one that covered male employees, also threatened the comparative advantage of southern industry seeking to attract business investment, the labor systems of low-wage agricultural employers in the

South and California, the vested interests of some unions, and the brotherhood of working-class masculinity that suffused the emerging mass-production manufacturing industries. Proponents of minimum wage legislation had to define the coverage of the FLSA narrowly in order to surmount these obstacles. Legal protection was limited primarily to a particular segment of unorganized workers who could not achieve living wages through collective bargaining.

In the past, the controversy between collective bargaining and state protection has been analyzed primarily as a "turf war" fought by the leaders of organized labor who feared that government involvement in wage setting would usurp their role. However, this is only one way of understanding the tenuous tightrope walked by advocates of a gender-neutral minimum wage. Another approach is to consider the gendered and racialized meaning of inclusion and exclusion in the legislation's provisions. Minimum wage laws had been associated with a discourse of weak and irrational workers who could not bargain for themselves – women and children. Such measures were difficult to reconcile with hegemonic concepts of masculinity. Extending state protection to some men led the relatively privileged craft workers represented by AFL unions to distance themselves and their members from protected classes of workers by differentiating among forms of masculinity. Union men who collectively bargained for wages were distinct from men who attained a living wage from the state, and a living wage for one group was not the same as a living wage for the other. Further, both of these groups were implicitly separate from those men and women exempted from coverage under the FLSA, especially African Americans.

Therefore, besides redefining the relationship between the state and the economy, the provisions of the FLSA constituted a series of social practices with the power to disrupt or maintain gender, class, and racial-ethnic hierarchies. In addition to debating the role of living costs, purchasing power, labor supply and demand, and productivity in setting wages, debates over the language in the FLSA reveal the process of redefining masculinities during this period of economic crisis. The New Deal extended the right to living wages and the perquisites of breadwinner status to new constituencies while excluding others from advancing these claims. This was accomplished by defining a multiplicity of living wages and a multiplicity of strategies for achieving them.

Policy in an era of economic crisis

The 1920s was a period of apparent prosperity, although underneath the booming stock market, stable prices, and soaring rates of production and consumption there were signs of economic vulnerability. Price rigidity was due, in part, to a wave of mergers and acquisitions from 1916 to 1929 that concentrated market power in large oligopolies in petroleum, steel, automobile manufacturing, food processing, and chemical industries, as well as privately held utilities, banks, and retail stores (DuBoff 1989). The distribution of income became more skewed. The wages of the highest-paid salaried employees rose far faster than those of low-income workers. For U.S. farmers (still one-fifth of the labor force), most of the 1920s were a difficult period. As a glut of food production forced prices down, costs of equipment and other manufactured goods held steady or rose. Consequently, farmers fell deeply into debt. Consumers and would-be stock market investors also borrowed heavily, while the fiscally conservative federal government did not. Balancing the federal budget was considered a priority.

Given these underlying conditions, it was not surprising that the U.S. economy was headed for a recession by the end of the decade. More unexpected was that a relatively normal downturn in the business cycle, coupled with a sudden plunge in the stock market in October 1929, became something else altogether. The Great Depression was virtually unprecedented in U.S. history in terms of the duration, depth, and diffusion of the economic downturn.

Economic analyses of the Great Depression focus on the major contraction from August 1929 to March 1933, a remarkable forty-three-month duration far longer than any other in the twentieth century. Despite positive growth rates beginning in 1933, the level of economic production (measured in terms of real gross national product or GNP) remained below pre-Depression levels until 1937 (Romer 1993: 35). This slow expansion period was followed by a second contraction, lasting thirteen months, in 1938. Thus, the entire period from 1929 to 1938 is often characterized as the depression era.

Nominal GNP declined by 49.6 percent during the first contraction, meaning that the value of goods and services produced in 1933 was half of the 1929 level. If the fall in prices is taken into account, real GNP declined by nearly one-third. The unemployment rate provides an even more vivid indication of economic hardship during this time. The percentage of workers who were seeking jobs but could not find any skyrocketed from 3.2 percent in 1929 to 24.9 percent in 1933. One in four members of the labor force was unemployed. Other "discouraged workers" were uncounted because they stopped looking for work, statistically dropping out of the labor force. The unemployment rate was still as high as 20 percent in 1938 when the FLSA was passed by Congress and did not fall below 14 percent before the end of the decade. The effects of the Depression were felt throughout the economy. Diffusion, the extent of the Depression's impact among nonfarm industries, reached 100 percent and 97 percent in each of the downturns (Moore 1980; Margo 1993).

One explanation for the persistence of the Great Depression (as opposed to why it started) emphasizes that the initial downturn occurred during a period of economic transformation (Bernstein 1987; see also DuBoff 1989). Mature industries that had dominated the economic scene for decades, and consequently employed a large percentage of the labor force, had saturated markets. In industries such as automobile manufacture and other fabricated metal products, there was little reason for additional investment by firms, even without the dramatic drop in consumption after the stock market crash. Textile manufacturing was already beginning to move overseas. Since these industries were in long-term decline, it would take an extraordinary economic surge (eventually triggered by World War II production) to jump-start private investment in new factories and equipment.

A few industries actually prospered throughout the 1930s. Unfortunately, they were in newly emerging sectors where overall employment levels were low. For example, during the 1920s the percentage of households with access to electricity rose dramatically. Coupled with women's increased labor force participation, this change in infrastructure fueled demand for household appliances. Processed and canned food was also a booming area. Yet these nascent industries could not absorb the massive numbers of unemployed workers.

Both women and men faced overwhelming job losses during the Great Depression. However, women's unemployment was somewhat sheltered by occupational segregation in the industries that were less hard hit (Mutari 1996). For example, auto workers were more likely to be male while women manufactured small appliances and processed foods. In some cases, there was also an "added worker effect" (Humphries 1976). Families increased the number of wage earners, sending wives and children into the labor force in order to compensate for the loss of a male breadwinner's wages. Unfortunately, such economic strategies contributed to the perception that women were taking jobs away from unemployed men. Hostility toward married women's employment escalated.

Herbert Hoover, a Republican with strong *laissez-faire* convictions about government, was president when the Depression began. By the 1932 election, the electorate clamored for a different approach. Franklin Delano Roosevelt, a Democrat, was elected, then re-elected three more times in 1936, 1940, and 1944. Roosevelt quickly began to implement a series of programs and policies to jump-start the economy, in what was termed the "New Deal." Although he himself was not wedded to a particular economic philosophy and retained at least a preference for balanced federal budgets, he was open to persuasion by advisors who believed in activist fiscal, labor market, and social welfare policies.[1] His administration began a series of policy experiments, some of which drew upon the legacy of state-level initiatives described in the previous chapter.

Frances Perkins goes to Washington

The story of Frances Perkins provides a vantage-point for seeing how the activism cultivated by a network of women reformers during the Progressive Era became translated into national public policy during the New Deal. One of two daughters of a small Massachusetts businessman, Perkins graduated from Mount Holyoke College, a bastion of women's education, in 1902. While she was at Mount Holyoke, Florence Kelley, founder of the National Consumers' League (NCL), came to speak on campus. Perkins was moved by Kelley's speech, later writing to a friend that it "first opened my mind to the necessity for and the possibility of the work which became my vocation" (quoted in Martin 1976: 52). After graduation, she moved to New York and devoted herself to the antisweatshop movement. Although she married and had a daughter, she was adamant in keeping the name Perkins throughout her career.

She entered the public sector in 1919 when Governor Alfred E. Smith appointed her to the Industrial Commission of the State of New York, a board within the Labor Department in charge of investigating working conditions. Smith was cognizant that women were new voters in the state and wanted to appoint a woman to political office, preferably one who was not the wife or sister of a male politician. According to her biographer, Perkins was concerned that her now-colleague and friend Florence Kelley might object to her entering a political administration rather than continuing to work for social betterment through the NCL. Governor Smith allegedly responded, "there'd better not be any of that separation much longer if we're to get good government. If you girls [*sic.*] are going to get what you want through legislation, there'd better not be any separation between social workers and the government" (Martin 1976: 144).[2]

When Franklin Roosevelt succeeded Smith in the governor's mansion, he promoted Perkins to Industrial Commissioner, the chief administrator supervising a largely male staff. Perkins then became Roosevelt's Secretary of Labor when he assumed the presidency in 1933, the first woman to serve in the Cabinet. In her memoirs of the politician whose career was so linked to her own, *The Roosevelt I Knew*, Perkins indicated that she accepted the post reluctantly, concerned that labor union leadership would object to her because she was not from their ranks. As the condition under which she would serve, she proposed an ambitious agenda that included the hallmarks of New Deal social welfare policy: an extensive public works program to combat unemployment (instituted in the Works Progress Administration and other programs), federal aid for unemployment relief and old-age insurance (accomplished in the Social Security Act of 1935), and a minimum wage/maximum hours law and a law banning child labor (both codified in the FLSA). Her background in the NCL and other Progressive Era women's organizations made wage and hour regulation and a ban on child labor her particular concerns – though she had many allies in the administration. When Roosevelt agreed to her conditions, she observed that such laws might be considered unconstitutional. She recollects Roosevelt's response as: "Well, that's a problem, but we can work out something when the time comes" (Perkins 1946: 152).

Plate 6.1 Secretary of Labor Frances Perkins, c. 1939

Source: courtesy of Franklin D. Roosevelt Library (photo no. 43–50:12)

Constitutional constraints

In order to understand the decisions that were made in writing the Fair Labor Standards Act, it is necessary to examine earlier attempts to institute wage and hours regulations during the 1930s. An important precursor to the Fair Labor Standards Act was the National Industrial Recovery Act (NIRA), passed in 1933 as part of Roosevelt's initial program to combat the depression during the so-called "first one hundred days." The NIRA, eventually declared unconstitutional by the Supreme Court, established a federal agency – the National Recovery Administration (NRA) – with the power to enact industry "fair trade" codes regarding wages, hours, working conditions, and union representation. Wage regulations were only one facet of this omnibus legislation, which included nonlabor trade practices as well. There was no peacetime precedent for this type of extensive intervention in economic affairs.

The NIRA was established as a temporary (two-year) measure. Through an analogy between the powers of the NRA and the government's prerogatives during a wartime emergency, the architects of the New Deal hoped to ward off the inevitable constitutional challenge. The codes set standards that businesses were expected to heed in light of the economic emergency. In coupling wage and hours standards, the NIRA linked a labor-supported movement for shorter hours with the social reformers' call for minimum wages. This was not the position favored by the American Federation of Labor. The labor federation preferred a thirty-hour week bill introduced by Senator Hugo Black of Alabama in 1932. The skilled craft unions that comprised the AFL sought shorter hours as a means of spreading the available work over a larger pool of workers, but they staunchly defended collective bargaining as the appropriate means of setting wages for male workers.

Secretary Perkins and her network of social feminists considered wages and hours to be inextricably linked. Without wage regulations, shorter hours could impoverish the lowest-paid workers. Perkins had been rebuffed when she proposed amending the Black bill to create industry boards setting minimum wages. Historian Landon Storrs observed that "what organized labor and some businessmen had accepted in the states for women workers they found unacceptable as part of a federal program that included men" (2000: 95). Perkins and her allies succeeded in coupling the two issues in the NIRA, however, because the labor movement was anxious for the favorable union organizing provisions incorporated into Section 7a of the NIRA; the unions traded off their opposition to wage setting by industrial boards for the right to unionize.

The labor standards section of the NIRA incorporated Perkins' three priority concerns: hours, wages, and child labor. As part of the NIRA program, employers voluntarily signed pledges to institute (1) work weeks between 35 and 40 hours; (2) minimum weekly wages of $12 to $15 (or 30 to 37½ cents per hour); and (3) bans on employment of youth under 16. The businesses agreeing to this code displayed decals with a "Blue Eagle" logo. Particular industries developed more specific codes of conduct, modeled on the industrial boards used in the states to administer minimum wage regulations. Industry representatives submitted proposed codes to NRA administrators who approved them after consulting with industry labor leaders and holding public hearings. The NRA also established Industrial, Labor, and Consumers' Advisory Boards to review each code, which, in addition, needed the approval of the head of the NRA and President Roosevelt.

Since adhering to the codes implied collusion and less industrial competition, the mandate of the NRA required a suspension of antitrust laws that was troubling to the Supreme Court. These were not the provisions that brought down the NIRA, however. The case of *Schechter Poultry Corp.* v. *United States* concerned the conditions under which kosher chickens were slaughtered and sold to butchers. On May 27, 1935, the high court ruled unanimously that the NIRA delegated legislative powers to an administrative agency (the NRA). It also ruled that the Brooklyn-based poultry business run by the Schechter brothers did not engage in interstate commerce and thus could not be regulated by the federal government. These two key factors, the separation of legislative and executive powers and federal responsibility for interstate commerce, thus became central elements to the construction of a federal wage and hours bill that could survive constitutional challenge.

One other important Supreme Court decision that influenced the construction of the FLSA involved a challenge to New York State's minimum wage law (see Ingalls 1974). New York, the birthplace of the National Consumers' League and Progressive Era battles against sweatshop conditions, had finally passed a minimum wage law for women during the trough of the Depression in 1933. Governor Herbert Lehman, Roosevelt's successor, was persuaded to support the bill as a means of boosting purchasing power and enhancing economic stability, a macroeconomic version of the living wage argument. Opposition was minimal, aside from some feminist organizations that opposed gender-specific protective legislation, such as the National Woman's Party and the National Federation of Business and Professional Women's Clubs (BPW).

Under the new legislation, one of the most notably low-wage industries, commercial laundries, was investigated almost immediately. African American and immigrant women in New York City toiled long hours for weekly wages of around $8 to $10. When the New York Department of Labor attempted to make the initially voluntary minimum wage for laundry workers mandatory in 1934, a legal challenge was elicited. Spotlight Laundry was managed by Joseph Tipaldo, who paid his nine laundry women $10 per week for forty-seven hours of work, less than the weekly wage floor of $14.88. When state inspectors uncovered the problem and demanded that the minimum be enforced, Tipaldo pressured his workers to endorse their paychecks back to the laundry in exchange for cash; the women were only given $10 although the face of the checks indicated the appropriate wage. To avoid criminal prosecution for fraud and other offenses, Tipaldo, the laundry owner James Giordano, and the bookkeeper challenged the constitutionality of the minimum wage law, citing the *Adkins* ruling as precedent. The laundry's legal costs were financed by the New York State Hotel Association, another low-wage industry with twelve-hour, seven-day work schedules.

The case, *Morehead v. New York ex rel. Tipaldo*, wended its way to the Supreme Court. On June 1, 1936, the Court voided the New York minimum wage by a 5–4 vote in a technical ruling that did not explicitly reaffirm *Adkins*. It was an extremely unpopular decision.[3] Newspapers and politicians from across the political spectrum lined up to criticize the court.

The "Big Switch"

Wage regulations with enforcement mechanisms would not have been possible had the Supreme Court not reversed its position of unrelenting hostility to market intervention. In March of 1937, the Supreme Court decided yet another case regarding a state minimum wage law, *West Coast Hotel Company* v. *Parrish*. A former hotel chambermaid, Elsie Parrish, sued her employer for $216.19 in back wages, claiming violation of the State of Washington's minimum wage statute. Parrish won in a 5–4 decision that explicitly reversed the *Adkins* decision. This ruling became possible because Justice Owen J. Roberts switched alliances, voting with three liberals and the moderate Chief Justice Charles Evans Hughes rather than with the block of four conservatives as he had in the *Tipaldo* case.

Historians have studied the complex set of factors leading up to this so-called "Big Switch." The political pressure wrought by the overwhelming economic hardship and Roosevelt's strategic maneuvers are generally credited with influencing Justice Roberts' change of heart. The year of the *Tipaldo* decision, 1936, was a presidential election year and Franklin Roosevelt had made the Court's opposition to social welfare and labor legislation a campaign issue. Roosevelt used the clout of his landslide victory (523 electoral votes out of 531) to exert political pressure on the Court. Following reelection, Roosevelt took an aggressively adversarial stance toward the conservative justices on the Court. In his January 1937 State of the Union address to Congress, he admonished the judiciary for serving as an obstacle to his programs (Roosevelt 1967a [1937]: 2832–3).

This criticism was followed by a proposal to reorganize the federal judiciary, expanding the number of sitting justices, and thereby allowing him to "pack" the court with those supporting his policies. A bill containing Roosevelt's court reorganization was submitted to Congress, but support evaporated after the Big Switch. The popular slogan used to summarize what happened was: "A switch in time saved nine." Yet there is strong evidence that the justices actually voted on the *Parrish* case before the court-packing bill was introduced, but delayed announcing the ruling for a variety of reasons. Historian John Chambers (1969) credits Justice Roberts with a genuine change of heart, embracing a new relationship between government and the economy following Roosevelt's re-election landslide. According to Chambers, "the people" legitimated minimum wage regulation through their political voice.

The historic ruling legitimizing the State of Washington's minimum wage law in the Parrish case signaled a change in legal doctrine that facilitated the development of a welfare state. The Court expanded the power of the federal government to regulate interstate commerce and "shifted the emphasis of the due process clause from protection of property to protection of civil rights" (Chambers 1969: 45). In the majority decision, Chief Justice Hughes questioned the doctrine of freedom of contract:

What is this freedom? The Constitution does not speak of freedom of contract. It speaks of liberty and prohibits the deprivation of liberty without due process of law. . . . [R]egulation which is reasonable in relation to its subject and is adopted in the interests of the community is due process.

(*West Coast Hotel Co. v. Parrish* 1937)

The door was open for the Roosevelt administration to introduce federal minimum wage legislation. And Frances Perkins was now free to pursue the legislative agenda that was the primary reason she came to Washington.

"That nice unconstitutional bill"

Perkins was prepared. Even as the constitutional challenge to the NIRA was being decided, flaws within the system it effected were becoming obvious. Domination of the National Recovery Administration by employers, implementation of low standards under the codes, and scanty enforcement had generated substantial criticism by and frustration for social feminists and labor unions even before the Court acted. In particular, sex and race discrimination were institutionalized in many of the industry codes (see Storrs 2000). Minimum wages for women were lower than minimum wages for men, for example. Perkins herself wrote that she believed at the time that the NRA "would blow up by internal combustion" (1946: 248).

Perkins resolved to work with legal strategists to draft a labor standards bill that might survive a constitutional challenge.[4] They developed a two-step approach: a public contracts bill, setting labor conditions for the manufacture of goods purchased by the government, and a general wage and hour bill. The strategy was to emphasize the federal government's power to regulate industries affecting interstate commerce. During the period of uncertainty over the fate of the NIRA, Perkins told Roosevelt that the bills were "locked up in the lower left-hand drawer of my desk against an emergency" (Perkins 1946: 249).

The first of the two bills, relating to public contracts, was quickly introduced in Congress as the Walsh-Healey bill and passed. It established a forty-hour week for government contractors, directed the Secretary of Labor to determine minimum wage rates for different jobs, and prohibited child labor in the performance of government contracts. Passage of the 1936 Walsh-Healey Act – along with the enactment the previous year of the National Labor Relations Act setting up a legitimate process for union elections, recognition, and bargaining – allowed Roosevelt to run in 1936 with some victories under his belt.

After re-election, Roosevelt encouraged Perkins to unlock the drawer, asking "What happened to that nice unconstitutional bill you had tucked away?" (Perkins 1946: 255). The White House then sat on it until after the Big Switch. The bill was sent to Congress on May 24, 1937, along with a message to Congress from President Roosevelt, referring to the "one-third of our population" that was "ill-nourished, ill-clad, and ill-housed."[5] It was known as the Black-Connery bill, named for its sponsors, Representative William P. Connery of Massachusetts as well as Senator Black, the sponsor of the 1932 thirty-hours bill.

The Black-Connery bill became the Fair Labor Standards Act, but with some significant changes. First, whereas the original bill provided for a statutory minimum hourly rate and maximum standard work week, universally assumed to be 40 cents per hour and 40 hours per week, the precise minimum and maximum were actually left blank. It also included the premium of "time and a half" for hours above the standard, a provision that survived in the final legislation. Second, Black-Connery designated a strong role for a Fair Labor Standards Board and for advisory committees that could set a minimum wage up to 80 cents per hour (or annual wage income of $1200) in specific industries or occupations. The Board would have the power to limit or prevent overtime in specific occupations or to lengthen the work week for seasonal or peak activity. Under the draft bill, like state-level protective legislation, broad powers were vested in the Board as an investigatory body. *As passed*, the FLSA established only a 25-cent minimum wage (rising in steps to 40 cents per hour by October 24, 1945), enforced by a new Wage and Hour Division in the Department of Labor. In the first years of implementation, there were also industry committees that could set higher minimums in specific industries, but not more than 40 cents per hour. The minimum wage quickly became a wage floor enforced by a complaint-driven litigation mechanism rather than by active investigation of labor conditions.

Coverage was limited from the start, but more and more exemptions were specified at each stage of the negotiations. The language of the act most clearly applied to wage workers in manufacturing, mining, wholesale trade, some transportation, and utilities. Agricultural work was exempted from the wages and hours provisions, although in the final law child labor in the fields was banned. Most retail sales occupations were omitted on the basis of the interstate commerce provisions. Executive, administrative, supervisory, and professional work were also unprotected, since the regulations were intended to apply to waged, not salaried, workers. Taken together, these restrictions excluded most female-concentrated jobs. Further, the two job categories that contained the vast majority of African Americans, farm labor and domestic service, were not covered by the FLSA, following the pattern set by most earlier state-level minimum wage laws.

Law and politics in FLSA passage

Obtaining passage of the FLSA was a long and arduous process. The Roosevelt administration, especially Secretary Perkins, worked with the pre-existing network of social feminists and legal strategists who had pioneered the state legislative experiments. They were opposed by a coalition of Southern Democrats in Congress representing the interests of Southern employers, anti-New Deal Republicans, the National Association of Manufacturers, and others. Labor union support was essential to overcome this coalition. The final wording of the act was the result of a series of amendments and compromises undertaken to garner political support and ward off constitutional challenges. The legislative process that led to passage of this compromised but nonetheless landmark legislation revived old alliances, generated new ones, and fomented divisions among expected allies.[6]

Consideration of the bill began in the summer of 1937. In June, the Committee on Education and Labor of the U.S. Senate and the Committee on Labor of the House of Representatives held extensive joint hearings on the original legislative proposal (see U.S. Congress 1937). The hearings continued for much of the month, with witnesses representing most of the key constituencies. Representative Connery passed away during the process. His position as Chair of the House Committee on Labor was assumed by Representative Mary Norton of New Jersey.

Divisions among allies

Organized labor eventually endorsed the FLSA but with varying degrees of enthusiasm. Sidney Hillman of the Amalgamated Clothing Workers' Union (ACWU) and David Dubinsky of the International Ladies' Garment Workers' Union (ILGWU) were strong supporters of labor regulations. Both men represented the garment industry, a prime site of sweatshops that employed large numbers of immigrants, many of them women. Both also had long-standing relationships with the social reformers advocating wage regulations.

Hillman testified in favor of a Labor Standards Board's power to set wages. He argued that higher rates would aid collective bargaining by protecting firms paying fair wages from wage-cutting competitors. In the garment industry, the unionized factories in the Northern states were threatened by competition from nonunion plants in the South. Equalizing wage rates across regions would diminish the problem of runaway shops. Therefore, he strongly opposed regional differentials that would permit southern employers to pay a lower minimum wage than in the north (U.S. Congress 1937: 943–58).[7]

In contrast, William Green, as president of the American Federation of Labor, represented the skilled craft workers who had the greatest clout in collective bargaining. Green's support for the legislation was lukewarm at best. Members of his executive board were more hostile, causing Green's position on specific provisions to waver during negotiations over passage. The AFL, Green included, specifically objected to taking wages "off the table" by vesting power in the industrial boards. While the union favored limits on hours, it vacillated in its position on a wage floor.

John L. Lewis of the of the United Mine Workers of America and the Congress of Industrial Organizations (CIO) – which was in midst of a two-year process of splitting from the AFL – took a middle ground. The United Mine Workers had national bargaining agreements and no substantial competition from nonunion companies, but the CIO as a whole organized the lower-skilled workers in mass-production manufacturing industries (automobiles, steel, etc.) that were targeted by the FLSA. The CIO used militant tactics such as sit-down strikes in which workers occupied the workplace (Zieger 1995). The AFL had long neglected these constituencies and eschewed these tactics. Lewis was more supportive of a flat minimum wage than Green, but agreed that the bill's coverage should be restricted to low-paid and unorganized workers. Neither Green nor Lewis wanted boards to have the power to raise wages above the 40-cent floor. Instead, they wanted to leave the field open for collective bargaining.

The women's movement was also divided. Although the National Woman's Party had long argued that their opposition to state minimum wage laws was based on their belief in gender neutrality, they withheld active support of the FLSA; it was not a women's issue as they defined it. They remained bystanders rather than taking the opportunity to heal the bitter rift that had been created by the division over gender-specific protective legislation. Social feminist groups, especially the National Consumers' League, actively supported the effort. The Women's Bureau did not testify at the hearings, perhaps because Secretary Perkins could represent their view, although it worked behind the scenes to ensure passage. The old split between labor-focused social feminists and the equal rights feminists who emphasized political rights and the Equal Rights Amendment continued through this legislative battle.

Regional economic interests also figured in the debate over a federal minimum wage. Southern legislators were intent on minimizing the law's impact so that Southern employers could maintain a comparative advantage in cheap labor. They opposed Black-Connery outright or insisted on regional differentials, citing a lower cost of living for workers and higher labor costs per unit because of lower levels of mechanization. Some Northern textile employers favored the bill (especially a flat minimum without wage boards), again because of concerns about low-wage competitors in the South.

The National Association of Manufacturers (NAM) sided against the legislation, based on a general objection to any and all forms of regulated labor standards (with the exception of the child labor ban). One NAM representative testified in opposition to the bill:

> It is impossible to inject an act of Congress into an economic machine and stop one major part of it – the free movement of prices – and expect the rest to go on as before. Once Government starts to interfere in direct economic control, it is difficult to stop doing so.
>
> (U.S. Congress 1937: 646)

A representative of the Ohio Chamber of Commerce was even more emphatic about his objection to federal government intervention: "South Carolina fired on Fort Sumter for a far less pretext than this bill affords" (U.S. Congress 1937: 866).

Legislative wrangling over FLSA provisions

The bill was worded to reassure unions that government regulation would not intervene in industries regulated by collective bargaining. Nevertheless, one of the first groups to chip away at the Black-Connery bill was the American Federation of Labor. The AFL proposed an (unsuccessful) alternative bill that limited the scope of the industrial boards so as not to interfere with collective bargaining. When it became clear that a separate bill could not gain sufficient support, the AFL sought to amend Black-Connery to the same effect. The labor federation insisted that the Senate drop the provision (section 5 of the bill) permitting the Labor Standards Board to raise wages or decrease hours in specific industries beyond the 40/40 standards. The Board could only set wages *lower* than the standard or *longer* hours.

The bill, thus weakened by the labor-sponsored amendment and added occupational exemptions,[8] passed the Senate July 31, 1937, by a vote of fifty-six to twenty-eight. Attention now turned to the House of Representatives. The House Committee on Labor reported it out on August 6 with additional occupational exclusions. Now, with the solid support of unions and the Roosevelt administration, the bill could have easily passed a vote in the full House of Representatives; but the House Rules Committee was controlled by an alliance between conservative Southern Democrats and the Republican members.[9] The summer session ended without a floor vote in the House.

That fall, Roosevelt issued a call for a special session of Congress to deal with wage and hours legislation and other New Deal proposals. When Congress reconvened in November 1937, however, the Rules Committee still blocked the bill from a vote in the full House. Further, Green faced more dissent from within his union leadership and began to demand new amendments. In particular, rather than simply limiting the power of the Labor Standards Board to set wages higher than the wage floor, the AFL strongly insisted that Congress abandon the Board altogether. Despite additional maneuvers, including moving administrative oversight to the Department of Labor, the bill remained dead for the remainder of the special session.

During the hiatus, several events crystalized the enthusiasm among the electorate for the New Deal in general and wage and hour legislation in particular. First, in an Alabama Democratic primary, New Deal supporter Senator Lister Hill beat back a challenger who ran in opposition to Roosevelt's policies. A major poll by the Institute of Public Opinion, a private and well-respected polling firm, indicated wide support for the Black-Connery bill throughout the country. The National Consumers' League, under its new General Secretary Mary Dublin, brought together a coalition of organizations, the National Labor Standards Committee, to galvanize support for the bill.[10] Thousands of individuals sent signed resolutions advocating the FLSA, one of several lobbying campaigns developed by the new committee. Finally, Senator Claude Pepper, another supporter of wage and hour regulations, won a Democratic primary in Florida against an opponent of the bill. Political mobilization was mounting.

When Congress reconvened in 1938, it was clear that the Black-Connery bill was going to pass, but in what form? The reformulated proposal finally adopted in the House of Representatives was far weaker than that passed by the Senate. A joint conference committee to reconcile the Senate and House versions of the bill faced the particularly stubborn issue of regional differentials advocated by southerners. In the final act, regional differentials were not explicitly mentioned but could be accommodated by the range between the 25-cent floor and the 40-cent maximum that the industrial committees could set. Once the 40-cent floor was reached in 1945, there would be no differentials. The Fair Labor Standards Act was approved by the Joint Committee on June 12, 1938.

Thirteen days later, on Saturday, June 25, 1938, President Franklin D. Roosevelt signed the historic act – along with 120 other bills passed by the recently adjourned Congress. In his radio "fireside chat" the night before, FDR admonished his listeners, "Do not let any calamity-howling executive with an income of $1,000 a day, . . . tell you . . . that a wage of $11 a week is going to have a disastrous effect on all American industry" (quoted in Grossman 1978: 22).

When the FLSA became effective on October 24, 1938, only 20 percent of the labor force met the narrow criteria of covered occupations and industries.[11] Of these 11 million covered workers, only 300,000 were earning less than 25 cents per hour (Andrews 1939: 53; Storrs 2000: 196). Advocates of wage regulations had settled for compromised legislation to enact the principle that workers were entitled to a living wage. They then turned their attention to three issues: (1) expanded coverage to include exempted groups such as agricultural workers; (2) maintaining and strengthening gender-specific minimum wage laws in the states for women in occupations that did not meet the interstate commerce standard; and (3) periodic battles to increase the wage floor specified in the FLSA.

Living wages for whom?

The Fair Labor Standards Act legitimated and institutionalized the idea that living standards and workers' needs mattered in setting wages. They mattered not simply in motivating workers to offer their labor power, but as the basis for government intervention in market mechanisms. Along with other legislation that constructed a system of welfare state capitalism in the United States, the FLSA posited a new relationship between production and consumption. Living wages were important not only normatively (as a matter of fairness and compassion) but analytically as a means of restoring prosperity

Plate 6.2 Women's Bureau exhibit advocating state minimum wage and maximum hours laws to supplement the Fair Labor Standards Act of 1938, c. 1938

Source: courtesy of National Archives (photo no. 86-G-4E-14)

and macroeconomic stability. Nevertheless, the attention to wages as a living did not preclude consideration of the link between wages and productivity. Again, a macroeconomic approach that viewed productivity as a function of wage rates, rather than vice versa, took precedence over more static conceptions of wages and productivity theory.

Ostensibly a gender-neutral piece of legislation, the FLSA nevertheless continued to reflect and construct appropriate gender relations. Given the coverage of the legislation, it was men's wages, lives, and identities, and specifically the masculine identity of unskilled and unorganized male workers, that was most at stake in formulating the new legislation. The tone of the discussion and the rationales for protection therefore shifted once the minimum wage was a male wage. As noted by historian Willis Nordlund, "the fervent rhetoric about low wages and morals that occurred during the debate of the prior five decades was absent from this debate" (1997: 32). Instead of the morals of mothers, the state's interest in macroeconomic stability and the ability of breadwinners to provide for their families were emphasized.

The minimum wage law was a racialized social practice as well. The FLSA reinforced the male breadwinner family as a marker of whiteness during this period. Our investigation indicates that the Fair Labor Standards Act was constructed so that white, male, unskilled workers could come closer to a male breadwinner wage.[12] Even though 40-cents per hour (and especially the initial 25-cent floor that actually passed) was below what proponents thought was a family-supporting wage, the language of breadwinning was integral to the debate. In fact, during this period the expansion of the male breadwinner model of gender relations was one of the institutional underpinnings of both a political economy based on mass-production industry and the Keynesian welfare state. The testimony offered at the 1937 hearings and other documents related to the process of the FLSA's passage reveal the implicit wage theories at play in constructing a federal minimum wage policy.

Living wages and market mechanisms

The "Declaration of Policy" in the opening text of the Fair Labor Standards Act stated that

> The Congress hereby finds that the existence, in industries engaged in commerce or in the production of goods for commerce, of labor conditions detrimental to the maintenance of the minimum standard of living necessary for health, efficiency, and general well-being of workers . . . constitutes an unfair method of competition in commerce.
>
> (Fair Labor Standards Act of 1938: 1060)

The declaration also asserted that such labor conditions were perpetuated and spread via interstate commerce, led to labor disputes, and interfered with the "orderly and fair marketing of goods." Quite strongly then, the advocates of a minimum wage countered the argument that competitive price mechanisms necessarily set wages fairly. In his message accompanying the original bill, President Roosevelt acknowledged that "exponents of the theory of private initiative as the cure for deep-seated national ills" were well intentioned; but their argument failed to account for "the inevitable minority of chiselers within their own ranks" (U.S. Senate 1937: 1).

There were certainly employer representatives, as well as economists, who asserted the sanctity of market mechanisms. For example, National Association of Manufacturers representative Robert Dresser testified at the hearings as follows:

> I believe that there are certain definite economic laws that cannot be denied. That, for example, in every returning period of prosperity, we

start with [low] prices as a result of low cost and low wages, which in turn stimulates buying, and as buying is stimulated, that puts more people back to work, starts new factories going, increasing the purchasing power, and you have the cycle of prosperity.

(U.S. Congress 1937: 669)

Dresser's comments reflect the faith in the self-regulation of markets that was the orthodoxy at the time of the Depression. If there was a temporary period of overproduction of goods, lower prices could stimulate consumers to buy them. If there was a temporary period of unemployment, lower wages could induce employers to hire back workers. It was this faith that was challenged by the depth and duration of the Great Depression, opening the door to acceptance of Keynesianism.

For those promoting *laissez-faire* markets, considering workers' needs was irrelevant to the process of wage setting. According to John Edgerton of the Southern States Industrial Council:

I have never thought of paying a man on the basis of what they need; that is, in a business. I therefore do not inquire particularly into what they need and what their idea of a standard of living is or what not. I pay them the best wage I can for the business that we have.

(U.S. Congress 1937: 791)

In response to relentless pressure by committee members about whether a family could live on less than a 40-cent wage (or $16 per week), Edgerton indicated that he "attends to those things in my church connections and in my philanthropic connections. That is an entirely different thing" (U.S. Congress 1937: 791).

Yet the lower cost of living in the South versus the North was integral to the argument for regional differentials. The discussion went beyond simply relative prices to encompass how workers lived. Since low-wage labor in the South was often African American, there were racialized tones to images of workers' lives. Testimony on whether to include workers who were employed by railroads to maintain the tracks is characteristic. One witness, Counsel for the Association of American Railroads, requested that these "maintenance-of-way men" be exempted from the bill. While acknowledging that the pay of some of the "colored labor" in these jobs was quite low, he argued that they were given "compensating advantages" such as a place to live. Specifically, he charged that "they have a garden, they have opportunities to raise vegetables, and things of that sort" (U.S. Congress 1937: 692). This reason was simply a variation on the contention that African Americans had fewer needs than white workers. Another employer association witness stressed that such differences in living styles justified North–South differentials; while Chicago workers commuted long distances, a southern factory worker "has a little garden and he walks to his job" (U.S. Congress 1937:

1072). Although geographic differentials were not explicitly written into the final bill, the exempted occupations and industries were fairly effective in accomplishing the same goals.

During this period, then, it was common for both price mechanisms and living costs to be invoked in discussions of wage setting. Even minimum wage proponents, who were clearly advocating a position based upon wages as a living, also considered the issue of prices. In particular, they advanced the argument that setting higher wages would induce employers to modernize to improve worker productivity. Low wages, it was contended, were symptomatic of inefficient firms who sought to compete by lowering costs rather than adopting new technologies and production methods. The issue was one of causality. For wages to reflect productivity, was it necessary to treat technology and productivity as given, or could they be a function of wage levels? Again, the highly competitive garment and textile industries were the focus of this debate, rather than oligopolistic sectors. Union spokesman Merle Vincent of the ILGWU proposed that "Better labor standards are not only a protection to labor, but they protect industry in stabilizing labor costs on a more fair competitive plane and increase the efficiency and productivity of workers" (U.S. Congress 1937: 265).

Of course, the primary economic argument made by minimum wage advocates was the importance of purchasing power. Raising wages would benefit the economy in depression by increasing consumption that would, in turn, stimulate production and restore employment levels. Although John Maynard Keynes' book *The General Theory* had only just been published, such macroeconomic arguments played a key role in defense of labor standards. While the phrase "purchasing power" is a recurring theme throughout the hearings, the testimony of Msgr. John A. Ryan, a pioneer of social economics and informal advisor to the Roosevelt administration, presented the most complete version of the Keynesian argument. In his opening sentence, Ryan avowed: "I favor this bill because it presents the only effective method of raising the wages of the underpaid and of bringing about full employment of our workers and full operation of our industries" (U.S. Congress 1937: 498). He continued by explaining that his reasons were based upon "certain economic facts and assumptions." After describing the potential productive capacity of the U.S. economy and how much of it had been unused since the 1929 crash, he put the blame on the unequal distribution of income: "The masses of the people could not buy more goods because they had not the money; the minority that could have bought more failed to do so because they already had enough" (U.S. Congress 1937: 498). Ryan (like Keynes) argued that the economy could not be self-correcting because lower prices could not induce those without money to buy. A minimum wage law could rectify this problem.

Others echoed this macroeconomic argument. Robert Johnson, President of Johnson & Johnson, was one of the Northern employers who testified in sympathy with the bill. His prepared statement was quite critical of employers who fought against higher living standards, but acknowledged that "it is difficult for men who are devoting every hour of their lives to the development of a private business to see clearly the relation between the prosperity of their own business and the prosperity of the Nation as a whole." The connection was purchasing power: "The prosperity for all American industry and commerce rests in the final analysis [on] the buying power of the masses and therefore we have a direct and selfish interest in the welfare of these people" (U.S. Congress 1937: 92).

In the hearings over the FLSA, alternative assumptions about the efficacy of price mechanisms were debated. Employer representatives warned against interference with economic laws and self-correcting markets, while proponents thought that higher wages might increase productivity and purchasing power, and foster economic growth. In light of the desperate poverty afflicting a substantial portion of the population, it seemed necessary to ensure some basic level of subsistence. Economic policy making also institutionalized social practices, however; gendered and racialized messages were prominent in debates over a federal minimum wage.

Brothers and breadwinners

The advent of mass-production manufacturing was associated with a process that has been referred to as "deskilling."[13] Autonomy and control in work processes were reduced as assembly-line workers tended machines that set the pace of production. Union membership and collective bargaining over wages became one means of forging a new masculine identity in a world of mass-production that stripped white male workers of the gender and racial identities as craftsmen that their "fathers" had established. This vision of masculinity is clearly articulated in a 1927 issue of *Auto Worker News*:

> One of the most priceless possessions still retained by modern man is what is called manhood ... would you be a MAN – free, proud, independent, POWERFUL? Then get together with your fellow worker, ORGANIZE YOURSELF, and you will be in a position to proudly look into the eyes of foremen, straw bosses, and all the world and say: I AM A MAN.
>
> (quoted in Lewchuk 1993: 824)

Employers such as Henry Ford preferred to center fraternal masculinity on the virtues of hard work, effort, and speed rather than union membership (Lewchuk 1993). Rather than focusing on the process of wage setting (through collective bargaining), employers emphasized the *level* of men's wages by linking being a wage earner to being a breadwinner. Both the level and the process of setting wages serve as emblems of masculinity and figured into the debates.

Although they considered it preferable for working-class masculinity to be grounded in a brotherhood of labor activism without the aid of government, organized labor found their resolve shaken by the Great Depression. Labor legislation came to be acceptable for circumscribed groups of male workers who were not union members. Using R. W. Connell's (1995) distinction between hegemonic working-class masculinity and subordinated forms helps us understand how masculinity for men with less economic power could be reconciled with state protection. For union leaders Green and Lewis, the demarcation between hegemonic and subordinate masculinities was based on the divide between organized versus unorganized labor. The discourse used to construct this demarcation occurred in two steps. First, a minimum wage floor was depicted as a means of raising wages for male breadwinners. Second, the inferiority of relying upon the state as opposed to collective bargaining was asserted.

For example, John L. Lewis drew upon the image of southern families with multiple earners in his testimony in support of the FLSA:

> It is possible, for instance, that a cotton-mill family, in which the husband, the wife, and say three adolescent children, are all employed in the mill, may obtain a very good income by their combined efforts. But this practice is destructive to all that we cherish most in our American institutions. Normally, a husband and father should be able to earn enough to support a family.
>
> (U.S. Congress 1937: 275)

Robert Johnson, the self-described "liberal-minded business leader," similarly invoked the male breadwinner ideal:

> As I understand it, the average family in America consists of a man and wife and two children. It would seem most improbable that any public official or responsible business man would come forward to propose that such a man could maintain his wife and children on less than $16 a week in 1937.
>
> (U.S. Congress 1937: 95)

Minimum wage legislation was thus advocated out of concern for men's wages in "substandard" jobs. Historian Bruce Schulman holds that one of the primary aims of policymakers was "to provide more secure, better paying employment for the men they assumed to be the heads of these desperate southern families" (1991: 65). Wages in the South were a primary, but not the sole, concern. Low-paid immigrants, sometimes utilized as "scabs" (or strikebreakers), had long been considered a threat to the standard of living of white, native-born workers. Economist Robert Cherry (2001) argues that during the early twentieth century a distinction evolved between "good" immigrants (settled family men) and "bad" immigrants (single men who sojourned briefly in the U.S. before returning to their homelands). Extending breadwinner status to married male immigrants could encourage and enlarge the first group relative to the second.

Establishing the minimum wage as consistent with masculinity was the first step. For labor leaders, the second step was to proclaim that dependence upon the decisions of wage boards was subordinate to collective bargaining. This inferiority was expressed using racialized language. In his testimony, Lewis compared reliance upon wage boards with "indentured servitude." In contrast, collective bargaining empowered "free men" (U.S. Congress 1937: 286). The choice of indentured servitude as a symbol perfectly represents the intermediate status conferred upon male workers covered by the FLSA. In the labor parlance of the early twentieth century, "wage slavery" was the term for underpaid, exploited labor (Glickman 1997). Coverage by the minimum wage did not imply slave status. The "whiter" concept of indentured servitude could be construed as a temporarily acceptable condition, although one that was still not fully free.

A more positive assessment of wage regulations that still asserted the same hierarchy was provided by the representative of a railway union, the Brotherhood of Maintenance of Way Employees (a union that represented African American as well as white workers):

> We much prefer, of course, to establish our wages, hours, and working conditions through the process of collective bargaining, to which our organization is committed. . . . At the same time we believe it to be both right and the duty of the Government to concern itself with unreasonably low wages or unjust working conditions when for any reason, whether it be lack of organization on the part of the men or ineffectiveness of organization, the wage earners find that they are unable to correct such conditions themselves through collective bargaining.
>
> (U.S. Congress 1937: 1149)

Roosevelt himself made the distinction between collectively bargained wages and those covered by regulation. In his 1938 State of the Union message as Congress was still debating the FLSA, he argued, "We are seeking, of course, only legislation to end starvation wages and intolerable hours; more desirable wages are and should continue to be the product of collective bargaining" (Roosevelt 1967b [1938]: 2836). The Report of the Senate Committee on Education and Labor, authored by Hugo Black, also hammered home the distinction: "It is only those low-wage and long-working-hour industrial workers, who are the helpless victims of their own bargaining weakness, that this bill seeks to assist to obtain a minimum wage" (U.S. Senate 1937: 4).

There was irony in asserting the compatibility of masculinity and state protection through an argument that the law was designed to enable men to support their families. Throughout the hearings, the legislators and some witnesses took note that the 40-cent minimum for forty hours per week, as specified in the initial bill, was not really thought to be sufficient for "a man and wife with two or three children" actually to support themselves. When directly asked about this contradiction, Sidney Hillman argued that "what is necessary is to lay as a foundation the principle that we are going to guarantee American labor a minimum" (U.S. Congress 1937: 953–54).

Racialized masculinity

Within the working class, if union men were hegemonic and state-protected would-be breadwinners were subordinate, those excluded from state protection – particularly black men – were subordinated still further (see Palmer 1995). The exclusion of agriculture and other provisions in the FLSA effectively defined African American males out of state-protected male breadwinner status. Another layer of hierarchy was created. The implicit exclusion of African American men was also linked to cultural acceptance of and economic dependence on African American women's paid labor. Since multiple earners were considered a norm – albeit an inferior one – for black families (especially in agriculture), the exclusion of minority-concentrated occupations from family wages under the FLSA did not trouble most policy makers. Robert Lieberman, in a study of New Deal social welfare policies, contends that:

> race-laden policies are not simply programs whose tendency to exclude by race is merely incidental or accidental. Race-laden policies, rather, reflect racially structured power arrangements – class conflicts, party coalitions, political institutions, and the like whose characters are shaped by racial distinction – that produce public policy.
>
> (Lieberman 1998: 7)

During the hearings, a representative of the National Negro Congress, John P. Davis, expressed concern that the FLSA would not offer protection to African American workers (U.S. Congress 1937: 571–6). Using the argument that low wages for African Americans threatened white workers, he admonished the Senators and Representatives that:

> This bill is supposed to be intended to help those workers whose lack of collective bargaining power renders them capable of exploitation by employers. As it stands it does no such thing. . . . It provides for all manner of exemptions through which hundreds of thousands of workers may be excluded from any meaningful improvement of their condition. . . . Once you permit employer-pressure groups to secure exemptions and differentials affecting half a million Negro workers, you will find that the very exploitative conditions you hope to cure by this bill will not be cured. Instead, the growing impoverishment of Negro workers will be the ugly cancer preventing the improvement of the lot of a much larger number of white workers.
>
> (U.S. Congress 1937: 573–4)

Davis argued forcefully but unsuccessfully for a unilateral wage floor without exemptions or deductions.

Again, the delineation of masculinities interacted with economic interests. In the south, agriculture was labor-intensive rather than mechanized. Tenant farms, the site of employment for many African American families, were based on paternalistic arrangements whereby labor services were directly exchanged for other goods and services. Southern employers argued that these paternalistic relationships substituted for welfare state intervention. Logically, then, if the minimum wage was an attempt to raise the wages of heads of households, male tenant farmers – both black and white – were denied this status because of their subordinate position in a paternalistic social structure. Agriculture was thus excluded from the FLSA partly on the basis of the subordinate masculinity of these men.[14]

Even with agricultural labor exempted from coverage, opponents expressed concern that higher wages in manufacturing industries would siphon off the supply of labor for farms (U.S. Congress 1937: 688; 762). Southern employers also claimed that Southern black labor was less efficient than white workers in the North, justifying wage differentials by occupation, region, and sometimes explicitly by race. For example, the president of a Houston, Texas, tool company defended unequal wages by race because "there are certain tasks that are colored, and there are certain tasks that are white," using occupational segregation to defend race-based wage differentials resulting from exclusion (U.S. Congress 1937: 248).

The ethnicity of different segments of white workers was rarely mentioned directly during the hearings. One brief discussion is instructive. During Hillman's testimony, several Congressmen criticized the perception by unnamed parties that immigrants and children of immigrants in northern factories were "a stronger and sturdier race" who were more efficient than the "old stock" in the south (U.S. Congress 1937: 951). Hillman disputed this contention, defending the productivity of southern workers in the ACWU. Racial-ethnic stereotypes about immigrants were apparently used to defend North–South geographic differentials.

Women's work and wages

Masculinity was not the only aspect of gender on the table. Legislating minimum wages elicited familiar debates over women's relationship to the labor market and, consequently, whether they should be paid at parity with men. The question facing policy makers was should living wages be equal wages – that is, should the FLSA, like the NIRA, permit different minima for men and women in the same industry?

Landon Storrs argues that, during the Depression, "The sheer scale of male unemployment triggered intense anxiety about the emasculation of American men. This preoccupation with manhood obscured both female unemployment and the increased importance of women's paid and unpaid labor to family survival" (2000: 90). Economic hardship intensified the aversion to married women's employment that was exhibited at the 1923 conference on women in industry described in Chapter 1. Married women were scapegoated for the problem of men's unemployment. The backlash was particularly strong in the professions, where a few college-educated women had made gains during the 1910s and 1920s. There was a virtual bar on married women's public-service employment, codified in a 1932 law that prevented the employment of two spouses by the federal government. Numerous states and localities, as well as private-sector employers, followed the model set by the federal government and restricted the employment of married women (Scharf 1980; Goldin 1990). Yet families needed extra earners more than ever.

As previously noted, many female-dominated jobs were located in firms that did not fall under the purview of the interstate commerce provisions of the bill. However, some women who worked in manufacturing were covered. For these women, the assertion of equal minimum wages was a crucial aspect of the bill. Above the minima, gender-based wage differentials would be legal (until the FLSA was amended with passage of the 1963 Equal Pay Act). Yet equal wages, even at the minima, was a difficult concept for many at the hearings, including both members of Congress and those who testified. Secretary Perkins was questioned three separate times about whether the bill permitted separate minima by sex, which she adamantly denied. The confusion may have been magnified by the labor union discourse that attempted to label the minimum wage a male breadwinner wage.

T. W. McCreary, of the Phoenix Glass Company in Monaca, Pennsylvania, a unionized company with over 500 employees, noted, as a matter of course, that his firm and the union representing his employees had set gender differentiated starting wages: "We have a minimum wage agreement with [our] own organization of 40 cents for male and 32 cents for female workers" (U.S. Congress 1937: 1167). He proceeded to express concern that the bill did not provide for lower wages for female employees. In his plant, he asserted, women do work that is "light, not dangerous, easily performed" (1168). McCreary continued:

> We do not believe female help should be placed at the same wage-rate basis as the male for the reason that they do not perform exactly the same work, and in cases where we have had experience of both male and female on the same line of work we have found they are not competent to perform the same work as efficiently as the male is.
>
> (U.S. Congress 1937: 1168)

Robert Luce, a Massachusetts Congressman and co-owner of the Press Clipping Bureau, took a slightly different tack. His company hired young girls to clip and categorize newspaper articles. Turnover rates, he argued, were high: "For all of them, it is a temporary occupation, as is true in the case of most women, to be terminated, naturally and wisely for the public good, by marriage" (U.S. Congress 1937: 845). With women, he maintained, revolving-door employees necessitated lower wages to compensate for training costs. Male workers were trained with the expectation of years on the job and a career ladder. Rather than request gender-based wage differentials, however, Luce proposed exempting young people under 21, foreshadowing the debate decades later on a youth sub-minimum wage.

Race also played a role in defining women's status. African American women's simultaneous *inclusion* in the labor market and *exclusion* from wage regulations constituted an important aspect of the way in which race was practiced. The two occupations in which African American women's employment was overwhelmingly concentrated, domestic service and agricultural labor, were both excluded from coverage. This pairing is ironic: domestic service was quintessentially women's work while arduous agricultural labor was quite the opposite (Jones 1986). Yet the legacy of slavery was that these two spheres remained open to African American women. Considered neither "mothers" under the state minimum wage laws nor "breadwinners" under the federal law, African American women were left to forge their own definitions of womanhood.

It can certainly be construed as a minor victory that the FLSA did not permit unequal minima by gender. Given the limited coverage for working women, however, the impact of the victory was slight. Moreover, activists maintained a two-pronged policy: advocacy of gender-neutral federal legislation and efforts to maintain gender-specific laws at the state level.[15]

Multiplicity of living wages

What is the relationship between legislated wage floors and the more elusive concept of a living wage? Are they synonymous? Does the phrase "living wage" refer to a subsistence wage or does it evoke a higher standard of living? The debates over the FLSA reveal that there were a multiplicity of living wages. The term living wage was used with different meanings when referring to the living standards of different groups of workers.

John L. Lewis, more than the other witnesses testifying about the Fair Labor Standards Act, devoted a substantial portion of his remarks to the meaning of the concept of a living wage. At one point in his testimony, Lewis seemed to endorse the idea that the legislated minimum, even though it was meager, could be considered a living wage. He remarked,

> The unskilled workers or those in the lowest grade of the scale of occupations in an industry are entitled to receive *the subsistence or living wage*, and above this guaranteed minimum, semiskilled or skilled employees are paid differentials established by precedent or through

collective bargaining, based on skill, experience, and productivity, and hazard.

> (U.S. Congress 1937: 275, emphasis added)

Nevertheless, a few moments later he disputed treating the minimum wage as equivalent to a living wage:

> But I think it would be a calamity if such a wage minimum as that referred to should in any way be construed as a living wage. The labor movement with which I am associated is interested in securing for every American unskilled or semiskilled worker a living wage – that is to say, a minimum income upon which he can maintain himself and his family at a level of healthy and decent living.
>
> (U.S. Congress 1937: 275).

William Green further confused the issue by referring to collectively bargained minimum wages:

> The American Federation of Labor has insisted from the beginning upon the establishment of a living wage as a minimum, and it has through the force of organized effort succeeded in establishing minimum wages far superior to those prescribed by wage boards of other countries.
>
> (U.S. Congress 1937: 219)

This ambiguity of meaning has led some historians to try to fix the meaning of the term "living wage."

A plural noun

As documented by Lawrence Glickman in his book *A Living Wage* (1997), the phrase became an important demand of the U.S. labor movement during the years following the Civil War. This first wave of the living wage movement represents an important ideological transition. In the late nineteenth century, working-class rhetoric shifted from a discourse where all proletarianization was regarded as "wage slavery" to a distinction between a living wage and "slave wages." Glickman (1993, 1997) emphasizes working-class agency in the construction of the ideology of the living wage. Specifically, he shows that the demand for a living wage became linked to the idea that there was an "American standard of living" that was the basis for living as a free citizen with a virtuous character. He observes that it was primarily skilled, white, male workers who articulated this ideology and who had access to high-paid jobs and rising consumption standards. Further, Glickman also argues that this ideology "was wielded against immigrants, blacks, and women" who were viewed as a threat to this standard and were blamed for their supposed willingness to work for lower wages (1993: 228). Thus, he implicitly recognizes that the nineteenth-century vision of a living wage embodied a particular vision of masculinity, whiteness, and nationalism.

In discussing the passage of minimum wage laws, Glickman suggests that they constituted a retreat from a more radical working-class vision of living wages. He polarizes the debate into two camps: working class versus middle class. The social reformers who lobbied for minimum wages at the state and federal level in the early part of the twentieth century are labeled as "middle class." Passage of the Fair Labor Standards Act, Glickman charges, institutionalized legislated minimum wages as subsistence wages, effectively supplanting the working-class definition of a living wage.

Despite acknowledging the importance of gender, race, and nationality, Glickman treats the white, native-born male wage and living standard as the true representative of working-class aspirations. This distinction treats the working class, as well as the working-class living wage, as a unified concept. The social feminist movement to (in the words of the NCL slogan) "investigate, agitate, legislate" is presented as a repudiation of the working-class living wage. Attention to the FLSA debates indicates that it is incorrect to view these shadings as either temporal or class differences; multiple meanings of the term "living wage" persisted into the twentieth century and were understood by working-class advocates. They reflected different visions of what constituted a living for different groups of workers and how these visions could be strategically achieved. For those workers deemed relatively powerless, state protection was necessary. A higher status, and thus a higher wage, was appropriate for those organized male workers who represented the hegemonic form of masculinity among the working class.

Conclusion

The Great Depression provided a climate in which the programs long advocated by social feminist reformers could be institutionalized as national policies. The New Deal legitimated the concept that wages were a living and some minimal standard should be enforced by the state. The big difference between state minimum wage laws and the Fair Labor Standards Act of 1938 was that the New Deal legislation was written to be applied equally to men and women. The legacy of the earlier state-level experiments was that labor legislation was stigmatized as appropriate only for weak members of the labor force. Although the FLSA established a gender-neutral minimum wage, it was primarily directed toward male workers, particularly unskilled and unorganized male workers in manufacturing. Economic debates about market mechanisms, purchasing power, and regional costs were accompanied by discourse attempting to reconcile protective legislation for men. This was accomplished by differentiating masculinities and establishing a hierarchy based upon occupation, union status, and race. Women's wages and their need for a living wage became marginalized in this process.

Passage of the FLSA did not bring an end to the battle for a living wage. Organized labor, strengthened by the symbolism of federal recognition of the right to bargain, focused on various strategies for raising wages for their (mostly male) members. Unions also remained at the forefront of periodic campaigns to raise the floor. Women's groups stuck with the increasingly ineffectual state laws, until 1969 when litigation resulted in a decision that gender-specific legislation violated Title VII of the Civil Rights Act.

FLSA coverage was extended to many new groups of workers through a series of amendments in the 1960s and 1970s. For example, a 1961 amendment to the FLSA greatly expanded the number of workers covered in the retail trade industry. In 1967, laundries, public schools, nursing homes, the construction industry, and some farm workers became covered (see Elder and Miller 1979; Nordlund 1997). These reforms were linked to President Johnson's War on Poverty and the civil rights movement, and they clearly benefited many African American workers. However, in the early 1970s, the minimum wage for farm workers was set below that of other covered workers; this differential was eliminated in 1977. Changes in 1974 were aimed at workers who were excluded on the basis of the interstate commerce requirements. Specifically, some categories of domestic workers (those with fairly regular employment) were now included. Employees of small retail establishments were added fairly late, in 1989. Thus, many once excluded workers are now included under the (living wage) umbrella offered by the FLSA.

The transition from the minimum wage as a state-level policy for women to a gender-neutral federal policy aimed at male workers illustrates the fluidity of the meaning of living wages as a basis for policy and wage setting. Living wages is an organic concept, evolving with changing circumstances. While setting the level for state minimum wage laws opened up discussions about how women should live, men's wages were clearly identified with a living for breadwinners. Different definitions of a living wage were utilized with respect to different groups of workers. Living wages is a plural, not a singular, idea. Hence, the movement in the U.S. in the twentieth century has been a movement for *living wages*, rather than *a living wage*. Nevertheless, while fighting for living wages, feminists and others also advocated policies that would offer similar living standards and life options to different groups of workers. This movement for *equal wages* existed contemporaneously with the movement for living wages, yet did not gain a strong foothold until mid-century.

7 Job evaluation and the ideology of equal pay

State-level minimum wage laws for women and the federal minimum wage statute resulted from efforts to guarantee living wages for marginalized groups of workers. Adherence to living wages was, and continues to be, one of two important wage-setting principles that have inspired social movements and public policy. The second principle is equal wages. In the next two chapters, we trace how equal wages became a social norm and the basis for federal policy.

Advocates for working women began the twentieth century relatively alone in carrying the banner for equal wages. Equal pay principles conflicted with wage-setting practices that instituted separate scales for male and female workers even when they worked in similar positions. To effect equal pay, the Women's Bureau openly supported wages based on job content, asserting: "A correct or suitable rate for a job can be established only by an analysis of the specific requirements of the job" (Women's Bureau 1942: 22). As the rhetoric of paying the job rather than the worker became managerial policy, the slogan of working women's advocates – equal pay for equal work – became codified as a personnel practice.

A critical aspect of this process was the adoption of job evaluation by large employers during the period from the 1920s to the 1950s. Job evaluation was both a wage-setting technique and an ideology about the proper basis for establishing pay relativities. As a wage-setting technique, job evaluation, like public policy, reveals the implicit wage theories of the economic actors who proposed and shaped its practice. As an ideology, job evaluation promoted a criterion of paying for job content rather than the individual traits of a worker. This criterion was a variation on the concept of wages as a price, grounded less in the fluctuations of supply and demand than in productivity theory. A specific job generated value for the employer, regardless of the occupant. This form of wages as a price discourse overtook a living wage discourse that focused on workers' needs.

Nevertheless, the *definition* of equal pay for equal work with respect to gender was subject to interpretation. As *equal pay* became an accepted principle, the meaning of *equal work* was contested, specifically before the National War Labor Board during World War II and in the mass-marketing of packaged job evaluation systems after the war. At this juncture, the institutionalization of job evaluation could have taken several forms. At one extreme, firms could have maneuvered their job evaluation systems to preserve separate salary scales by gender, a lawful practice prior to the federal Equal Pay Act of 1963. Or, there could have been the broad institution of equal pay for work of equal value, what we now know as comparable worth, since job evaluation made comparisons of jobs performed by men and women more feasible.

Instead, a compromise emerged. Job evaluation contributed to the abolition of separate pay scales for men and women in the same job. In many big businesses, explicitly separate pay scales for men and women in the same job were eradicated. Yet at the same time, the prevailing job evaluation systems reproduced gendered pay practices in new ways, institutionalizing unequal pay between predominantly men's jobs and female-dominated occupations. Equal pay for equal work became an ideological basis for wage practices although women continued to be underpaid when they performed comparable work. Job evaluation, in this guise, was a social practice. That is, it was a means of institutionalizing particular sets of class, gender, and racial-ethnic relations.

The development and rhetoric of job evaluation

Nearly all organizations rank the relative value of jobs. The procedures for ranking jobs can be very elementary or extremely complex. Job evaluation formalizes the process. It is a procedure that hierarchically orders a set of jobs in terms of their characteristics or content. Simply put, the greater value or "worth" of a job within an organization, the higher the wage. Once a level of value of a job has been determined, a specific wage or salary is based on that value. Wages are set according to "the rate for the job." Proponents such as job evaluation pioneer Eugene Benge argued strenuously that "work should be paid for in direct relation to its value and not according to who does the job" (cited in Lytle 1946: 288). As the International Labour Office conveys, "Job evaluation rates the job, not the man [*sic*]" (1960: 8).

Although not widely adopted at the time, the earliest evaluation systems can be traced back to the U.S. Civil Service Commission in 1871. "Modern" job evaluation likely originated in 1912 with the Civil Service Commission of Chicago, followed shortly thereafter by Commonwealth Edison Company of Chicago (Patton and Smith 1950: 4). Beginning with the Classification Act of 1923, employees of the federal government received a uniform salary for each grade and class of work, that is, the rate for the job irrespective of sex, race, or any other individual characteristic.

With the growth of the size of enterprises in the 1910s and 1920s, job evaluation moved to the private sector. Four major job evaluation methods were developed: (1) ranking, (2) grade description, (3) factor comparison, and (4) point factor. The simplest methods, ranking and grade description, tended to employ "whole job analysis." Decision makers used their impressions of overall job content to rank or grade jobs. In an effort to reduce the subjectivity inherent in determining such rankings, there was a shift over time towards more "rational" and "scientific" methods of rating, including factor comparison and point factor systems.

In essence, these new forms of job evaluation applied the principles of scientific management to wage setting. Key individuals in the development of job evaluation techniques were management specialists and industrial engineers. The point factor job evaluation plan and the factor comparison method, a modification of the point factor plan, were developed and introduced by Merrill R. Lott and Eugene J. Benge respectively (Benge, Burk, and Hay 1941: 13–15; Beatty and Beatty 1984: 67). As Frederick Taylor promoted the reorganization of production techniques to improve efficiency by standardizing motions (scientific management), these advocates promoted the scientific organization of compensation systems.[1] Lott introduced point factor job evaluation in a 1925 article in *Management and Administration* entitled "Wage Scales with a Reason." The following year he expanded on the topic in his book, *Wage Scales and Job Evaluation*. The same year, 1926, Benge modified the point factor scheme, originating the factor comparison method (see Benge, Burk, and Hay 1941: 13–15; Patton and Smith 1950: 33; Lanham 1963: 108; Livy 1975: 13; Beatty and Beatty 1984: 67).

How job evaluation works

The *a priori* point factor method became the most common method of job evaluation. Edward N. Hay developed the most widely used "canned" or "off-the-shelf" *a priori* system, the Hay Guide Chart-Profile Method, and marketed it through the consulting firm that, to this day, bears his name. Here is how a point factor job evaluation system works. First, an organization selects job attributes that it believes are valuable. These are referred to as *compensable factors*. The most common categories of compensable factors are *skill* (including years of education and training requirements as proxies for skill); *effort* (primarily physical); *responsibility* for machinery, money, or people; and *working conditions* (what economists might call compensating differentials). The earliest plans included only the first three: skill, effort, and responsibility. Remuneration for difficult or hazardous working conditions was integrated later, largely at the behest of labor unions and industrial relations specialists. The relative weight of each compensable factor is determined in advance (or *a priori*) by determining a range of points that can be accumulated for each. Usually skill is weighted the highest.

The second step is to rate jobs or job classes. Job descriptions, detailed questionnaires, and interviews with employees and/or their supervisors are used to rate jobs on each compensable factor. Total point scores are then tallied for each job or job class. The third step assigns a wage rate, using a salary scale to relate a specified point score (or range of points) to a specific wage level. The greater the points, the higher the wage. Usually these salary scales come from wage surveys for key (or benchmark) jobs. As a hypothetical example, if a machinist is rated at 4600 points in a firm's job evaluation system, and a salary survey indicates that machinists earn a wage of $25 per hour in local markets, then the machinist and other jobs with similar point scores will be paid a comparable wage. Benchmark jobs are supposed to be those with clear comparators in external labor markets. Therefore, market wages influence the outcome of job evaluation systems.

Even though job evaluation explicitly focuses on establishing *internal* wage relativities, it was also viewed as a strategy for maintaining lower *absolute* wage levels. Advocates specifically portrayed job evaluation as either a preferable alternative to collective bargaining or a means of limiting negotiated wage increases. For example, Benge, Hay, and another co-author emphasized that job evaluation provides a "defensible" basis for setting relative wages (Benge, Burk, and Hay 1941). Wage rates set by collective bargaining were depicted as "unstable and subject to fluctuation, depending upon economic and labor conditions at the time when labor contracts are up for renewal," according to their 1941 manual (19). Comparing collective bargaining to wage determination by fiat or individual negotiations, they labeled all of these alternatives to job evaluation "unsystematic" (18). Hay noted that job evaluation "permits of considerable control over salary costs" (1940: 22).

This entailed a conscious rejection of labor's efforts to base wages on living standards – what we refer to as "wages as a living." Supporters of job evaluation viewed labor's effort to link wages to the cost of living as a fruitless quest that would be undermined by inflation. Specifically, Benge, Burk, and Hay asserted that "Wage scales which are geared to the cost of living, and move up or down in accordance with some accepted cost of living index, . . . start an upward or downward spiral in the cost of living itself" (1941: 16–17). Further, these industrial engineers expressed concern that competition between employers in tight labor markets ("piracies of employees by employers") put upward pressure on wages. Job evaluation was also supposed to reduce pay disparities across departments and divisions of the company and lessen employee grievances and spiraling wage costs due to competition between groups of employees or even individual employees within the organization. Job evaluation could thus "stabilize labor rates for the community" (179). The discourse used to promote job evaluation thus indicates a rising macroeconomic concern with inflation.

Although one intent was to reduce wage disparities, gender-based wage differentials were not the initial focus. The pioneers of early job evaluation did not raise the issue of gender in their writing. Overall, their key objective was to rationalize personnel policy.

Why employers adopted job evaluation

As they adopted job evaluation techniques, employers echoed the management specialists who developed them. Job evaluation was both "rational" and a means of reducing wage costs. Groups such as the American Management Association professed that job evaluation was a device to "maintain management control of the wage structure under collective bargaining" (Slichter, Healy, and Livernash 1960: 561). The largest and predominant business lobby, the National Association of Manufacturers, advocated job evaluation as "but one of a series of man-job controls" (NAM 1957: 3). The National Industrial Conference Board in the U.S. added that, at the bargaining table, job evaluation helps vindicate existing pay rates: "A sound system of compensation is particularly helpful at times of negotiation for higher rates of pay" (1940: 3). According to labor economist Herbert R. Northrup: "Job evaluation was used by management partly to deter or prevent unionization, partly to rationalize its wage scales prior to unionization . . . and partly to stabilize the wage structure and eliminate continuous bargaining over particular rates after unionization" (quoted in Hutner 1986: 25; see also Gomberg 1947).

Why were employers so concerned about stabilizing wage costs and disempowering unions? The evolution of job evaluation was contingent upon the economy, institutions, and gender relations in the relatively short time period from the 1920s to the 1950s. Widely adopted by the large manufacturing firms that constituted the dynamic sector of U.S. industry, job evaluation helped to restructure relations between management and labor. As described by David Gordon, Richard Edwards, and Michael Reich in *Segmented Work, Divided Workers* (1982), mass-production was replacing craft production. As a result of the new production methods, the number of varied yet relatively unskilled occupations had increased sharply.[2] Employers sought to pay their workers on the basis of this "deskilled" job content.

With the shift from craft to mass-production came a de-emphasis on individual ability: "while skilled craftsmen may be said to be paid in accordance with what they were able to do, semi-skilled and unskilled workers tend to be paid according to what they are actually doing" (ILO 1960: 7).[3] In the words of an industrial engineer at U.S. Steel, the goal was to "dissociate the individual from the job" (King 1938: 98). Managers in fast-growing industries argued that job evaluation was the best method of aligning rates of pay in industrial jobs, as the traditional craft wage structure based upon master, journeyman, apprentice, and helper was no longer applicable.

In the place of the old craft structure were new hierarchies based upon "internal labor markets." Institutional economists developed the concept of an internal labor market to describe the distribution of positions within large firms during the middle of the twentieth century. In a firm with an internal labor market, employees are hired into positions that are considered ports of entry. Upward mobility is then governed by a set of administrative rules and procedures. For example, a worker may receive on-the-job training to qualify for advancement.[4] In 1940, job evaluation expert Edward Hay wrote: "At first sight [job evaluation] seems to place a severe limit on individual earning power. Actually, however, it concentrates the attention of each employee on the necessity for qualifying for a higher position in order to deserve a further increase in salary" (Hay 1940: 22). In fact, the clear line between mass-production and traditional craft jobs had become blurred. Pay on the basis of job content, not personal attributes, complemented this system of labor relations.

Large firms were also replacing the paternalistic business leaders of an earlier era with a professional managerial class; the transition to paying the rate for the job coincided with this bureaucratization process. Job evaluation was designed to eliminate management practices that evaluated a worker's family circumstances, work history, and other personal considerations in determining wages. As firms grew and the personnel function became depersonalized, such discretion was discouraged (Edwards 1979).

For employers, job evaluation was a not-so-subtle repudiation of union bargaining power because evaluation determined "the rate for the job" on the basis of internal hierarchies and market wage surveys rather than collective negotiations. The rise of (militant) industrial unionism in big businesses was therefore also central to the story. The 1930s were marked by sit-down strikes as new unions mounted initial organizing drives in automobile manufacturing and other related industries. Labor turned their attention from the AFL's traditional base among the skilled crafts to the growing numbers of "semi-skilled" factory workers. In fact, unions were highly skeptical about job evaluation. From the traditional class perspective of predominantly male unionized workers, job evaluation practices represented a threat, a managerial strategy to control wage-setting practices and limit wage increases. While there was no singular voice of opposition in the U.S. from the AFL, CIO, or later the AFL-CIO, there certainly were objections raised by many individual unions. In their 1954 manual, *What's Wrong with Job Evaluation*, the International Association of Machinists (IAM) presented job evaluation as a direct threat to the union and its members. In its view, job evaluation pitted workers against one another, jockeying for better ratings within the system (cited in ILO 1960: 104–5). This undermined their unified voice in opposition to management.

Further, labor felt that management took advantage of workers' lack of understanding of all the techniques involved in point factor job evaluation. Metal workers called job evaluation so complex as to be largely incomprehensible (see ILO 1960: 103–8; Livy 1975: 140). The process placed wage issues in the hands of so-called management experts. Evaluation plans were often drawn up and "presented to the unions." A nationwide survey by the Bureau of National Affairs revealed that among companies that had unions at the time job evaluation was introduced, about one-half developed plans *without* active union participation (1956: 8–9).

Job evaluation before World War II

Job evaluation techniques were launched in two of the leading industries representative of the sectoral changes in the economy, the metal fabricating and electrical equipment industries. The National Metal Trades Association (NMTA) and National Electrical Manufacturers Association (NEMA) developed industry-wide point factor evaluation plans and encouraged their members to adopt them.[5] The NEMA plan was the first to utilize skill, effort, responsibility, and working conditions as categories of compensable factors (Treiman 1979: 6). An article in *Factory Management and Maintenance* promoting the NMTA plan was entitled "How to Rate Jobs and Men [*sic*]" (Kress 1939).

Table 7.1 lists some of the major companies that adopted job evaluation relatively early, that is, prior to 1940. Steel rolling mills, other metal trades, and electrical appliance manufacturers were well-represented, responding to the support of the trade associations. Three major retailers, Marshall Field, Montgomery Ward, and Sears, Roebuck had implemented job evaluation. Eight of the firms in Table 7.1 were among the thirty listed companies comprising the Dow Jones Industrial Average at that time – an indicator that they were considered dominant market leaders. Job evaluation was on the rise.

Table 7.1 Some major companies adopting job evaluation by 1940

For manufacturing and wage-earning jobs

American Optical Company – Metals Division	International Harvester*
	Kimberly-Clark Corporation
American Rolling Mill Company	Leeds and Northrup Company
American Telephone & Telegraph*	Marshall Field & Company
Atlantic Refining Company	Montgomery Ward
Carnegie-Illinois Steel	Revere Cooper and Brass Incorporated
Cheney Brothers Company	Sears, Roebuck and Company*
Cincinnati Milling Machine Company	Socony-Vacuum Oil Company
Firestone Tire & Rubber	Standard Oil of Ohio
Frigidaire Corporation	US Steel*
General Electric Company*	Westinghouse Electric and Manufacturing*
General Foods Corporation*	
Goodyear Tire and Rubber Company*	Wright Aeronautical Corporation
Hammermill Paper	

For salaried jobs
Atlantic Refining Company
General Electric Company*
General Foods Corporation*
The Pennsylvania Company
Westinghouse Electric and Manufacturing*

Sources: Riegel (1937); Walters (1938); National Industrial Conference Board (1940)

Note
*Indicates that the company was included in the Dow Jones Industrial Average as of March 14, 1939; the composition of the DJIA did not change again until July 3, 1956.

A group of employers who were beginning to pioneer "rational" wage administration procedures gathered at a series of conferences hosted by the Bureau of Industrial Relations at the University of Michigan in 1936. The purpose was to examine and discuss wage policies and practices. The forty-eight participating companies were among those who were the backbone of the industrial heartland, with the addition of large utility and retail employers, including: Carnegie-Illinois Steel, Firestone Tire & Rubber, General Electric, Hammermill Paper, International Harvester, Kimberly-Clark, Marshall Field & Company, Sears, Roebuck and Company, Standard Oil of Ohio, and Westinghouse Electric and Manufacturing.[6] As a sequel to the conference, the Bureau of Industrial Relations surveyed salary determination policies and procedures in forty top U.S. companies, including manufacturers, public utilities, retailers, banks, insurance companies, plus one each of educational institutions, consultants, and civil service commissions.

The information gathered at the University of Michigan conferences and in the subsequent study was assembled into two volumes by Bureau Director John Riegel in 1937 and 1940. Riegel favored job evaluation as an improved method of wage determination. He viewed the conference as a means of promoting the practice:

> The leading companies whose experience has been reviewed state that their aim is to adjust wages according to reasonable and open methods. They intend to graduate and adjust the wages of their employees fairly, and to avoid unwarranted wage discrimination against any divisions of their companies, against any grades of work in a division, and against any persons in a given occupation.
>
> (Riegel 1937: 118)

Thus, the emphasis was on internal equity in pay practices. However, these employers were also interested in mirroring market wages within their organizations, and the early chapters of Riegel's first report emphasize the importance of wage surveys to establish rates of pay for key jobs within organizations.

Gender and job evaluation before the war

Neither of Riegel's two volumes devotes more than passing attention to the issue of pay rates by gender. Nor did Riegel raise the issue of gender in a major address on job evaluation to the Detroit chapter of the Society for the Advancement of Management in 1945 (Society for the Advancement of Management 1945). In part, this is because gendered pay practices were so prevalent as to generate little comment.

A two-tiered wage structure for men and women was not only taken for granted culturally, it was a perfectly legal workplace practice. Unequal wages derived from the faulty assumption that men were breadwinners who deserved a family wage and that most women were secondary earners, primarily supported by husbands, fathers, or brothers. Hiring rates (the starting salaries at a firm) were generally lower for women than for men. In wage surveys, the gender composition of the job – "sex of the operators" – was a key variable when gathering information in the salary surveys that were used to determine pay rates for benchmark jobs. If an employer was surveying the prevailing wage for, let us say assemblers of electric appliances that were mostly female, they would only be compared with the wages of female assemblers in other firms. The sex of the job incumbent was as important as job content in defining comparators. Salary surveys treated men and women as existing in separate labor markets: men's wages reflected market rates for men and women's wages reflected market rates for women. Even those women who did identical work to men earned lower pay for that work.[7]

In the second of Riegel's volumes, *Salary Determination: Common Policies and Selected Practices in Forty American Corporations*, it is noted that employers' policies on men's and women's wages still followed the practice of unequal pay for equal work, except in rare instances:

> Most of the companies visited have separate salary scales for men and women. The salary scale for men is priced with reference to prevailing rates in the community for men's positions, and the women's salary scale is priced with reference to prevailing rates in the community for women's positions. In junior clerical positions, the "equal pay for equal work" rule is often followed. Many young men in such positions, however, are in training for higher positions filled only by men.
>
> (Riegel 1940: 42–3)

Riegel also reported that executives challenged the notion that women and men would do comparable work or the same work. One pointed out that even in the same jobs, women "do not deal with the more difficult cases" (1940: 43). Some positions were filled by women in the day shift and men in the night shift; the day shift was priced according to the "women's scale" and the night shift to the "men's scale."

Of course, it was still relatively uncommon to find men and women in the same jobs. According to Riegel, "The conferees noted with approval that most occupations in their companies were filled respectively by men or by women throughout. The conference favored the segregation of men's jobs and women's jobs for valuation purposes" (1937: 21). In the written survey, some companies openly reported on their policy to fill any position exclusively with men or exclusively with women. Companies also resorted to changing the designation of an occupation: "When a company finds that a particular position can be filled by women as well as by men, there is a tendency to substitute women for men and apply the [cheaper] rates in the women's scale" (Riegel 1940: 43).

At this time, prior to World War II, job evaluation was attuned to structural economic trends and early systems were reconciled with the pre-existing practice of separate pay scales for men and women. Where men and women performed similar work, unequal pay for equal work remained a common, legitimate practice. Many employers clung to separate pay scales for men and women in the same job. The principle of equal pay for equal work by gender conflicted with generalized social norms. It took the influx of women into formerly male job enclaves during World War II and active state involvement in wage setting to dislodge these gendered practices.

Further, the ideology of equal pay for equal work, although put forward in order to stabilize class relations, *destabilized* the prevailing logic of gender wage differentials. Job evaluation textbooks, written for employers and personnel specialists, were beginning to cite the principle of "equal pay for equal work":

> Job evaluation deals with jobs impersonally and is not concerned with the race, creed, color, age, or sex of the employee unless in some way these personal variations become pertinent to the jobs. Equal pay for equal work is the very essence of job evaluation.
>
> (Lytle 1946: 287)

> The purpose of job evaluation is to find out exactly what each job is and to measure its true value in relation to all other jobs in the company. When this measure has been determined, the pay rates for all jobs can be established on the basis of equal pay for equal work.
>
> (Johnson, Boise, and Pratt 1946: 1)

However, it was not until World War II that equal pay for equal work began to be institutionalized as ideology and, less completely, as practice.

The legitimation of equal pay for equal work

During the 1940s, as working women entered newly available manufacturing jobs in war industries, the issue of women's wage rates became a pressing policy issue. The Women's Bureau took an active role in documenting the extent of pay equity and inequity. In a key study, *"Equal Pay" for Women in War Industries* (1942), the Bureau defended equal wages using the discourse of wages as a living, wages as a price, and wages as a social practice. It argued that women's health and morale depended upon earning living wages. Women's responsibility for supporting dependents, alone or in conjunction with other family members, was another recurring theme. Further, pay differentials for the same or comparable work were unfair since the price of labor should reflect the value of the work performed. Finally, the Bureau asserted that if wage standards in manufacturing were eroded by paying women less than men earned before the war, this would be disruptive to the morale of men in the armed forces.

Management had other uses for job evaluation. There is no evidence of a shift in employer attitudes towards equal pay for women – whether they were in men's jobs or traditionally female industries. As noted by industrial relations scholars Baker and True (1947: 62), wage administrators were resistant to eliminating gender-based wage differentials, citing competition. Since common practice in job evaluation did not *lower* any worker's wage to correct imbalances, pay equity could only be achieved by *raising* women's wages, increasing wage costs relative to discriminating employers.[8]

However, there was a new alliance between labor and management. One reason was management and union efforts to increase wages by any means during wartime stabilization policies. The Wage and Salary Stabilization Law of 1942 authorized the President to issue a general order stablizing prices, wages, and salaries. Faced with labor shortages during the war, management, ironically, sought to use job evaluation techniques as a way of justifying wage increases under these wage and price controls. "The popularity of job evaluation swelled during World War II," argued personnel experts John Patton and Reynold Smith in their textbook on job evaluation (1950).

Under the wage stabilization policies, there was a new actor taking a stronger role in wage determination: the state. The National War Labor Board (NWLB) during World War II, modeled partly on its World War I predecessor of the same name, was charged by President Roosevelt with resolving any impasse in wartime labor relations. (Unions had generally agreed to a "no-strike pledge" for the duration of the war.) The War Labor Board was comprised of an equal number of management and labor appointees, plus representatives from the public.[9] The decisions of the Board hoisted job evaluation, especially analytic point-factor methods, into the spotlight. Under Executive Order No. 9250 issued October 3, 1942, the National War Labor Board would not approve any increase in the wage rates prevailing on September 15, 1942, unless such increase was necessary to correct maladjustments or inequalities, to eliminate substandards of living, or to aid in the effective prosecution of the war (National War Labor Board n.d.: v. 1, xix). The Board was hesitant to intervene on the basis of "substandards of living," that is, the lack of a living wage. Very few increases were granted on this basis (NWLB n.d.: v. 1, 211).

According to the Board, an employer could conduct a job evaluation and use the findings to argue that certain jobs were underpaid. Anomalies and inequities in the wage structure – "scientifically" determined by job evaluation studies – were admitted by the War Labor Board as grounds for granting wage increases. Industrial relations scholars have pointed out that the Board did not order job evaluation, per se, but "it frequently required the parties to bargain out inequities within the framework of an order setting up certain guides and controls" stimulating formal or informal evaluation (Slichter, Healy, and Livernash 1960: 562). Unions, who had few opportunities to obtain raises for their members during the war, went along with the practice.[10]

The use of job evaluation to reduce inequalities and legitimate wage increases opened the door to its application for the purposes of equal pay for equal work. In fact, the War Labor Board strongly endorsed the principle of the rate for the job. This support is perhaps best illustrated by a statement by its Chairman, George W. Taylor. Taylor was a Professor at the Wharton School at the University of Pennsylvania and would return there after the war. In a speech before the American Management Association, the Chairman revealed:

> One of the most striking impressions I have of American wage rate structures is a failure of a large part of industry to develop properly aligned wage schedules in the plants – with jobs defined, rates standard for those classifications and rates for particular jobs compensating with reasonable accuracy for the skill involved. Too many wage scales have what I call "random rates" based not on the job but on the individual.
>
> (quoted in NWLB n.d.: v. 1, 243)

According to sociologist Ruth Milkman, a case brought to the board in 1942 by the United Automobile Workers (UAW) and the United Electrical Workers of America (UE) was regarded as a "milestone" because it helped to firmly establish equal pay for equal work as government policy. The September 26, 1942, decision stated that "Wages should be paid to female employees on the principle of equal pay for equal work" (quoted in Milkman 1987: 74).[11] On June 5, 1943, the Board issued an opinion in a dispute over pay differences based upon race in the Southport Petroleum Company and affirmed equal pay by race. In what the Board itself called a "small but significant case," separate classifications for "colored laborer" and "white laborer" were combined and all laborers were brought up to the higher wage level. The opinion asserted that this ruling was justified by "the democratic formula of equal pay for work equal in quantity and quality in the same classification" (NWLB n.d.: v. 2, 339).[12]

On November 24, 1942, the Board issued General Order No. 16 providing for pay adjustments "which equalize the wage or salary rates paid to females with the rates paid to males for comparable quality and quantity of work on the same or similar operations" (NWLB, n.d.: v. 1, 290).[13] The Board noted that "identical jobs, under this policy, may not be remunerated at different rates on the basis of the sex of the occupants of the job."[14] Their primary concern, however, was with women moving into men's jobs: "The analyst should bear in mind the fact that General Order No. 16 does not apply to jobs historically assigned only to women" (v. 2, 1015).

Thus, although equal pay for equal work gained legitimacy during this period, those who sought the broader interpretation, that is, equal pay for work of equal value or comparable worth, were less successful. Throughout the war, considerable disputes ensued over comparable worth. The United Electrical Workers of America took a strong stand in favor, arguing that it was not enough to demand equal pay for equal work: "The guarantee of equal pay for equal work does nothing whatsoever to remove or cut down the inequalities between rates for men's and women's jobs" (UE 1943: 91). In an NWLB case that demanded equal pay for work of equal value, the UE challenged the job evaluation systems at General Electric and Westinghouse that still assigned different pay rates by gender of a job's incumbents. Management responded that these gender-based rate differentials were long-standing, accepted by the union during bargaining rounds, and in line with industry practices (NWLB n.d.: v. 1, 295). To pay women more would put the firms at a competitive disadvantage. If one assumed that market wages reflected the value of the job (a core premise of wages as a price), an employer who paid more would have to raise prices, thus losing customers, or lose profits. Also, the employers made arguments that reflected wages as a social practice, saying that the Board should consider "sociological factors," that is, women's different social and economic roles.

On December 12, 1945, the Board ultimately decided this case in the union's favor, albeit on very narrow grounds. Women in the plants were granted small wage increases and the employers were urged to use a single evaluation system and wage scale for all jobs. The G.E.-Westinghouse opinion elaborated specific principles regarding the Board's equal pay policy. First, equal pay for equal work was defined to cover women in the same jobs as men, in jobs formerly performed by men, and jobs which differed "inconsequently" from men's jobs. Intangible cost factors that employers claimed were associated with hiring women were not a legitimate reason to reduce women's wages. Second, the Board determined that "The rates for jobs which have historically been performed by women only, and which differ measurably from the jobs performed by men, are presumed to be correct" (NWLB n.d.: v. 1, 296). Job evaluation could be used to justify lower wages for women. Therefore, the union's victory was both pyrrhic and short-lived.

Milkman notes that employers largely ignored the positive aspects of the decision; to replace separate pay scales, gendered concepts such as the distinction between "light" and "heavy" work became a basis for unequal pay (Milkman 1987: 80–1; see also Steinberg 1984). Intra-occupational segregation, for example, hiring men and women in different plants, was also a way to maintain wage differentials. The final report of the War Labor Board is clear that the Board favored job evaluation as a method of reducing conspicuous intra-plant inequalities, but it permitted interplant wage disparities by gender (NWLB n.d.: v. 1; Parrish 1948).

Although women's advocates continued to assert both dimensions of equal pay, they faced an uphill battle, as we shall see in the next chapter. Comparable worth remained a more contentious principle than equal pay for equal work. In fact, job evaluation methods were used to institutionalize unequal pay for work of comparable value.

Postwar job evaluation as a gendered compromise

The active promotion of job evaluation by the NWLB reverberated during the postwar period. Between the end of World War II and 1957, "it is probable that no other practice of business management has gained so rapidly in acceptance as the use of job evaluation" (Patton and Littlefield 1957: vii). Some percentages prior to and after the war are revealing. In 1940, about 13 percent of firms in industry used job evaluation, according to a survey of personnel practices by the National Industrial Conference Board; another Conference Board survey found that the percentage had multiplied to 59 percent by 1948. Firms were more likely to use job evaluation for hourly-paid and salaried employees than for supervisory or executive positions (Quaid 1993: 30). Job evaluation was nearly universal in large firms and was quickly reaching medium and small firms. A national "Personnel Policies Forum" survey of 132 personnel and industrial relations executives by the Bureau of National Affairs (BNA) in 1956 confirmed: "Some kind of job evaluation plan is in use in six out of seven of the larger companies and three fourths of the smaller firms" (1956: 1). One estimate indicated that about two-thirds of the labor force was covered (Livy 1975: 136).

The techniques were introduced to more and more managers through information bulletins from the National Association of Manufacturers and through the American Management Association "handbooks" in 1950, 1952, and 1954. Handbook chapters were authored by both scholars and industry practitioners. An extensive survey published by the American Management Association in 1961 confirmed that job evaluation had a firm stronghold. More than 90 percent of companies affirmed they would initiate a job evaluation plan if they did not have one (Patton 1961: 75).

Wages and science: selling job evaluation

Many job evaluation textbooks in the postwar era specified that the plan must be sold to employees as well as to managers themselves. With the war-era wage and price controls lifted, organized workers, especially white males, had little reason to continue supporting the practice.[15] Most companies made attempts to enlist support for new job evaluation plans through meetings with workers, union representatives, letters and flyers (BNA 1956). Therefore, popular publications aimed at workers flourished in the 1950s. The appendix to the 1950 American Management Association (AMA) *Handbook of Wage and Salary Administration* (Dooher and Marquis 1950) contains a reproduction of an entire "comic book" given to employees of the Armstrong Cork Company summarizing and explaining how job evaluation affects their hourly pay rate. Booklets with titles such as *You and Your Wages* led to what management called "effective results" (Patton and Smith 1950: 206–7). A later survey completed for the AMA concluded that the success of job evaluation depends upon the way the program is explained (Patton 1961).

For employees, including line managers who generally rose from the ranks,
job evaluation advocates utilized the language of "wages as a living." In a
1960 handbook for line managers published by the American Management
Association, readers were reminded that "the 'price' of employee services
represents income to employees as well as part of the cost of doing business"
(Sibson 1960: 15). The "market approach" to wage setting ignored one of the
three faces of wages – that for workers wages represented the means to
acquire a standard of living. Business understood this. They appealed to
workers by presenting job evaluation as an alternative to a cold and
indifferent market:

[The market approach] rests primarily on the proposition that managers
need merely pay the "going rate" for workers in various categories, and
market forces will automatically result in equitable pay. This may have

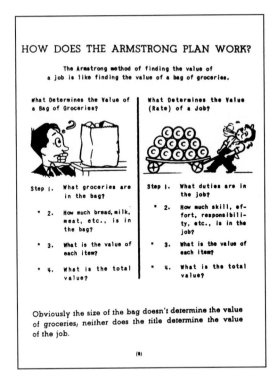

Plate 7.2 "How Does the Armstrong Plan Work?" A page from the former Armstrong Cork Company's (later Armstrong World Industries, Inc.) pamphlet, *Your Hourly Rate*, explaining job evaluation to its employees

Source: reprinted from *The AMA Handbook of Wage and Salary Administration* edited by M. Joseph Dooher and Vivienne Marquis. Copyright 1950 by American Management Association, New York, NY. Used with permission. All rights reserved

been a practical method of solving company pay problems at some time in the dim past, but it is completely unworkable as a basic approach under current conditions. Labor markets are not that clearly defined and many jobs are unique to individual companies. Furthermore, the application of the "natural laws of supply and demand" may be too harsh to be acceptable to employees, the business, or the community.

(Sibson 1960: 19)

Eventually, union resistance was worn down. Organized labor cautiously and gradually accepted job evaluation and began to solicit more of a voice in the process. Some unions began to seek ways of integrating job evaluation with collective bargaining. Basically, a bargain was struck between labor and management. Unions accepted job evaluation as a means of establishing relative wage rates within the firm, so long as collective bargaining over wage increases could continue. Management also moved toward accommodation. Job evaluation was not used to deter union organizing, but it did limit the scope of collective bargaining. This type of deal making was characteristic of the early postwar period. Labor and management formed an uneasy alliance as unions embraced a philosophy of what has been termed "business unionism" (see Moody 1988).

In order to sell job evaluation, there was no end to descriptions of the technique as "rational," "scientific," "systematic," "logical," "consistent," "sound," "providing hard data," "reasonable," "impartial," "less subjective," "reliable," "a sharper tool," and "superior." For example:

> Job evaluation follows the principles of scientific management. The scientific method of approaching a business problem is based on a systematic way of thinking. It is not necessary that we have laboratory-devised and control-tested formulas in order to establish such a system. But it is necessary to establish a uniform, inflexible framework for thinking about jobs, so that the plan administrators and the supervisors will use the same factor values.
>
> (Johnson, Boise, and Pratt 1946: 275; see also Smyth
> and Associates and Murphy 1946: 4–5)

As feminist scholars have noted, this science-based terminology served to legitimate the wage structure because of cultural associations between rational science and masculinity, in opposition to supposedly feminine subjectivity (Ferber and Nelson 1993).

Economists and job evaluation

Labor was sold on the practice of job evaluation through a combination of strategic maneuvers and rhetorical arguments. The stability and objectivity of job evaluation were posited as beneficial to workers. Ironically, these claims of objectivity were either ignored or contested by most academic economists. For neoclassical wage theorists, any wage-setting practices that deviated from market rates would be corrected by market forces; therefore, the institutions used for setting wages could conveniently be ignored. Economist Frank Pierson, writing in 1957, observed in fact that labor economists lagged in their incorporation of job evaluation techniques into wage theory. A search for articles by subject in the *Index of Economic Journals* from the 1920s through the 1960s, a reference publication listing journal articles in ninety economics and industrial relations journals (similar to today's *Journal of Economic Literature*), revealed a general neglect of the topic of job evaluation. This contrasts markedly with management journals such as the *Harvard Business Review*, which regularly discussed new techniques in personnel administration, job analysis and classification, and wage policies.

A few labor economics texts in the early postwar period did tackle the issue of job evaluation. These economists were more open to the role of institutional and administrative factors in labor markets, while generally defending market forces. Most challenged proponents' claims of the objectivity of job evaluation. For example, Lloyd Reynolds (1971 [1951]) argued that "it is not possible to 'measure' the relative worth of different jobs with the precision and impersonality of a thermometer. The ranking of jobs continues to rest on a multitude of qualitative judgments" (263). Although not rejecting job evaluation outright, Reynolds had reservations. Similarly, Harvard professor Robert Livernash wrote that "job evaluation is not a rigid, objective, analytical procedure." However, he adds that "Neither is it a meaningless process of rationalization" (1957: 163). In *The Economics of Labor*, E. H. Phelps Brown (1962) asserted: "job evaluation . . . may rest upon the direct observation of different jobs; but this observation cannot provide objective measurement – only subjective assessments that are private to each observer, even though at any one time consensus prevails" (129). On a related note, he is also suspicious of wage regulation because it is at variance with "the facts of the market" (206).

Despite acknowledging the importance of decision making within firms, institutional economists were also wary of job evaluation. For example, Clark Kerr and Lloyd Fisher (1950) argued that job evaluation was "compounded of many nonobjective elements" (88). Kerr and Fisher were particularly concerned about the undercompensation of job hazards and physical exertion, the compensable factor of working conditions. They were also suspicious of its use by management to reduce the bargaining power of unions. According to Kerr and Fisher, internal wage structures neglect "external considerations" (1950: 77). These external considerations include market wages, which they defend in the following manner: "The fact remains that the failure of a [job evaluation] plan to account for recognized wage levels is an open invitation for employee dissatisfaction and labor union strife to arise" (78). Looking through the lens of skilled labor, the traditional constituency of labor unions, they saw market rates as determined, in part, by the bargaining power of scarce labor.

Nevertheless, Kerr and Fisher suggested that other constituencies might benefit from job evaluation. While organized labor could rely upon bargaining strength to lift market wages, "weaker groups are better served by an evaluation plan than by the market; the former places the emphasis not on force but on equity" (1950: 93). They listed among the weaker groups janitors, nurses, and typists. Whereas job evaluation was inimical to skilled craft workers, for workers in undervalued, female-dominated and minority-concentrated jobs, the process of internal job rating held promise. Market wages for these occupations tend to be lower than their relative rankings in job evaluation plans.

The "scientific" basis for unequal pay

To reconcile pre-existing gender wage hierarchies with the principle of paying the job and not the person, job evaluation itself was used to rationalize
pay inequities. Specifically, job evaluation practitioners maintained the gender of the job class as an element in wage determination. In this section, each
of three common practices is discussed: (1) the separation of job evaluation
by gender of occupation, (2) the priority given to the attributes of male-
dominated occupations, and (3) the procedures used to link point scores to
salaries. All of these practices were adopted by various employers and job
evaluation practitioners.

For example, Baker and True (1947) cited one company's job evaluation
administrators who suggested all of these as alternatives to pay equity. These
practitioners explicitly recommended excluding female occupations from
the job evaluation plan, excessively weighting "male characteristics" such as
"strenuousness," or using different wage scales for converting points to pay
(62). In job evaluation textbooks written in the 1940s and 1950s, there were
overt recommendations to separate job evaluation for clerical jobs and factory jobs. One early text advised that a committee evaluate clerical and technical occupations such as typist, tabulating machine operator, and librarian
separately from blue-collar, production jobs, and further that this evaluation
be completed after key factory jobs are selected and evaluated. The rationale:
"Clerical and technical grades can then be set up so they are in line with
factory standards, which determine the relative pay rates of the great majority of employees. Otherwise the selection of key clerical and technical jobs is
based on the same principles as apply to key factory jobs" (Johnson, Boise,
and Pratt 1946: 27). Managers were directed to give corresponding labor-
grade numbers to office jobs whose pay was equal to that of factory jobs,
adding additional grades at the top and the bottom of the scale (the top for
jobs with specialized education and the bottom presumably for undervalued,
feminized jobs).

Feminist scholars have found that characteristics traditionally associated
with women's jobs remain invisible in traditional job evaluation schemes
(see, for example, Steinberg 1992). In fact, separate job evaluation systems
meant that male and female jobs could be evaluated according to slightly
different factors or factor weights. On the one hand, the separation of job
evaluation procedures was justified by pointing to the "physical effort" and
"unusual hazards" compensable factors as "unnecessary" or "not ordinarily
included" for evaluating clerical and technical jobs (Johnson, Boise, and Pratt
1946: 21, 22).[16] Union staff member Solomon Barkin, Director of Research
for the Textile Workers Union of America, CIO, criticized the hypocrisy of
job evaluation practices regarding the value of education. In systems for
factory workers, education was highly weighted. This meant that manual
labor jobs were undervalued, given the onerous working conditions. While
his intent was not to point to gender bias, he nevertheless opined that despite

the education needed for clerical jobs, "we know that the present labor market does not tend to pay as high a rate of pay to the clerical white collar jobs as to the production jobs" (cited in Gomberg 1947: 67).

On the brighter side, those same textbooks argued that clerical and technical jobs had extra responsibilities that should be valued in their own right, including responsibility for contacts with others, responsibility for errors, and responsibility for confidential data. Some job evaluation experts also suggested inclusion of a "mental and visual demand" factor. These are precisely the types of factors that feminist pay equity advocates fought to include in comparable worth job evaluations in the 1980s (Figart and Kahn 1997: ch. 5; Steinberg 1999).

As feminist social scientists who are pay equity proponents have argued in their research, the very nature of what constitutes job complexity is itself socially constructed and culturally specific. In early evaluation systems, the existing wage rates for jobs were used as the basis for determining what types of job content were complex. In other words, if a high-paying job involved responsibility for control of budgets, budget responsibility was treated as involving high levels of job complexity. Job evaluation systems assigned high point values to such job content. By contrast, if a lower-paying job involved responsibility for client well-being, this responsibility was treated as involving low levels of job complexity. It, thus, received a low point value. Then, once a hierarchy of job content complexity had been constructed, any references to the wage structure on which it was based were dropped (Schwab 1980; Treiman and Hartmann 1981).

The feminist literature on pay equity has devoted less attention to the racialized content of compensable factors. For example, the prototypical undervalued female-dominated occupations were largely the domain of white women until the 1960s. However, minority-concentrated occupations also possess skills that are unrecognized and undervalued. Several occupations that are both female-dominated and minority-concentrated involve cleaning. Like child care, knowing how to clean is often viewed as either a natural ability or a general, not specialized, skill, justifying lower compensation. Further, there has been less attention to disparities in the cultural valuation of compensable factors other than skill, that is, effort, responsibility, and working conditions. Adverse working conditions, including exposure to disease, in minority-concentrated health occupations such as nursing aides, orderlies, and attendants are not recognized and awarded compensation equivalent to that received by white, male road construction workers who endure the outdoors (see Figart and Lapidus 1998).

According to job evaluation's defenders, internal hierarchies were to be determined through point-factor and other classification methods. Then, wage surveys were utilized to determine the appropriate salary scale for a given evaluated point score/classification. Here too gender bias was incorporated into the process. In a chapter of the 1950 AMA *Handbook of Wage and Salary Administration* on "How to Conduct a Wage Survey," a sample questionnaire is included as an example. On the first page of the form, after occupation, grade, and code, just prior to hours and pay rates, there is a column for "Sex" of the job (Dale 1950: 96). In another job evaluation text, on a sample wage survey form to be completed in an on-site interview with a participating firm, the second question asks the minimum company hiring rate for a male and a female (Patton and Smith 1950: 140). One company was found to use separate wage curves for male and female jobs with identical evaluated point scores (Lytle 1946: 287–8).[17]

Thus, wage administrators utilized a variety of methods to maintain gender wage differentials. The Director of the Management Engineering Department of the International Ladies' Garment Workers' Union, AFL, William Gomberg, noted that these practices contradicted the basic principles of job evaluation:

> if "the job carries the rate," as proponents of job evaluation insist, the question arises why then have some well known evaluation manuals provided differentials between "male" and "female" rates? There is no logical answer to this criticism. The excuse may be offered that such discriminatory differentials were imbedded in the wage structure long before job evaluation was introduced. Nevertheless it seems necessary that such obvious inconsistencies should be eliminated if the claims of job evaluation are to be taken seriously.
>
> (Gomberg 1947: 15; see also Baker and True 1947: 62)

At another point in his union manual on job evaluation, Gomberg focused on the issue of *occupational segregation*, which he noted was more prevalent than unequal pay for equal work. Advocating job evaluation as a means to pay equity, Gomberg asserted, "There is no logical reason why women whose jobs have the same point value as men should not be paid the same rate as men" (1947: 61).

The principle of paying the job, not the person, opened the door for working women at the same time that the implementation of job evaluation stymied women's progress. In the words of University of Michigan economist Z. Clark Dickinson:

> The slogans "equal pay for equal work" and "the rate for the job" both express too narrowly the real objective of equality of economic opportunity between the sexes, for they concentrate attention too exclusively on the rather few occupations which are common to both sexes in peacetime, or in which women replace men during wartime. An adequate programme of job evaluation attempts to make proper allowance for all compensable factors, to the end that wage rates shall be equitable, not merely within but as between all occupations.
>
> (Dickinson 1943: 711)

The full potential of job evaluation thus was not realized. Job evaluation was constructed as a gendered social practice. The narrow interpretation of equal pay for equal work that emerged from World War II was ultimately institutionalized in federal wage policy, a process described in the next chapter.

Conclusion: from equal pay to equal value

The widespread institution of job evaluation by industry during and immediately following World War II was an important moment in the history of wage determination. From a purely class perspective, job evaluation was clearly a regressive development. The practice was cultivated and implemented as an end run around labor unions, taking wage relativities off the bargaining table. Ideologically, the battle over the adoption of job evaluation was a contest between labor's view that the level of wages should be bargainable and job evaluation experts' view that wages were a cost to employers that needed to be stabilized. This contest revolved around issues of how wages as prices should be determined rather than the demand for a living wage.

From a gender perspective, the practice is more complex. On the one hand, it opened the door to equal pay for equal work and even equal pay for work of equal value. Job evaluation trumpeted the phrase "equal pay for equal work," establishing a precedent for contemporary equality discourse. Paying the rate for the job became construed as a form of fairness. Women's advocates thus grounded their argument for equal wages on the conviction of getting prices right. However, with the door to equal pay ajar, job evaluation came face-to-face with the pre-existing practice of separate pay scales for men and women. Resistance to equal pay was justified on the basis of costs and prevailing social relations. The dissonance had to be resolved.

The concept of equal wages had different meanings to different constituencies. A narrow definition, that came to be synonymous with equal pay for equal work, required men and women to work side by side, performing identical tasks for the same employer in the same plant or location. This idea that men and women who do equal work deserve the same pay has since become a generalized social norm. In the opening address to a 1952 conference hosted by the Women's Bureau, Secretary of Labor Maurice J. Tobin spoke of equal pay as a social norm and an economic practice:

> Ask the average businessman, the laboring man, and the public servant whether he believes in equal pay, and you will get virtually unanimous agreement. They are for it just as they are against sin. And it is a pretty general assumption that women *do* get equal pay. But the reality is often a denial of general belief.
>
> (Women's Bureau 1952: 7; emphasis in original)

Even the National Association of Manufacturers' Board of Directors approved a recommendation by its Industrial Relations Committee in support of equal pay for equal work on April 24, 1942. Popular acceptance of the principle of equal pay for equal work appeals to a fair-play ethic, yet the principle remains stronger than the practice. Several studies find that women's earnings are fairly close to men's earnings when they are employed by the same establishment and are in the same, narrowly defined, occupation (Sieling 1984; Gunderson 1989; Petersen and Morgan 1995).[18] Wage differences of only 5–10 percent are typical. In other words, within-job wage discrimination is lower than wage differentials based upon occupational segregation. Nevertheless, these estimates indicate that unequal pay for equal work still persists and ongoing implementation is imperative.

Broader concepts of equal pay have focused on substantially similar, rather than identical, work. These broader meanings, though, were shunted aside. Job evaluation, since it was designed to compare the relative value of different jobs, could have been utilized to compare the wages of men's and women's jobs. Instead, the most common job evaluation plans institutionalized pay differentials focused on the gender of the job class. Under the veil of a supposedly more scientific approach to wage determination, traditional gender hierarchies have remained an important arbiter of pay scales. Most job evaluation systems incorporated the gender bias of the early twentieth century, perpetuating and rationalizing the existing two-tiered wage structure without explicit reference to the gender of individual incumbents. As illustrated in Chapter 9, it was not until the 1980s that job evaluation was extensively criticized by feminist scholars and then utilized by activists and policy makers as a practical means of implementing equal pay for work of equal value.

8   Legislating equal wages

> The fight for equal pay, i.e. "the rate for the job without regard to sex" lacks
> the glamour of the battles waged in the United States by the feminists earlier
> in the century which finally won women the vote. No "equal pay" parade has
> yet taken place. No newspaper has reported a single brick thrown through a
> window, nor the name of one woman worker willingly dragged off for a night
> in prison to dramatize the economic injustice to women.
>
> (Women's Bureau 1952: 1)

The principle of equal pay for equal work, legitimated by the National War
Labor Board and institutionalized through job evaluation in industry, gained
acceptance after World War II. However, adopting the principle of equal
wages and passing legislation mandating equal wages were different matters.
Further, the version of equal pay endorsed by the National War Labor Board
(NWLB) and employer associations was not what many advocates had
wished for. It was only a very narrow conception of equal pay – for virtually
identical work – not equal pay for comparable work. Job evaluation methods
effected in the decades surrounding World War II reproduced unequal pay
for work of equal value.

As a result, wage gaps were maintained, or even widened, *between* traditionally "women's work" and "men's work." Women's wages remained
below men's, even when comparable work was performed by both sexes
(Women's Bureau 1952, 1963). Although differences between men's and
women's wages *within* detailed occupational categories were small relative to
the gap between men's occupations and women's occupations (Sanborn
1964), even the more limited definition of equal pay for equal work was not
enforced.

In a study of the Board's decisions for a Master's thesis at American
University, Ella Joan Polinsky commented that the NWLB was shy
about overtly ordering equal pay for men's and women's jobs. The Board's
reticence had an impact on the way equal pay was implemented:

> In summary, it may be said that while the equal-pay principle has been

recognized as national policy, it has not been applied on a national basis. It has been applied to jobs where women have replaced men or where they do the same work as men. It has not been applied on women's jobs or on jobs where the rates for the same job vary from plant to plant. The task of extending the equal-pay principle to these areas by narrowing or removing sex differentials still needs to be done.

(U.S. Senate 1946: 212)[1]

According to Marguerite Fisher, a political science professor who published a 1948 article on equal pay legislation in the *Industrial and Labor Relations Review*, "Sentiment in favor of equal pay was not strong enough, nor were women sufficiently organized, to see to it that the War Labor Board's policy was carried out in practice" (1948: 51). Therefore, following the war working women's advocates turned to the federal and state governments to legislate equal pay. Their proposals resurrected the vision of a policy based upon comparable rather than equal work.

In this chapter, we document the movement to seize upon the gains made during World War II and secure an expanded federal policy of equal pay for work of equal value. These efforts ebbed and flowed from 1945 through 1963. The drive for equal wages culminated in a compromised piece of legislation, the federal Equal Pay Act of 1963. Its wording narrowly defined gender-based wage discrimination as unequal pay for equal work rather than unequal pay for work of comparable value. Further, the implicit wage theories used to advance and critique equal pay legislation reveal that the three facets of wage setting were embraced by proponents, while opponents narrowly invoked wages as a price.

Legislative experiments: state equal pay laws

Equal work was only one of several alternative constructions of the basis for equal pay debated throughout the twentieth century. Rather than a unifying principle, equal pay for equal work was compromise language that was long resisted by advocates for working women. Ultimately, "equal pay for equal work" legislation prevailed because the language drew upon the precepts of job evaluation that, by the 1960s, had become standard practice for establishing relative wages within large organizations and upon implicit wage theories that treated wages as a price. Although many of the concessions embedded in the Equal Pay Act have been identified in the past, discussion of the process that led to the weakened legislation is often brief.[2] Accounts give little attention to the efforts of feminist advocates, with the support of some trade unions, to legislate a broad equal pay principle: equal pay for work of comparable quantity and quality.[3] Like minimum wages, our story begins at the state level, since this is where the earliest experiments with equal pay laws took place.

Equal pay legislation was pioneered by the states, which served as a testing ground for alternative wording and compromises. Michigan and Montana passed the first laws applying to private employment in 1919. During World War I, as in World War II, women performed war work in formerly male-dominated enclaves, prompting fear among male workers and their unions that employers would make the substitution permanent in order to lower costs. The Michigan and Montana statutes were passed as men returned to their jobs on the home front, foreshadowing the wave of legislative activity on equal wages following World War II.

During the interwar period, the movement for equal pay legislation stagnated. As discussed in Chapter 7, industry was implementing job evaluation and the concept of paying the rate for the job was gaining credence. There was strong resistance, however, to extending the equal pay principle to women. The atmosphere changed once the War Labor Board took its stance in favor of equal pay for equal work by issuing General Order No. 16 in late 1942. By the spring and summer of 1963, when the U.S. Congress ultimately passed the Equal Pay Act, twenty-two states (including the two pioneers) had enacted equal pay laws. These states, along with the effective dates and coverage of equal pay legislation are enumerated in Table 8.1.

Several waves of activity are evident from Table 8.1. Three states, Washington, Illinois, and New York, enacted equal pay legislation during World War II, following the War Labor Board decree. A flurry of new equal pay laws was then passed immediately following the war. Of twenty-two in total, eight took effect between 1945 and 1949, and four more were enacted during the early 1950s. According to the Women's Bureau, twenty-one states introduced equal pay bills between 1957 and 1963 (Women's Bureau 1963); as Table 8.1 indicates, just five were actually passed during this period. The final five state laws were passed between 1959 and 1962.

Unable directly to lobby state legislatures because it was a federal agency, the Women's Bureau aided the equal pay movement by drafting a model state bill after World War II, leaving coalitions of labor groups and women's organizations to pressure state legislators. For example, in New York key advocates included the state American Federation of Labor (AFL), the state Congress of Industrial Organizations (CIO), the Women's Trade Union League, the League of Women Voters, the Federation of Business and Professional Women, and the Women's City Club of New York (Fisher 1948: 52). Many of the states passing equal pay laws were highly unionized, indicating the importance of organized labor in pursuing this issue (Steinberg 1984: 9).

The 1940s laws, especially New York's, were patterned after the Women's Bureau model. The Bureau recommended charging a Commissioner of Labor with equal pay enforcement. Such a Commissioner and designated agents would have the right to enter workplaces, inspect payrolls, question employees, and compare their responsibilities. This approach stemmed from the legacy of women reformers' investigations of factories for sweatshop conditions during the Progressive Era. The New York law created an Equal

Table 8.1 State equal pay laws as of January 1, 1963 (in order of passage)

State	Effective date	Coverage
Montana	July 1, 1919	All public or private employment
Michigan	August 14, 1919[a]	Manufacturing employer; amended to cover any employer of both males and females
Washington	June 9, 1943	Employers employing both males and females
Illinois	July 1, 1944	Manufacturing employer of 6 or more persons
New York	July 1, 1944	Any employee, except domestic service, farm labor, and specified types of nonprofit organizations
Massachusetts	October 10, 1945[b]	Any employee, except domestic service, agriculture, and specified types of nonprofit organizations
Rhode Island	April 25, 1946	Any employee, except domestic service or specified types of nonprofit organizations
New Hampshire	July 1, 1947	Any employee, except domestic service, agriculture, temporary or seasonal employment, and specified types of nonprofit organizations
Pennsylvania	January 7, 1948[c]	Any employee
Alaska	May 7, 1949	Any industry, trade, or business
Maine	August 6, 1949	Any employer
California	October 1, 1949[d]	Any employer employing males and females in the same establishment
Connecticut	October 1, 1949[e]	Any employer
New Jersey	July 1, 1952	Any employee, except hotel workers, domestic service, farm labor, or those performing volunteer work for nonprofit organizations or corporations
Colorado	April 7, 1955	Public and private employment, except domestic service, farm and ranch labor
Arkansas	June 9, 1955	Any employee, except domestic service, agriculture, temporary or seasonal employment, or specified types of nonprofit organizations
Oregon	August 3, 1955	Any employer, except state, municipal and federal civil servants, persons providing personal services under a fixed rate
Hawaii	May 21, 1959	Any employer
Wyoming	May 23, 1959	Any industry, trade, or business
Ohio	July 16, 1959	Employers of 10 or more, except domestic service and farm labor
Wisconsin	October 10, 1961[f]	Any employer, except specified types of nonprofit organizations and individuals employed by his/her parents, spouse, or child
Arizona	June 21, 1962	Any employer

Sources: U.S. House of Representatives (1948); U.S. Senate (1963)

Notes
a Re-enacted in 1931, amended in 1962.
b Amended in 1947 and 1951.
c Repealed and replaced with a new law in 1960.
d Amended in 1957.
e Amended in 1953.
f Amended in 1962.

Pay Bureau within the Department of Labor that was responsible for investigating complaints. In Washington, it was the State Industrial Welfare Committee. In contrast, some of the earlier equal pay laws, including those in Michigan, Montana, and Illinois, simply entailed a "declaration of law" without any administrative oversight or significant penalty (Fisher 1948). In Michigan and Montana, wage discrimination was only a misdemeanor, punishable by a small fine for each offense.

The state laws varied greatly in their coverage. The original Montana law was broad in scope, including all public and private employment. However, many of the laws enacted after the war excluded a number of categories of workers, most often domestic employees, farm workers, and employees of charitable or religious groups (see Table 8.1). Others also exempted hotel employees (New Jersey), public employees (Oregon), or temporary or seasonal employees (Arkansas and New Hampshire). As with the state minimum wage laws described in Chapter 5 and the Fair Labor Standards Act described in Chapter 6, these exemptions were particularly detrimental to African American women and other people of color, whose employment was concentrated in agriculture, domestic service, and, to a lesser extent, hotels. Finally, the original laws in Michigan and Illinois applied only to manufacturing. In 1930, only 8.4 percent of employed African American women worked in manufacturing. This contrasts with 21.2 percent of European American women and 24.7 percent of Chicana women (Amott and Matthaei 1996: 335). Thus, the coverage of state equal pay laws implicitly circumscribed which women were eligible for equal pay.

In addition to variations in coverage, there were also differences in the way states specified the basis for equal pay and thus the legitimate bases for wage differentials. The language of some state laws invited a narrow interpretation, limiting equal pay to women and men in the same job titles, with similar duties, working for the same employer. Others left the door open for comparable worth, that is, comparisons of the value of men's and women's jobs. The Michigan statute, one of the two earliest, read, in part:

> Any employer of labor in this State, employing both males and females in the manufacture or production of any article, *who shall discriminate in any way in the payment of wages as between sexes* . . . shall be guilty of a misdemeanour; provided, however, that no female shall be given any task disproportionate to her strength, nor shall she be employed in any place detrimental to her morals, her health, or her potential capacity for motherhood.
>
> (quoted in Dickinson 1943: 701, emphasis added)

This language on wage discrimination was potentially broad and comprehensive, although its application was open to interpretation. This quote also reflects what we term "wages as a social practice." Even while resolutely passing legislation asserting wages as gender-neutral prices for labor, the

Michigan legislature felt a need to emphasize their belief in women's essentially different nature, including images of women's physical weakness, moral frailty, and calling to become mothers. Montana, the other forerunner, prohibited employment of women for "salary, wages, or compensation less than that paid to men for equivalent service or for the same amount or class of work or labor in the same industry, school, establishment, office, or place of any kind or description." Other states using fairly general language in prohibiting wage discrimination included Colorado, Connecticut, Illinois, New Jersey, New York, Washington, and Wisconsin. Table 8.2 lists these states, as well as those using alternative language.

Five states incorporated the term "comparable" as the basis for equal pay. For example, Massachusetts prohibited wage discrimination for "work of like or comparable character, or work on like or comparable operations." Pennsylvania's wording was "work under comparable conditions on jobs requiring comparable skills. . . ." Arkansas' statute simply mentions "comparable work." "Same quality and quantity" was the phrase favored by Arizona, California, and Hawaii. This language also permitted comparisons between men's and women's jobs. Only in a few states – Maine, New Hampshire, Ohio, Rhode Island, and Wyoming – was the basis for equal pay limited to work that was "equal," "identical," or the "same." Thus, the majority of the state equal pay laws went beyond the concept of equal pay for equal work and legislated a broader meaning of pay equity.

Most of the state equal pay laws contained provisions indicating that pay differentials based upon factors other than sex would be considered valid (see Table 8.2). In Pennsylvania, for example, the legitimate bases for unequal pay included "seniority, experience, training, skill, or ability or difference in duties and services performed, or difference in the shift or time of the day

Table 8.2 Language of state equal pay laws

Wage discrimination	Comparable	Same quantity and quality	Equal work
Colorado	Alaska	Arizona[abc]	Maine[abc]
Connecticut[b]	Arkansas[abc]	California[abc]	New Hampshire[abc]
Illinois[abc]	Massachusetts[b]	Hawaii[b]	Ohio[d]
Michigan[c]	Oregon[bc]		Rhode Island[abc]
Montana	Pennsylvania[bc]		Wyoming[d]
New Jersey[c]			
New York[c]			
Washington[c]			
Wisconsin[c]			

Notes
a Exempts disparities based on skill and/or other listed compensable factors.
b Exempts disparities on the basis of seniority.
c Exempts disparities based on any factor other than sex.
d In lieu of "equal" Ohio uses "identical work" and Wyoming uses "same work."

worked or any other reasonable differentiation except difference in sex" (quoted in Fisher 1948: 53). The most common exemptions, later appearing in the federal statute, were for skill and other compensable factors such as training or experience and for seniority. The majority of states, fourteen of twenty-two, exempted wage disparities based on any factor other than sex. This language also appears in the Equal Pay Act of 1963. Equal pay laws, both at the state and federal level, were constructed to target gender, not race, inequity. Unequal pay on the basis of race could continue as a legitimate practice. In part, this emphasis on sex rather than race derived from the identification of equal pay regulations with the issue of women's war work.

As Tables 8.1 and 8.2 make clear, the states with equal pay laws were concentrated in the West, industrial Midwest, and the Northeast. States in the Southeast or agricultural Midwest remained unregulated prior to federal action. Advocates of federal legislation noted that this provided an unlevel playing field. According to James B. Carey, President of the International Union of Electrical Workers, the lack of a national law gave "an advantage to an employer in a state where no state law exists or where the state law is ineffective." Reflecting the distance traversed since the constitutional controversies over minimum wage laws, he also argued, "It has become a firm and recognized principle that in order to deal equitably on problems affecting interstate commerce, it is necessary to have the same law apply on a nation-wide basis" (quoted in BNA 1963: 5).

Of course, in these states without equal pay laws, women were protected from wage discrimination in cases where they were organized and won equal pay clauses in their collective bargaining agreements, or where individual employers voluntarily paid equal pay. In the early 1950s, the Bureau of Labor Statistics conducted an analysis of 2,644 collective bargaining agreements and discovered that only 17 percent included a clause asserting equal pay as a principle (cited in Women's Bureau 1952: 4). A few years later, the Women's Bureau found that the percentage had increased to 38 percent. Some union contracts explicitly perpetuated separate pay rates, separate evaluation processes, or different wage increases for men and women (BNA 1963: 5–6).

At the same time that feminist activists were pursuing state-level legislation, they were also working on passage of a federal equal pay bill. When Congress began deliberating the first federal bill, only six states had already adopted equal pay legislation: Michigan, Montana, Washington, Illinois, New York, and Massachusetts. It took many years and multiple revisions to find language that could muster sufficient Congressional support for passage. The state laws provided precedents for these ongoing efforts, offering examples of alternative language for legislators.

The fight for federal legislation begins

A federal equal pay bill (S. 1178), termed the "Women's Equal Pay Act of 1945," was first introduced in the 79th Congress in 1945. It was called the

"Pepper-Morse" bill, after Senators Claude Pepper of Florida and Wayne Morse of Oregon, the bill's sponsors – although it was actually drafted by Mary Anderson, the Women's Bureau director from 1920 to 1944 (Deslippe 2000: 45). The proposed federal equal pay law began with fairly broad wording:

> It shall be an unfair wage practice for any employer engaged in commerce or in transactions or operations affecting commerce to discriminate between the sexes . . . by paying wages to any female employee at a rate less than the rate at which he pays or has paid wages to male employees *for work of comparable quality or quantity.*
>
> (U.S. Senate 1946: 1, emphasis added)[4]

Not only did the original bill permit comparisons between comparable jobs, it also contained language that deliberately limited substitution as a cost reduction strategy through the use of the past tense: " . . . or has paid. . . ." Administration of the law would be given to the Women's Bureau of the U.S. Department of Labor, under the jurisdiction of a newly created Equal Pay Division. The bill called for every employer to keep and maintain records of persons employed by sex, job classification, wages, and other terms and conditions of employment. Inspectors would have the right to analyze jobs to determine comparability. It would have applied to any employer engaged in interstate commerce with eight or more employees. This original proposal would have been more far-reaching with respect to equalizing wages than the Equal Pay Act that finally passed.

The Women's Bureau, as a federal agency, was not directly involved in activities designed to influence Congress. Yet, through its consistent documentation of unequal pay and facilitation of dialogue between different constituencies, the agency played a critical role in supporting the Women's Equal Pay Bill. Active lobbying was done by major women's organizations and clubs, who educated their membership, lobbied legislators, and testified for the bills. Some, but not all, sectors of organized labor also lent support. The *principle* of equal pay was endorsed by both the AFL and the CIO at their 1944 conventions, although the AFL lagged behind the CIO in support of federal legislation.[5] The same year, the conventions of the United Electrical Workers of America (UE) and United Automobile Workers (UAW) endorsed the federal legislation. This support was, in part, motivated by the unions' concern, especially on the eve of victory in the war, over preservation of jobs for men. But it was also the result of diligent work by women union members who maintained pressure on union leadership. Both the Democratic and Republican parties supported equal pay policies in their 1948 platforms, but only the Democrats specified that they endorsed legislation "assuring that workers of our Nation receive equal pay for equal work regardless of sex" (Women's Bureau 1952: 5).

Despite support for the *principle* of equal pay for equal work, major business groups resisted *legislation*. The National Association of Manufacturers (NAM) had issued a statement recommending equal pay principles as sound practice in 1942:

> In the matter of wage policies we advocate the principle of equal pay for equal performance by women. In effectuating this policy it is essential that consideration be given to methods whereby "equal work" may be measured. In this connection we recommend that industry give thought to the wider use of such techniques as job analysis and evaluation to determine the precise nature of the job and the elements comprising it.
>
> (quoted in U.S. Senate 1946: 35)

This support for equal pay for equal work in job evaluation systems did not translate into an endorsement of federal regulation to enforce the practice.

During almost twenty years of debate over federal equal pay legislation, there were never any proposals to mandate equal pay by race. None of the organizations or clubs for women of color testified at any of the federal hearings on equal pay, nor did they join the coalitions advocating for pay equity. The absent voices of African American women and other women of color on this issue indicates that they did not perceive the definition of the equal pay problem as inclusive of their experience.

A subcommittee of the Senate Committee on Education and Labor held hearings on the Pepper-Morse bill in 1945. Officials from the U.S. Department of Labor, the Women's Bureau, organized labor, and women's groups testified at the hearings. A statement submitted to the Senate subcommittee by former Women's Bureau Director Mary Anderson listed forty-two organizations in support of the bill. Tables 8.3 and 8.4 list the women's and labor organizations that testified or submitted written statements in favor of the original equal pay bill at the 1945 hearings, as well as two sets of subsequent hearings.[6] Business organizations and other opponents of the bill did not testify at the original hearings, presumably excluded by the Democrat-controlled committee chairs.

During the 1945 hearings, the Senate first called upon the U.S. Secretary of Labor, Lewis B. Schwellenbach. Secretary Schwellenbach relied upon three key, overarching arguments in support of the legislation, arguments that were echoed in much of the subsequent testimony. First, equal pay is fair and just. He interjected that

> There is an old saying that "the laborer is worthy of his hire." I see no basis for making a distinction between men and women workers, in this connection. If they turn out the same quantity and quality of work, they should receive the same compensation.
>
> (U.S. Senate 1946: 5)

Second, women support dependents, just as men do. Finally, equal pay preserves wage standards, consumer purchasing power, and thereby helps the

Table 8.3 Women's organizations in favor of equal pay bills at hearings in 1945, 1948, and 1963

Organization	Date of hearings		
	1945	1948	1963
American Association of University Women	✓	✓	✓
Congress of Women's Auxiliaries of CIO	✓		
Consumers' League of New York	✓		
Council of Catholic Women, Green Bay Diocesan		✓	
Council of Catholic Women, St Louis Archdiocesan		✓	
General Federation of Women's Clubs	✓	✓	
League of Women Shoppers, Inc.	✓		
League of Women Voters	✓	✓	
National Consumers' League	✓	✓	
National Council of Catholic Women	✓	✓	
National Council of Jewish Women	✓	✓	
National Federation of Business and Professional Women's Clubs, Inc.	✓	✓	✓
United Church Women, National Council of Churches			✓
Young Women's Christian Association	✓		✓

Sources: U.S. Department of Labor, Women's Bureau (1955); U.S. Senate (1946, 1963); U.S. House of Representatives (1948)

economy run full steam. The third argument drew upon Keynesian economic thought and was vital to those who remembered the Great Depression.

The Women's Bureau Director, Frieda Miller, used her testimony to try to elaborate on what equal pay for work of comparable value is and is not. She argued that it did not entail comparing apples and oranges, but comparing women's jobs and men's jobs in the same workplace. Job evaluation provided a method for such internal job comparisons. Enacting equal pay legislation would not require business to adopt new procedures, since most major employers already had evaluation systems in place. According to Miller's testimony, the already widespread adoption of job evaluation did not guarantee equal wages because employers could still use separate, lower pay scales for women (U.S. Senate 1946: 26). To support this assertion, Miller then read directly from an issue of the American Management Association's *Management News*, on how sex differentials can permeate wage setting, even under job evaluation:

> The fact that in normal labor markets women are willing to accept lower wages than men for work of similar content tends to give rise to the setting of wage rates on a basis that smacks of sex discrimination. Similarly, any group of jobs which, in normal situations, is filled mainly by women tend to lower the wage scale for the type of work in the industry and the area for all workers regardless of sex.
>
> (quoted in U.S. Senate 1946: 26)

Table 8.4 Labor organizations in favor of equal pay bills at hearings in 1945, 1948, and 1963

Organization	Date of hearings		
	1945	1948	1963
Amalgamated Clothing Workers of America	✓	✓	
American Federation of Labor	✓		
AFL-CIO			✓
[International Brotherhoods of] Boilermakers, Iron Ship Builders, Blacksmiths, Forgers and Helpers	✓	✓	
Communications Workers of America	✓	✓	
Congress of Industrial Organizations		✓	
Food, Tobacco, Agricultural and Allied Workers' Union	✓	✓	
Hotel and Restaurant Employees' International Alliance; and Bartenders' International League	✓		
National Education Association	✓		✓
National Federation of Telephone Workers	✓		
National Women's Trade Union League	✓	✓	
[Brotherhood of] Railway and Steamship Clerks, Freight Handlers, Express and Station Employees	✓	✓	
Office Employees International Union			✓
Retail Clerks International Association			✓
United Electrical, Radio, and Machine Workers	✓	✓	
United Rubber, Cork, Linoleum and Plastic Workers	✓	✓	
United Automobile Workers	✓	✓	✓
[United] Textile Workers of America (AFL)	✓		

Sources: U.S. Department of Labor, Women's Bureau (1955); U.S. Senate (1946, 1963); U.S. House of Representatives (1948)

Despite the efforts of equal pay advocates, the bill failed to garner sufficient support for passage. The bill was reported out of the Education and Labor Committee in June 1946. But Senator Pepper's attempt to have the bill considered on the Senate floor was defeated by an effort from Senator Robert Taft, the infamous architect of the anti-labor Taft–Hartley Act of 1947.

The long road to the Equal Pay Act of 1963

It would take another eighteen years of laborious effort to enact a federal equal pay law. In the interim, the wording, coverage, and administration of the act changed substantially. A measure that sought to remedy wage discrimination against female-dominated occupations with strong investigative and enforcement mechanisms was transformed into a clause of the Fair Labor Standards Act that narrowly focused on equal pay for equal work. How did the original vision get lost? In what follows, we present a concise summary of the legislative history that led to passage in 1963.[7] It shows that the bill was watered down in a stepwise fashion, as different bits of wording were changed in order to garner Congressional support.

A political stalemate

At least one equal pay bill was introduced in every subsequent session of Congress until passage. Advocates in the House of Representatives held four days of hearings in February of 1948 on a bill, modeled on Pepper-Morse, cosponsored by Congresswomen Helen Gahagan Douglas of California and Margaret Chase Smith of Maine. The 1948 hearings indicate that support for a broader interpretation of equal pay was already fragmenting. Secretary of Labor Lewis B. Schwellenbach, for example, expressed disagreement with Women's Bureau Director Frieda Miller over the scope of comparable work. While endorsing the concept of work of a "comparable character," he was reticent about empowering the Women's Bureau to undertake comparisons of jobs within workplaces (U.S. House of Representatives 1948: 83). He argued that coverage and enforcement should be similar to the minimum wage provisions of the Fair Labor Standards Act. As we will see, this suggestion turned out to be prophetic.

Testimony was heard on both sides of the debate during these hearings (see Table 8.5 for a list of business organizations who testified or gave statements in opposition to the equal pay bill). George F. Kohn, a member of NAM's Industrial Relations Committee, insisted that the National Association of Manufacturers had long advocated the principle equal pay for equal performance. But they opposed legislating equal pay, favoring voluntary acceptance by employers, collective bargaining, and expansion of job evaluation. In Kohn's view, legislation was unnecessary because "The wisdom and necessity of establishing equitable rate structures based on job evaluation" was already promoted by NAM, the American Management Association, the National Electrical Manufacturers Association, the National Metal Trades Association, the Society for the Advancement of Management, and many other management organizations (U.S. House of Representatives 1948: 256).

This time, the bill was not even reported out of the House Committee on Education and Labor. This pattern – bills introduced but remaining in committee – continued until 1962.[8] Seventy-two bills were introduced over the decade of the 1950s, from the 82nd through 86th Congress (BNA 1963: 4). Conservative opposition was strong, and images of deserving "Rosie the Riveters" who had helped win the war were being lost in the haze of the 1950s glorification of domesticity (Harrison 1988; Deslippe 2000).

Meanwhile, the Women's Bureau continued to document the ongoing problem of pay inequity and to assist the groups and individuals pressuring Congress to pass legislation. The agency convened a working conference on equal pay on March 31 and April 1, 1952 (Women's Bureau 1952). The stated purpose of the conference was to bring together individuals within

Table 8.5 Testimony or statements in opposition to equal pay bills, as proposed in 1945, 1948, and 1963

	Date of hearings		
	1945	1948	1963
American Pulp and Paper Association			✓
American Retail Federation			✓
Armstrong Cork Company		✓	✓
Association of American Railroads		✓	
Electronics Industries Association			✓
General Electric Company		✓	
Illinois Manufacturers' Association		✓	
International Association of Ice Cream Manufacturers			✓
National Association of Manufacturers		✓	✓
National Retail Merchants Association			✓
Owens-Illinois Glass Company			✓
State Chambers of Commerce			✓
Thatcher Glass Manufacturing Company			✓
U.S. Chamber of Commerce			✓

Sources: U.S. Department of Labor, Women's Bureau (1955); U.S. Senate (1946, 1963); U.S. House of Representatives (1948)

Note
Corning Glass Company testified in favor of the bill.

organizations concerned with the issue. Legislation, education leading to voluntary action on the part of "enlightened employers," and collective bargaining were all posed as strategies. The report of the conference indicates that the majority of, but not all, attendees endorsed equal pay legislation; some participants from labor and business preferred the other strategies or keeping legislation confined to the states. Clearly, a subtext in the conference was to persuade those who merely endorsed the principle of equal pay to support federal and additional state legislation. The attendees were presented with recommendations from a "Committee on Findings"; these recommendations stressed the need for a federal equal pay law.[9]

The Findings Committee also recommended the establishment of an ongoing committee to "further the objectives agreed upon," including the enactment of legislation. The creation of this independent group, the National Committee for Equal Pay, in 1953 enabled the Bureau to provide "fact-finding" and "technical advice" (Women's Bureau 1952: 19; see also Kessler-Harris 1990: 101). Members included representatives of women's organizations, unions, and civic groups; the committee served as a means of coordinating the efforts of these different organizations (Women's Bureau 1955: 11). Despite this new coordination, equal pay legislation remained entangled in Congressional committees through the end of the decade.

"There can be no doubt that disagreements over enforcement provisions contributed to lack of Congressional action on equal pay legislation until 1963," chronicles Kathleen Laughlin in a history of the Women's Bureau and its postwar activism (2000: 57). In the 1950s, a fracture materialized among feminist supporters. The National Federation of Business and Professional Women's Clubs (BPW), a pro-business feminist organization, tried to negotiate a viable alternative to the old Pepper-Morse model bill. BPW drafted a bill that weakened the enforcement mechanism by attaching equal pay provisions to the pre-existing Fair Labor Standards Act. Under the new administrative process implied by this change in jurisdiction, the Department of Labor would have far more limited authority than had been envisioned by the Women's Bureau. The FLSA, as noted in Chapter 6, did not have proactive enforcement.

After nine years of directing the Women's Bureau, Frieda Miller was replaced when Republican President Dwight D. Eisenhower appointed Alice Leopold. Leopold was the first director who gained her experience in party politics rather than the activism of women's social reform organizations (Laughlin 2000). Leopold's Women's Bureau did not draft or lobby for legislation, but saw itself as providing services to individuals. Leopold and Eisenhower quietly supported the BPW version of equal pay enforcement,[10] but most women's activists resisted this compromise.

The political tide turns

In 1962, during the end of the 87th Congress, the tide began to turn. Ronnie Steinberg (1982) suggests that the revival of the equal pay movement was in large part due to the active support of the Kennedy administration. This support was payback for labor's efforts in electing John F. Kennedy and a Democratic majority in Congress (see also Deslippe 2000: 60). Additionally, women's organizations had supported Kennedy's candidacy and the so-called "second wave" of the women's movement was budding (Chafe 1991: ch. 11). Kennedy appointed Esther Peterson, a former lobbyist for the AFL-CIO's Industrial Union Department, as Director of the Women's Bureau; Peterson steered the administration's efforts to secure passage (Cobble 1994: 66).

An equal pay bill, introduced with the backing of the Kennedy administration, was reported out of committee to be voted on by the full House of Representatives. The bill was passed, but only after accepting two amendments offered by Republicans from the House floor. The first amendment struck the word "comparable" and substituted "equal"; the revised language required equal pay for "equal work on jobs the performance of which requires equal skills." The second amendment would have made it possible for employers to reduce the wages of their male employees to correct for inequity. The latter amendment was clearly designed to undercut the support of male workers and organized labor. This amended version of the equal pay bill also passed the Senate as a rider to an appropriations bill. However, it was held up over procedural issues and time expired as the 87th Congressional session ended.

Both amendments were resisted by many feminists. One of the sponsors of the Kennedy administration's bill, Congresswoman Florence Dwyer of New Jersey, strenuously objected that the amendments would greatly reduce the effectiveness of the act. In reintroducing her bill the following year, she reflected that the 1962 amendments set too high the standard for proving discrimination. Absolute equality is impossible to measure; only comparability can be ascertained with certainty. Further, said Dwyer, the equal work language provided a large loophole: "An employer who wished to continue discriminating between men and women employees could simply make a slight and insignificant change in a woman's job description or activity and thus be relieved of paying the woman an equal wage" (U.S. House of Representatives 1963: 27).

Nevertheless, unequal pay for equal work was clearly a problem and women's advocates needed to break the legislative stalemate. In a study released in 1963 entitled *Economic Indicators Relating to Equal Pay*, the Women's Bureau documented the wide disparities in pay between men and women in the same occupations. For the economy as a whole, the ratio of women's wages to men's wages among full-time workers actually declined between 1955 and 1961, from 0.64 to 0.59, the 59 cents for every man's dollar that became a rallying cry for activists (Women's Bureau 1963: Table 2). Table 8.6 is based upon data from this report and indicates the ratio of men's to women's wages in occupations requiring at least a college degree. Two years after graduation, when differences in experience and continuity of employment should be minimal, women earned less than men in the same occupation.

Even entry wages were frequently lower for working women. Table 8.7 focuses on advertised wage rates for job openings requiring less education, advertised in public employment offices. In each of these cases, employers explicitly specified a lower hiring rate for women than for men. For example, the entry rate for a clerk-typist in a hospital was $45 per week for a woman and $54 for a man. Bank tellers also have a $10 discrepancy in their weekly wages. The 1963 Women's Bureau study also provided evidence of unequal wages for clerical workers (accounting clerks, payroll clerks, tabulating machine operators, etc.) employed by the same establishment and school teachers in states that did not require equal pay for comparable teaching positions. It is indicative that the opening sentence of the study refers to the "principle of paying men and women equal rates for equal or comparable work" – indicating the ambivalence about the basis for equal wages at the time. In contrast, the 1952 conference was described in its foreword as addressing simply "equal pay for comparable work" (Women's Bureau 1952: v).

During the first session of the 88th Congress, Congresswoman Dwyer reintroduced her version of the equal pay bill (H.R. 4022). Dwyer's bill, along with the companion Senate bill introduced by Clifford Case of New Jersey, was essentially the original Pepper-Morse bill – with a slight change

Table 8.6 Annual salaries of male and female 1958 college graduates in 1960, by occupation and degree

	% Female	$ Women	$ Men	Ratio (%)
Bachelor's degrees				
Social and welfare workers	57.7	4,180	4,470	93.5
Chemists	19.6	5,540	5,960	93.0
Mathematicians	31.5	5,520	6,090	90.6
Research assistants	33.7	3,940	4,920	80.1
Personnel workers	30.6	4,290	5,400	79.4
Accountants	4.4	4,290	5,490	78.1
Pharmacists	10.2	5,500	7,060	77.9
Writers	48.3	3,990	5,380	74.2
Artists	38.6	3,720	5,100	72.9
Master's degrees				
Librarians	73.8	5,080	5,170	98.3
Social and welfare workers	57.8	5,340	5,710	93.5
Psychologists	43.9	5,000	5,690	87.9

Sources: Authors' calculations based on data from Bureau of Social Science Research, Inc. in U.S. Department of Labor, Women's Bureau (1963: Table 19)

Table 8.7 Advertised weekly wage rates in public employment offices, selected occupations in cities across the U.S., 1963

Job title	Industry	Hiring rate – women ($)	Hiring rate – men ($)
Accounting clerk	Insurance	51.00–58.00	55.00–60.00
Billing clerk	Textile	50.00	55.00–60.00
Cashier	Dairy	55.00	60.00–65.00
Clerk-typist	Hospital	45.00	54.00
Cook	Cafeteria	30.00	45.00
Dishwasher	Restaurant	18.00	20.00
Machine operator	Publishing	46.00–50.00	54.00–60.00
Order clerk	Machinery	56.00–60.00	100.00
Sales clerk	Retail trade	35.00	75.00
Stock clerk	Meatpacking	65.00–70.00	70.00–75.00
Teller	Banking	50.00	60.00

Source: U.S. Department of Labor, Women's Bureau (1963: Table 1)

toward gender-neutral language. That is, it prohibited employers from paying "any employee at a rate less than the rate at which he pays wages to any employee of the opposite sex" for comparable work (S. 882).[11] Another change since the 1940s was that the new bill had no lower boundary for the size of employers. The bill still encapsulated the original feminist vision that would subsequently be sacrificed via a lengthy process of debate and revision.

For the Dwyer-Case bill was not the only bill under consideration. There were many more versions floating through the halls of the Capitol during the

88th Congressional session.[12] The Kennedy administration's bill (H.R. 3861) was introduced by Congresswoman Edith Green of Oregon, who was also a member of the President's Commission on the Status of Women. In the Senate, the administration's bill was S. 910, sponsored by Senator Pat McNamara of Michigan. The administration conceded the substitution of equality for comparability as in the previous year's amendment, although the bills did not incorporate the ability to lower men's pay. This version also limited coverage to establishments with twenty-five or more employees.

Jurisdiction moved

A major shift occurred with the introduction of a new version by Congressman Charles E. Goodell, a Republican from New York. Goodell revived the old Republican-backed draft that was circulated by BPW. Goodell's bill, H.R. 5605, placed jurisdiction for equal pay under the Fair Labor Standards Act (FLSA). This administrative change was cited on the House floor as "the catalyst that had been needed" (BNA 1963: 107). Virtually all of the provisions of Goodell's bill became incorporated into the Equal Pay Act of 1963 (H.R. 6060).

In a statement clarifying the difference between this bill and that of the Kennedy administration, supporters argued that their approach would avoid "the creation of a vast new bureaucracy" (BNA 1963: 98). Rather than charging the Secretary of Labor with regulatory authority and endowing a new division with the power to investigate and administrate complaints, equal pay administration would be given to the existing Wage and Hour Division, already authorized to enforce the minimum wage and overtime provisions of the FLSA. For enforcement, the Secretary of Labor could bring a lawsuit for back pay, the Department of Justice could bring civil action, or the employees themselves (with the assistance of a union or employee organization if they had one) could lodge a lawsuit.

Circumscribing the bill as an amendment to the FLSA enabled sponsors to secure support for the bill, ostensibly because it did not create a proactive investigatory division. During the hearings, witness after witness representing employers decried the bureaucracy the original bill would create. The discourse of opposition to bureaucracy provided cover for substantially reducing the effectiveness of the proposed legislation and taking enforcement out of the hands of the feminist activists at the Women's Bureau. Instead of proactive enforcement from the executive branch – what conservatives referred to as "arbitrarily through an all-powerful administrative body" – women would rely primarily upon the federal courts to enforce the provisions of the bill (BNA 1963: 108). Unfortunately, litigation depended upon the initiative and resources of employees themselves, which was often limited unless supported by a local or national union.

Because the equal pay bill would be incorporated into pre-existing minimum wage legislation, all of the exceptions in the FLSA applied. In the early

1960s, these industries still included agriculture, hotels, motels, restaurants, and laundries. As with the state laws that exempted these industries, the effect was to exclude people of color from coverage. Uncovered occupational categories included professional, managerial, and administrative positions, as well as outside salesmen.

Equal, not comparable, work

Goodell's bill also adopted the language of equality rather than comparability. In a speech on the floor of Congress, Congressman Goodell opined:

> Last year when the House changed the word "comparable" to "equal" the clear intention was to narrow the whole concept. We went from "comparable" to "equal" meaning that the jobs involved should be virtually identical, that is, they would be very much alike or closely related to each other.
>
> (U.S. House of Representatives 1963: 83)

He continued by noting that Congress did not want the Department of Labor to "go into an establishment and attempt to rate jobs that are not equal" (U.S. House of Representatives 1963: 83). Job evaluation was to remain the province of employers, not the government.

The Labor Subcommittee of the Senate Committee on Labor and Public Welfare held hearings on the alternative proposals in April 1963 (see Tables 8.3, 8.4, and 8.5 for some of the participants). In light of concerns raised at the hearings, the subcommittee Chair, Senator McNamara, decided to endorse Goodell's language and introduced a companion bill S. 1409. McNamara thus abandoned his earlier bill, arguing that the new proposal was simpler than previous versions.

Although most of the business organizations who testified against the bill opposed any form of legislation, Corning Glass Company and the Electronic Industries Association were willing to accept a bill with alternate wording. Specifically, Ezra Hester, Director of Industrial Relations and Research at Corning testified that "Skill alone, as a criterion, fails to recognize other aspects of the job situation that affect job worth" (U.S. Senate 1963: 102). To address this issue, the primary clause of the new bills focused on equal pay "for equal work on jobs the performance of which requires equal skill, effort, responsibility, and are performed under similar working conditions." Wage differentials based on any factor or factors other than sex would be permitted. Rather than exclusively focusing on jobs requiring equal skills as the Kennedy proposal did, this version listed all the compensable factors. McNamara's report when the bill was submitted to the floor of the Senate indicated that the administration supported his changes. In his report, McNamara also argued that the sense of the Senate was that the jobs did *not* have to be identical to be considered equal work.

Several members of the House subcommittee who supported the bill asserted that the four compensable factors "are the core of all job classification systems and the basis for legitimate differentials in pay" (BNA 1963: 98). Adam Clayton Powell, Chairman of the House Committee on Education and Labor, said that the bill's language stemmed from valid differences in pay based upon compensable factors. He anticipated that a bona fide job evaluation program would be a valid defense against charges of wage discrimination (U.S. House of Representatives 1963: 44). Thus, the pre-existing practice of job evaluation helped to construct the basis for equal pay institutionalized in the legislation, while job evaluation itself remained a management prerogative.

More exemptions were added before eventual passage of the Equal Pay Act. Modeled after many of the state laws, the final wording specified some of the alternative compensation practices that would be exempted from the principle of equal pay for equal work. Rather than simply the broad exemption for factors other than sex, the revisions specified seniority, merit systems, and piecework payment as legitimate rationales for inequality. A merit system need not be formally written down to be a valid reason for pay differences.

Congressman Paul Findley of Ohio proposed an amendment to the House version that would have also provided an exemption based on the alleged added cost of employing women. (The debate over the cost of hiring women is discussed in detail later in this chapter.) Findley's amendment was rejected; however, Goodell noted that there was nothing in the legislation to prohibit differentials based upon specific and ascertainable costs associated with hiring women. Further, Findley wanted to ensure that employers could offer higher wages to the head of a family. From the floor, he inquired whether the language of the legislation "would permit employers to provide higher pay to the head of a family, say a fellow who has eight or nine kiddies at home" (U.S. House of Representatives 1963: 87). After some discussion, the sponsors agreed that a gender-neutral policy of differentials for heads of families would be permissible under the existing language, although Congresswoman Green (the original sponsor of the Kennedy administration bill in the House) noted that such differentials might be used as "obvious subterfuge" to undermine the spirit of equal pay. She reiterated the idea that pay should be based upon the work performed.

The House and the Senate bills (H.R. 6060 and S. 1409) were reconciled without a conference and the Equal Pay Act of 1963 passed on June 10; it became effective one year later. The body of the Equal Pay Act as passed read:

> No employer having employees subject to any provisions of this section [Section 6 of the FLSA] shall discriminate, within any establishment in which such employees are employed, between employees on the basis of sex by paying wages to employees in such establishment at a rate less

than the rate at which he pays wages to employees of the opposite sex in such establishment for equal work on jobs the performance of which requires equal skill, effort, and responsibility, and which are performed under similar working conditions, except where such payment is made pursuant to (i) a seniority system; (ii) a merit system; (iii) a system which measures earnings by quantity or quality of production; or (iv) a differential based on any other factor other than sex.

The Act also contains a provision prohibiting employers from lowering the pay of any employee to meet the requirements of equal pay. Since there was a time gap between passage of the bill and its effective date, adjustments that lowered pay were legal during this period. To qualify for coverage, the firm must be engaged in interstate commerce; a minimum dollar volume of sales was also specified.

Plate 8.1 President John F. Kennedy signing the Equal Pay Act of 1963 in the White House Oval Office on June 10, 1963. Standing fifth from the left (in white suit with dark trim) is Esther Peterson, Director of the Women's Bureau from 1961 to 1964. Others in the photo include Secretary of Labor Willard Wirtz (partially obscured), Ethlyn Christenson of the YWCA, Representative Martha Griffiths (D-Michigan), and Vice President Lyndon B. Johnson

Source: photograph by National Park Service Photographer Abbie Rowe. Courtesy of Abbie Rowe, National Park Service/John F. Kennedy Library, Boston (image no. AR 7965-F)

In sum, passage of the Equal Pay Act was accomplished only after a series of compromises that vastly limited its scope and effectiveness. Nevertheless, the members of Congress themselves disagreed about which types of pay comparisons were permissible under the newly passed legislation. While Congressman Goodell, the House sponsor, felt the jobs should be "virtually identical," Senator McNamara, the Senate sponsor, took a broader view. The precise interpretation of the compromised language used in the law was left to the Labor Department as the enforcement body, and to the courts.

Administration of the Equal Pay Act was placed in a pre-existing division of the Department of Labor that was not under the jurisdiction of the Women's Bureau. And employers were given multiple justifications for pay inequity to protect them from litigation: seniority (always a problem for marginalized groups who were last hired); merit systems (subject to bias and favoritism); and, most importantly, a job evaluation system that rationalized gendered pay practices. By placing the Equal Pay Act under the Fair Labor Standards Act for "simplicity," the institutionalized exclusion of many people of color from access to living wages was perpetuated in new legislation.

Industry, although opposed to legislating equal pay, was glad to have the language narrowed. According to the National Association of Manufacturers Law Department summary of the law, "The word 'equal' is a key term in the bill. The legislative history indicates that it was intended to mean something less than identical but more than merely similar or comparable" (NAM 1963: 3). Industry was also pleased that, compared to early drafts, the enforcement mechanisms were weakened. The Secretary of Labor could not issue "interpretative regulations," only write "interpretive bulletins" which would serve as practical guides to employers.

The compromise legislation that was finally enacted would have minimal impact on the wage gap since the devaluation of tasks and activities differentially found in women's work and undervalued by traditional job evaluation was left intact. In fact, as was shown in Chapter 2, the gender-based wage ratio did not change between 1965 and 1970; it remained 59.4 percent. It was only when women, especially white women, began to shift into better-paid occupations that substantial improvement in the wage ratio took place. Yet even a limited victory can be construed as a form of victory. The Equal Pay Act set in place a process for redressing the most blatant forms of wage discrimination and legitimated a basic feminist precept. "Equal wages" was now a matter of national policy.

Gender versus race discrimination?

The Equal Pay Act only addressed wage discrimination based upon sex. It was silent on discrimination based upon race. This neglect was experienced by black women and other women of color who worked alongside white women. In contrast, race discrimination in labor markets was legislatively defined as a lack of access to particular jobs. Race discrimination was the provenance of separate equality legislation passed the following year, the employment provisions of the Civil Rights Act of 1964. The equal opportunity policies incorporated in Title VII of this legislation were primarily designed to address discrimination by race, religion, and national origin (Burstein 1985).[13] "Sex" was added to protected classes at the last minute. Many argue that the amendment mandating equal treatment by sex was an attempt by conservatives to sink the legislation. The proposal to include sex discrimination was made by Representative Howard Smith of Virginia, an opponent of civil rights legislation and was met with laughter. Women's advocates, some of whom had planned to seriously propose such an amendment, seized upon the opportunity (Robinson 1979: 514–19; Giddings 1984: 299–300; Burstein 1985: 22–3).[14]

Blankenship (1993) argues that the primary *raison d'être* of Title VII was to break down occupational barriers for black men so that they could assume their role as head of household. In this light, we can see this legislation as partly a response to the attitudes embodied by the 1965 report on "The Negro Family" authored by Daniel Patrick Moynihan. In this controversial study, Moynihan characterized black families as matriarchal. Although he also examined institutional racism, he viewed this "pathological" family structure as one of the roots of black poverty.[15] African American women were not the primary focus of either equality policy, although they did eventually benefit from them. By clearly outlawing race discrimination, Title VII assisted black women in gaining access to female-dominated jobs formerly held exclusively by white women, especially clerical work (Giddings 1984; Jones 1986).

The administrators charged with enforcing Title VII of the Civil Rights Act initially focused exclusively on racial discrimination. According to Giddings, the first director of the Equal Employment Opportunity Commission (EEOC) regarded the inclusion of sex discrimination in Title VII as a "fluke" because it was proposed by civil rights opponents (1984: 300). Title VII contained a loophole permitting certain types of discrimination when sex or religion could be considered a *bona fide occupational qualification* (for example, rabbis, ministers, and priests or actors and actresses). Many states still had gender-specific protective legislation on the books, so there was an explicit conflict between these restrictions on when and where women could work and the new legislation guaranteeing equal opportunity. Gradually the courts ruled in favor of equality rather than protection (Deitch 1996). In fact, Phyllis Wallace notes that up until 1969, "sex discrimination in employment could be permitted where it was reasonably necessary to the normal operation of a business" (1982: 4). Although race and gender discrimination were initially addressed in separate legislation and through separate enforcement mechanisms, the distance of this estrangement narrowed. Administration and enforcement of the Equal Pay Act was transferred from the Labor Department to the EEOC in 1979. Protection from pregnancy discrimination and sexual harassment, for example, now fall under Title VII.

Contours of debates over the Equal Pay Act

We now turn from "how" to "why." That is, we explore the contours of the debates and discussions that led to the Equal Pay Act. In particular, we focus on the participants in the 1945, 1948, and 1963 Congressional hearings on equal pay. How do their arguments for and against the Equal Pay Act reflect the different dimensions of wages as a price, living, and social practice?

Advocates for working women used a variety of arguments to pursue their cause. Some were strongly felt while others may have been more strategic in nature. Some arguments for equal wages emphasized women's individual achievement and worth, while others focused on family units and community living standards. All were meant to invoke commonly accepted precepts about what constituted a fair or just wage. Opponents of legislation frequently focused on other issues such as the expansion of bureaucracy and federal encroachment on the prerogatives of states. But their arguments also addressed fairness in wage setting, often fairness to small and struggling employers. While supporters of equal pay legislation underscored the reasons workers deserved similar wages – the rate for the job, equal pay for comparable or equal work – opponents stressed the legitimate bases for wage differentials.

In her book of essays, *A Woman's Wage: Historical Meanings and Social Consequences*, Alice Kessler-Harris (1990) argues that the unifying power of "equal pay for equal work" derived from the double meaning of the phrase itself. As a slogan for feminists, especially the more middle-class and individualistically oriented groups such as the National Woman's Party, it signified a cry against difference and an assertion of men's and women's equality. Using our constructs, these arguments assert *wages as a price* over *wages as a living*, emphasizing the value of the work in order to undercut comparisons between women's and men's needs. Women who performed the same work as men should be paid the rate for the job. Defending equal pay legislation also required proponents to redefine the concept of a living wage to include working women. Kessler-Harris also notes that the labor movement, especially in male-dominated unions, used "equal pay for equal work" specifically as a defensive measure to ward off substitution. If women employees were cheaper than men, employers would have an incentive to replace male workers. If wages were equal, there would be little incentive to hire women except in jobs that were already deemed women's work. This interpretation of equal pay for equal work "could be read as the final defense of a sexually segregated work force" (Kessler-Harris 1990: 84; see also Deslippe 2000: ch. 2). In our framework, this reading implies that equal pay for equal work was a *social practice* that reinforced existing gender relations.

In this section, we expand upon Kessler-Harris' study of the rhetoric on equal pay, examining how the arguments proffered reveal implicit theories about wage setting. We focus on the testimony and statements offered during three sets of hearings in 1945, 1948, and 1963 and incorporate several Women's Bureau studies and other materials from the period. Wages as a living, price, and social practice are treated separately for analytical purposes, although the use of multiple layers of argument by the proponents of equal pay regulations indicates that these constructs are not mutually exclusive. In fact, Labor Secretary Lewis B. Schwellenbach seamlessly shifted between wages as a price and wages as a living during his 1945 testimony: "Pay is for work done rather than the number of dependents of the worker. It should be noted, however, that many women who work for a living do so because they have dependents" (U.S. Senate 1946: 5).

Wages as a living

As we have seen in previous chapters, the concept of a living wage, directly contrasted with labor as a commodity, had long been articulated by organized labor and social reformers. From this perspective, allowing wages to be set solely by supply and demand equated human beings with other commodities and was therefore dehumanizing. Employers were ethically obligated to pay no less than a living wage; to underpay was to be a social parasite (Power 1999). Some of the supporters of equal pay used this opportunity to remind their audience that wages served other economic purposes besides the allocation of resources. Wages were also a living, a means of supporting oneself and one's dependents. This entailed asserting women's right to economic independence and their work in supporting their families. From a macroeconomic perspective, wages were also more than a price; they were an essential determinant of the level of demand for goods and services. Inadequate wages would translate into inadequate consumption, leading to recession or depression.

During the 1945 hearings, the testimony by Women's Bureau Director Frieda Miller contains a fascinating long-winded digression on the commodification of labor. According to the transcripts, Senator Wayne Morse, one of the two sponsors of the legislation, interrupted Miller's testimony to engage in a discussion with Senator James M. Tunnell, the subcommittee chair. Morse noted that during the war, when labor was scarce, employers embraced the principle of equal pay for equal work as a rationale for raising wages and attracting women workers to fill vacant jobs. Now that labor markets were no longer tight, employers sought to return to discriminatory practices. As Morse put it, "we have got a problem here of deciding whether it is fair and right to discriminate against women in times of surplus of labor and not discriminate against them in times of scarcity of labor." In his view, basing wage policies on the supply and demand for labor treats people as commodities, that is, solely as a factor of production. He rejected this, implicitly asserting that wages should be determined by more than market forces (U.S. Senate 1946: 11):

SENATOR MORSE: We are right up against it, as I see it, in this bill, as to whether or not we are going to recognize this problem in this country and say to American employers quite frankly: "Legislatively you cannot treat women in the labor market as a commodity; you have got to pay them on the basis of the quality and quantity of their work, a pay comparable to the pay that you give to men." . . . I am one who thinks we have got to say: "We are going to support this competitive system, but you are going to have to operate your competitive system on the basis of a policy that once and for all eliminates the notion that labor is in any sense, be it woman labor or man labor, a commodity." I think this bill is a blow in the direction of eliminating the idea that labor is a commodity.

SENATOR TUNNELL: Doesn't it come to this question: "Are wages paid as compensation for work or are they paid as a social obligation?"

SENATOR MORSE: That is it.

In fact, the answer to Tunnell's question appears to be: "Both." According to Morse's statement, women should be compensated for their work, on terms that were comparable with men, an argument that suggests wages are a price. He also invokes the idea that employers had a social obligation not to take advantage of groups with less bargaining power, the classic position of living wage reformers.

In addition to this traditional conception of living wages associated with organized labor, the feminist version of this discourse promoted women's rights as wage earners to support themselves and their dependents. Proponents offered evidence that women were responsible for dependents too. In fact, young women were often more likely than their brothers to contribute to family income, yet a Women's Bureau report noted, "One never hears the argument advanced that a young unmarried man should be paid a reduced wage because of his status, though usually he assumes less financial responsibility for the home than does his sister" (1942: 15). Representatives of the Women's Bureau reiterated their research findings each time they had the opportunity to testify in support of equal pay on Capitol Hill.

In 1948 hearings, one of the bill's sponsors, Representative Helen Gahagan Douglas, graphically illustrated the need for equal wages. As noted in Chapter 5, it was often argued that women's needs were less than men's, therefore their wages could be lower. Douglas used the imagery of market prices to assert the equality of needs:

When a woman buys bread, she pays the asking price – the same to all persons. No baker reduces the price of his bread because a woman is buying it. There are no price differentials based on sex when a woman buys cigarettes. Meat and potatoes, milk and eggs – whatever she needs – she has to pay exactly the same rate as a man does whether she is buying for herself alone or for her family, or whether she has to pay all her living expenses or whether she shares them with her husband.

(U.S. House of Representatives 1948: 13)

Citing Women's Bureau studies about the importance of women's wages to their families, Douglas argued: "So it is no good saying to women, 'You better stop working and go home.' There are too many who will not have any home to go to unless they continue working, because they either have to support it themselves or they have to contribute to its support" (U.S. House of Representatives 1948: 13). Not only did women support families whose incomes were otherwise inadequate, the war had left widows and wives of disabled veterans who had to work, noted a UAW spokesperson (U.S. House of Representatives 1948: 180). Whether or not women's presence in the labor force was desirable, it was acknowledged by proponents as a necessity. Women worked because they had to.

There was a third, macroeconomic version of the living wage argument. A high standard of living and prosperous business conditions could not exist without equal pay (Women's Bureau 1952: 2). In her 1945 testimony, Director Miller reasoned that continuing to allow wage differentials by sex would drag down men's wages and thereby the American standard of living (U.S. Senate 1946: 17). The argument was repeated in the 1948 hearings by Senator Douglas:

The unfair advantage the employer obtains who scales down the standards of living of his workers is short-lived, because as their living scale goes down, as competition forces similar industries to cut wages, the buying power of the people is reduced. They cannot buy back the things they make. Depression and unemployment, with all the attendant tragedy, is inevitable.

(U.S. House of Representatives 1948: 14)

A Keynesian economist could not have explained the downward spiral of the multiplier effect any better.

By the 1963 hearings, fear of recession had diminished, so the countercyclical benefits of raising women's wages was no longer used to defend the proposed bill. However, *sustaining economic growth* was a concern. A few observers noted the importance of women's labor in achieving this goal. A Vice President from the Retail Clerks International, not incidentally a union representing service sector workers, maintained:

Our economy cannot function at its present levels without the direct participation of women in economic activity. The urban explosion, the growth of suburbia, changes in technology, the rise of government as an employer, wars, depressions, changes in our social values, the lengthened span of life have all contributed to the revolution in the work pattern now pursued by women.

(U.S. Senate 1963: 105)

Not only did women need employment, employers needed women workers.

Opponents of equal pay legislation did not choose to debate proponents on the question of wages as a living. In the postwar era, unlike the early part of the twentieth century, few openly asserted the rationale that women needed fewer calories or could be assumed to be someone else's dependents in order to justify wage differentials. While full-time homemaking was still posed as an ideal, the reality of many women's paid employment was increasingly apparent. Differences in productive value and therefore the price of labor, rather than differences in needs and living standards, formed the heart of the opposition to equal wages. Therefore, the definition of women's needs and living standards belonged to the advocates of equal wages. There were three constructions of the living wage argument, one based on a broad critique of market mechanisms, another upon women's responsibilities, and the last based on the erosion of working-class living standards. The latter arguments touched on the implications of equal work for men's wages. This theme has ramifications for gender relations and thus for wages as a social practice.

Wages as a price

In seeking to legitimate specific wage-setting practices, both proponents and opponents also drew upon the concept that wages were a type of price. For proponents, this meant that wages should be paid according to the work performed. They asserted that equally productive workers, male or female, should receive equal wages. This assertion directly challenged wage-setting practices that treated men, as presumptive breadwinners, differently than women. The touchstone of neoclassical economics, remuneration as a reflection of marginal productivity, was thus embraced by feminists. Feminists merged this with neo-institutional economists' emphasis on relative wages for jobs within organizations. Wages, according to equal pay advocates, should be based on the rate for the job.

Critics of equal pay likewise focused on productivity and the generation of revenue. However, they disputed that women's work was equal to men's. In particular, they argued that the costs of hiring women were higher and their output was lower than men's. These costs were not characteristics of the job itself – as captured by the compensable factors of skill requirements, effort, responsibility, and working conditions. They were based on the characteristics of individuals, as captured in neoclassical economics by human capital theory. Human capital characteristics were considered a primary determinant of productivity. Both proponents' and opponents' conceptions of wages as a price were debated throughout the federal legislative process.

Equal pay was cited by advocates as a principle of justice or fairness because pay should be based upon the job performed rather than familial status. For example, Al. Philip Kane, the General Counsel for the National Federation of Telephone Workers (later called the Communications Workers of America or CWA) testified in 1945 that:

> In fighting for equal pay for equal work the women of the country are not attempting to achieve some vague or lofty goal. Rather they are pressing for the adoption of a simple principle of fundamental justice. The workman should be paid what his or her job is reasonably worth. The wages received by labor should not depend on age, marital condition, dependency, or sex.
>
> (U.S. Senate 1946: 131)[16]

Witnesses pointed out that most employers simply let gender stand as a proxy for whether someone was a breadwinner rather than examining individual cases. The Director of the National League of Women Voters, Mrs Harold A. Stone, noted this hypocrisy in her assertion of the doctrine of wages as a price:

> If wages were paid on a basis of need, bachelors should receive less money than widows supporting children. Such is not the case. Our wage system is based on the theory of pay according to ability, rather than pay according to need. We would like to see this theory put into practice insofar as women are concerned.
>
> (U.S. Senate 1946: 146)

The Women's Bureau offered a similar argument: "in this country . . . the wage is paid for the job done and not according to the number of dependents" (1942: 15–16).

Opponents felt comfortable on the terrain of discussing wages as a price. As has been noted, many argued vigorously that they accepted the principle of equal pay for equal work but disputed the contention that women did equal work. Individual characteristics were brought back into wage discussions, not based on the differential *needs* of breadwinners and supplemental earners, but based on how these gender roles affected *productivity*. In summarizing the issues raised during passage of the Equal Pay Act, a study by the Bureau of National Affairs paraphrased the logic of opponents as:

> Women are not inherently unequal to men. But because they are inher-

ently different, the cost of employing them is inherently greater. There-fore (the syllogism continues) a pay differential between men and women doing the same work is justified on the basis of differential cost of employment.

(BNA 1963: 54)

For example, during the 1963 hearings the representative from the Cham-ber of Commerce of the United States, William Miller, argued that women have higher rates of absenteeism due to "physiological differences" and their responsibility for children, and higher turnover because they quit when they marry, become pregnant, or follow their husbands' jobs (U.S. Senate 1963: 70–1). The problem of greater costs was echoed by W. Boyd Owen, Vice President of Owens Illinois Glass Company. In those same hearings, Owen cited the expense of "special facilities" for female workers. The amenities supposedly required by women but not men included more elaborate lounge areas and additional toilet facilities. He also argued that maintenance costs rose with women employees. Employers also warned that there would be disemployment effects if wages were equalized. Women's employability, it was implied, depended upon being cheaper than male workers.

The alleged costs of hiring women had already been addressed by the Women's Bureau in their earlier studies (see Pidgeon 1938; Pidgeon and Mettert 1939; Women's Bureau 1942). In their 1942 study of war industries, the Bureau argued that changes were only minor and inexpensive and could not be used as a legitimate reason to lower pay. Adding locker rooms, toilets, and larger eating facilities were part of the necessary costs of an expanding labor force, regardless of which sex was hired. Similarly, the supervision required was no more than would be required to take on any further group of workers. Regarding women's reliability as employees, the Bureau argued that turnover, illness, and absenteeism were products of the job and working environment, not the individual worker. Absenteeism, for example, was lower when measures – such as shortened hours, precautions against speed-ups, and adequate rest periods – were enacted to prevent excessive fatigue.[17] Repeatedly responding to the assertion that women induced cost increases, the Women's Bureau subtly turned attention from gender stereotypes to institutional characteristics. Yet their aim was to reassert that a particular job had a specific value to an employer that should be reflected in the wage, regardless of who did the job.

Wages as a social practice

The participants in these legislative debates clearly and overtly acknowledged that wages reflected and influenced gender relations. The assertion that women contributed to family income and supported dependents, and thus deserved a living wage, countered the traditional notion that equated men and breadwinners. Thus, equal pay was a way of recognizing the social and economic shift away from a male breadwinner model of the household. As suggested by Al. Kane of the National Federation of Telephone Workers,

> The theory of family income may have been appropriate enough in a simpler economy and in times and places where the husband and wife were regarded as one person before the law. It has no place at all in an economy such as we have developed during the past 100 years.
>
> (U.S. Senate 1946: 131–2)

The defense of equal wages was also predicated on the view that unequal pay was a threat to male wages. Wages, in this guise, were also related to identity, to ideas about masculinity and femininity. As discussed in Chapter 6, the so-called "American Standard of Living" was, in fact, accessible only to a part of the working class. It was linked to a living wage for men, especially organized white male workers in what were considered skilled jobs. Earning a living wage was a badge of masculinity and whiteness. Preserving men's wages therefore preserved a particular definition of masculinity linked to being a breadwinner. It is the seemingly contradictory relationship between the assertion of new horizons for women (as in Kane's quote above) and the preservation of men's identities (in the following excerpts) that Kessler-Harris (1990: ch. 4) describes as the "double meaning" of equal pay.

Arguments reflecting concern over men's unemployment and the loss of a male breadwinner wage were particularly strong in the 1940s, with the Depression still fresh in memories and in light of men's return from the front lines. Testimony by labor officials and questioning by Senators Tunnell and Morse asserted that equal pay policies during World War II helped to stabilize labor/industrial relations by preventing work stoppages, labor unrest, and confusion. Union men did not want to be replaced in jobs by lower-paid women and would take action to prevent perceived threats (U.S. Senate 1946). A patriotic tone, in lieu of fear, was articulated in the Women's Bureau's (1942) wartime study. The Bureau insisted that men in the armed forces must not feel that women in industry were being forced to undercut established wage standards. Similarly, Bertha Nienberg of the Business and Professional Women's Clubs of the District of Columbia evoked the specter of male unemployment during peacetime in her 1945 testimony:

> The performance rendered by women war workers leaves no doubt that, with modern labor-saving devices, women can do as satisfactory work as men in a large number of occupations in almost all industries. It becomes essential, therefore, to protect the employment of men as well as women by requiring the fixing of wages on the basis of service rendered rather than on the sex of the worker.
>
> (U.S. Senate 1946: 149)

By the 1963 hearings, the emphasis on technology remained, even though the period of women's war work had faded in memory. According to James B. Carey, Secretary-Treasurer of the Industrial Union Department of the AFL-CIO and President of the International Union of Electrical Workers, automation was replacing muscular strength. He expressed concern about the creation of a low-wage economy built on automated jobs held by women. An economist commissioned by the American Nurses' Association, the National Consumers' League, the National Council of Catholic Women, and the National Council of Jewish Women, also argued that automation would lead to the displacement of higher-paid men. In the same hearings, Esther Peterson, Assistant Secretary of Labor and Women's Bureau Director, presented a more sanguine image of the same trends. She pointed to projections of shortages for technologically trained workers "with higher skills," arguing that raising women's wages to reflect the rate for the job would encourage women to train for these positions (U.S. Senate 1963).

Further, during this period the demarcation of gender began to shift. Women's, especially white married women's, increasing labor force participation and attachment belied the association of masculinity with breadwinning and earning a living wage. Therefore, rather than defining gender in terms of whether or not one had a job, the type of job one held was increasingly a marker of masculinity or femininity.[18] Within manufacturing, the distinction between "light" and "heavy" work was frequently used to delineate women's and men's jobs. Physical strength was associated with masculinity. Manual dexterity was attributed to women. By valuing the masculine traits more highly, wage practices maintained a gendered hierarchy in the face of women's increased employment.[19]

The representative of the Chamber of Commerce used his testimony at the 1963 hearings to warn that occupational segregation might increase as a result of the Equal Pay Act. Secretarial work was cited as an example. Acknowledging that men are hired into these positions primarily as an entry position leading to promotion and are paid more as a result, William Miller intimated (threatened?) that employers would cease hiring male secretaries if they had to equalize wages. Beyond this specific example, Miller suggested that employers would "divide all jobs into men's and women's jobs" in response to passage of the act. Their explicit motivation would be to avoid government investigation of their wage structure: "There will be a strong compulsion upon employers who do not want the Department of Labor looking over their shoulder to establish separate 'men's' jobs and 'women's' jobs and never to hire a person of the opposite sex in these jobs" (U.S. Senate 1963: 72). The subtext was that gender differentiation by job assignment would be more important if gender differentiation by wages within jobs were eliminated. Employers would continue to pay women less than men, according to Miller; they would simply adjust their hiring strategies to further segregate their workforce.

Conclusion: a narrow view of equality

This chapter traces the legislative history of equal pay. A number of states pioneered the earliest examples of equal pay legislation. These state laws varied in their enforcement mechanisms, the extent of coverage, the legitimate basis for pay comparisons between jobs, and the exemptions permitted to employers. They provided a range of alternative models for legislators and lobbyists crafting federal legislation.

Early drafts of federal equal pay legislation supported by labor unions and women's groups called for paying men and women equally for work of comparable character. This comparable worth standard met with staunch opposition from big and small business. Congressional leaders appeased business and passed a bill mandating simply equal pay for equal work. Thus, the Equal Pay Act was limited to men and women working side-by-side doing identical, virtually identical, or essentially similar work – a small minority of the labor force. As important as this change in language was the decision to limit the coverage of the Equal Pay Act by proposing it as an amendment to the Fair Labor Standards Act (FLSA). A large number of industries where women (especially women of color) were employed were exempted from the FLSA. Further, the administrative mechanisms for enforcement were folded into the Wage and Hour Division of the Department of Labor instead of a proactive division within the Women's Bureau dedicated to equal pay. These efforts contained the scope of the legislation and reduced its effectiveness in solving the problem it was intended to correct.

The tension between viewing wages as a price and wages as a living can be seen in the arguments over passage of the legislation. While the proponents of equal pay legitimated their arguments with reference to the rate for the job, they also defended women's need to earn a living and support dependents. Opponents preferred to debate only price, arguing that women's relative cost necessitated lower wages, or to focus attention on bureaucratic intervention in the work place.

However, implicit in all of these discussions was the proper scope of women's economic roles and how to signal gender differences. Wages – even, ironically, equal wages – were a social practice that could be utilized either to preserve men's labor market privilege and, thereby, their masculinity, or to enhance women's economic status. The Equal Pay Act, as passed, did both. College-educated women, especially white women, increased their labor force participation and attachment and moved into occupations considered careers rather than jobs. These momentous shifts belied the association of white masculinity with breadwinning and earning a living wage. The assertion, explicitly made by proponents of equal pay, that women contributed to family income and supported dependents, and thus deserved living wages, countered the traditional notion that equated (white) men and breadwinners. Equal pay was a way of recognizing the social and economic shift away from a male breadwinner model of the household.

Nevertheless, the Equal Pay Act was limited by its emphasis on equal pay for substantially equal work. Acceptance of a narrow view of equality, while assisting women in nontraditional occupations, institutionalized a divide between these women and workers in female-dominated job ghettoes. The jobs in which most women were employed were not subject to its provisions. Many of these female-dominated jobs – serving meals, running cash registers, cleaning buildings, and assisting health-care providers – were in expanding sectors of the economy. Ironically, African American women were gaining access to these expanding female-dominated occupations that were excluded from equal pay regulations by the narrow definition of equal work. Thus, the division between women in men's and in women's jobs took on a race as well as a class dimension. The fight for pay equity for the latter group turned back to the states, giving rise to the comparable worth movement of the 1980s.

Part III
The century ahead

9 Living wages, equal wages revisited

Contemporary movements and policy initiatives

At the end of the twentieth century and in the beginning of the twenty-first, the quest for living wages and equal wages has once again been reconfigured. Movements for living wages have broadened their constituency, incorporating workers initially left out of minimum wage legislation. Similarly, the fight for equal wages, initially settling for a narrow conception of equal pay for equal work, returned to a broader definition of equal pay for work of equal value. Both of these revived movements have at their very center the people who have been left behind in the wage regulations we have discussed so far: people in female-dominated and minority-concentrated jobs. These two precepts, living wages and equal wages, have become increasingly intertwined. Further, the debate about these issues indicates widespread (but by no means universal) acceptance of the idea that women as well as men support dependents. More than seventy years after the Women's Bureau attempted to expand the concept of breadwinner to include women, the new living wage movement is centered around the need for a gender-neutral family-sustaining wage.

Consider the story of Sammie Sims. In 1996, an article appeared in the *Christian Science Monitor* profiling Sims, a maid on Chicago, Illinois' "south side" who worked in a city-sponsored retirement home. Earning the then-minimum wage of $4.25 per hour, Sims expressed her frustration and sense of injustice about her situation. "I've just about had it; I'm paid next to nothing," she is quoted as saying. "The city has got to start paying us a wage we can live on." While some might view working as a maid as inherently low-skilled work, Sims did not see it that way. She defined her work in terms of the care she gave the pensioners: "I love taking care of my elders and I work hard and do the best I can. But right feelings and hard work should pay something I can live on" (Tyson 1996: 1).

The narrative implicitly told by the reporter who profiled her is as interesting as the story of Sammie Sims herself. Writing about the efforts of Sims and other Chicago workers to pass new laws that would raise their wages, staff reporter James Tyson described those initiatives as ones that "would enable *a breadwinner* to earn an annual income above the federal poverty line . . . for a family of four" (Tyson 1996: 1, emphasis added). Sammie Sims

– a woman in a dead-end, female-dominated, minority-concentrated occupation – was rightfully portrayed as a breadwinner. This simple designation of breadwinner status marks the distance that was traversed over the century. The problem of women's employment had been redefined. In 1923, it was seen by all but a few as a scourge to be avoided whenever possible; it signaled the failure of the economy and society to provide men with the means to be breadwinners. By 1996, although the acceptance of women as breadwinners was far from universal, the problem of women's employment was largely discussed as the lack of living wages as well as the lack of equal wages.

The limited coverage and effectiveness of minimum wage and equal pay legislation gave rise to new movements in the last decades of the twentieth century. In this chapter, we describe two grassroots policy measures that emerged in the context of massive economic and social upheaval during a period in which state intervention in the economy was increasingly under fire. The pay equity movement that captured the headlines in the 1980s and the revived living wage movement of the 1990s promoted policies that specifically targeted those workers who had not benefited from prior wage regulations. Though both strategies still hold great promise, each has had relatively limited impact, especially since they have not been institutionalized in national legislation.

New breadwinners in a new economy

The end of the twentieth century was a period marked by dramatic changes in the political economy, in the social consensus on the proper role of the state, and in attitudes toward family structure. The economy underwent a period of restructuring, as new technologies and industries combined with globalization to challenge the institutions that had fostered stability during the postwar period. A prolonged period of economic instability beginning early in the 1970s was followed by an apparent boom in the mid-to-late 1990s that still left many behind. The demise of active state policy coincided with a return to *laissez-faire* principles regarding market forces. And the male breadwinner family described an ever-decreasing subset of households.

From bad times to boom times

The 1970s were the turning-point in the U.S. political economy, a period marked by sluggish growth rates, deteriorating overall wage rates, and declining productivity. The manufacturing sector that once formed the heart of the postwar economic prosperity appeared unable to compete with Japan, Western Europe, and, eventually, other newly industrialized economies. For example, in 1950 the U.S. auto industry built three-quarters of all the cars and trucks produced worldwide. By the 1980s, the industry had lost more than half of its world market share (Bluestone and Bluestone 1992). The term "deindustrialization" was coined to describe the widespread, systematic disinvestment in manufacturing infrastructure that characterized this transformation. Unemployment among industrial workers skyrocketed. Wages did not keep pace with inflation, especially for men without a college education who once held these well-paid manufacturing jobs. Income inequality among families rose as the rich grew richer and the middle class and poor struggled (see Levy 1998; Mishel, Bernstein, and Schmitt 1999).

However, for working women the picture was somewhat more complex. The service sector, which had been expanding for decades, continued to grow. Occupations in this industry constituted roughly half of U.S. employment following World War II and grew to three-fourths by the mid-1980s (Herzenberg, Alic, and Wial 1998). Demand for women's labor expanded, since many of these jobs – for example, serving meals (82 percent female), running cash registers (82 percent female), and assisting health-care providers (83–8 percent female) – were female-dominated.[1] Unfortunately, many of these jobs had little job security, few benefits, and meager prospects for promotion. Approximately one-third of working women held clerical jobs. These jobs were generally more stable than service work and likely to provide benefits, but still offered limited promotional opportunities (Power and Rosenberg 1995). And, of course, women's occupations, both in service and clerical work, paid less than the disappearing male-dominated manufacturing jobs.

At the same time, college-educated women found the barriers to professional and lower-level managerial positions somewhat diminished. Such formerly male enclaves as public relations, personnel management, management of local bank branches, real estate sales, pharmacy, and book editing became more integrated by gender (Reskin and Roos 1990). As a result, aggregate measures of occupational segregation, that is, utilizing broad occupational categories across the overall economy, declined. But this progress is deceptive for several reasons. The pace of the improvement decelerated after 1990 (Jacobs 1989; King 1992; Blau, Simpson, and Anderson 1998). Within managerial hierarchies, some specialities became feminized "ghettoes." Women concentrated in "soft" areas – human resources and marketing, for example – had less mobility than managers in typically male fields such as finance and production.

The economic fortunes of women polarized, by race, by educational achievement, as well as by class. Women in middle management still encountered "glass ceilings" limiting their access to promotions. Worse, women in female-dominated occupations, especially women of color, were stuck in jobs with low wages and even less upward mobility (Wagman and Folbre 1988; Badgett and Williams 1994; Albelda and Tilly 1997; Cherry 2001). Some women did well. Many did not.

By the middle of the 1990s, macroeconomic indicators began to rebound. Growth, as measured by Gross Domestic Product, was moderate but steady.

Productivity once again began to rise; real wages also rebounded, though more slowly. Low-wage workers saw an increase in their real earnings for the first time since 1973, in part due to increases in the federal minimum wage and state minimum wages. While the stagflation of the 1970s had hinted at ever-worsening inflation and unemployment, the conservative economists who blamed government for this trend were chastened by a combination of low unemployment and low inflation in the mid-to-late 1990s. Technological innovations, especially those involving computers and the internet, sparked the emergence of new industries and the restructuring of mature ones. Consumer confidence was high, stimulated in part by heightened media coverage of a booming stock market.

Yet the 1980s had left the United States with problems similar to those diagnosed by John Maynard Keynes regarding the 1920s. Slow wage growth combined with high stock market dividends redistributed income towards the wealthy, who had a lower propensity to consume (spend their income). Demand for the economy's goods and services was propped up by credit cards and other private debt (see, for example, Manning 2000). Consumption levels were also maintained by working longer hours and increasing the number of household members in the labor force – a cycle of work and spend. Where once the macro economy was stabilized by active fiscal and monetary policy, government no longer "primed the pump." As federal budget deficits were attacked and nondefense programs slashed, individual consumption financed by credit cards and the optimism wrought by increasing stock portfolios fueled economic growth. In other words, personal debt replaced public debt. The size and mandate for government had been curtailed and replaced by a renewed faith in the power of markets. Business mergers and acquisitions went largely unchallenged in the pursuit of competitiveness. Nineteenth-century *laissez-faire* capitalism had re-emerged, this time on a global scale.

The stereotype of the typical worker in the "go-go" nineties was the youthful high-tech employee with stock options, who retired wealthy by age 30-something. However, not all of the jobs in this "New Economy" were high-technology, professional positions. Low-wage jobs assembling motherboards, writing code, and entering data were just as much a part of the restructured economy as the glamorous jobs and entrepreneurial opportunities in the so-called "dot-coms." Service sector jobs continued to replace activities once performed in the home. Many expanding job categories were female-dominated and/or concentrated with racial-ethnic minorities or staffed by new immigrants. These jobs kept workers in poverty at the same time that the booming stock market and skyrocketing executive salaries and perks raised living standards for the wealthy. The number of people in both tails of the income distribution grew.

From male breadwinning to shared breadwinning

The 1970s to 1990s also delivered massive changes in family structure and lifestyle attitudes. The women's movement, along with demographic, sociological, and economic shifts, prompted the collapse of the male breadwinner norm. A nationwide survey of women and men conducted by the polling firm, Louis Harris and Associates, for the New York-based Families and Work Institute asserted:

> Traditionally, the responsibility for meeting families' material and emotional needs was divided along gender lines. Men were seen as the main economic providers whereas women were the primary nurturers. However, data from this attitudinal survey confirm what demographic studies have been showing: that such assumptions no longer govern the daily lives of women and men in the United States.
>
> (Families and Work Institute 1995: 20)

Instead, the study found that women expected to combine breadwinning and caregiving roles. Nine out of ten women surveyed also believed that most girls anticipated combining paid work and a family. Despite the breakdown of male breadwinner social norms, other studies have clearly documented women's continued responsibility for most of the unpaid work in the home. Combined hours of paid and unpaid work have increased dramatically, especially for women (see, for example, Leete and Schor 1994; Heath and Bourne 1995; Heath, Ciscel, and Sharp 1998; Bluestone and Rose 2000).

The U.S. has become increasingly a work-focused society, with Americans caught in a cycle of working and spending. In fact, rising consumption and debt pressures were among the forces contributing to the prevalence of dual-earner families. As middle-class and working-class families found they could not maintain the coveted standard of living without women's wages, wives and mothers continued to work longer and longer hours for pay. Families received little support from the public sector or their employers for balancing work and family. According to *The 1997 National Study of the Changing Workforce*, dual-earner families were stressed out by time pressures, inadequate child-care arrangements, and job insecurity (Bond *et al.* 1998).

The pressures on dual-earner families have had repercussions for attitudes toward single mothers, especially poor ones. Female-headed households became a common, if not entirely acceptable, way of living in the late twentieth century. At the same time, the social consensus that had fostered income replacement programs (however meager) for single mothers unraveled. As married women were no longer supported by male breadwinners, social welfare programs that took the place of male heads-of-households lost legitimacy (see, for example, Fraser and Gordon 1994). Passage of the Personal Responsibility and Work Opportunity Act of 1996 (welfare reform) signaled the demise of a key dimension of the welfare state that social reformers in the Progressive Era had worked so hard to establish. The Temporary Assistance for Needy Families (TANF) program established under the act basically offered single mothers two alternatives: marriage or employment. State support for caring virtually evaporated. This conservative turn in social policy brought new attention to the kinds of jobs available to former welfare recipients and the need for family-sustaining wages. In the words of Minneapolis-area living-wage activist Mary Jo Maynes: "If we are going to kick more and more people off welfare, we need to guarantee that they'll be able to find jobs that pay enough to keep them out of poverty" (quoted in Macek 1997).

The fight for equal pay continues

These economic and social conditions provided an impetus for the revival of movements to raise wages for women's jobs in the 1980s and 1990s. As we saw in Chapters 5 and 6, the quest for living wages consisted of multiple strategies, including a fight for a legislated minimum wage, from early state legislation to a national Fair Labor Standards Act (FLSA). The FLSA was intended to support breadwinning, assumed at the time to be primarily a male activity. Prior to the 1970s, the minimum wage had steady support in the U.S. Congress, and across party lines. It was raised regularly, especially in periods of high inflation. Although declining political support for the minimum wage became most apparent in the Reagan era of the 1980s,[2] the ratio of the minimum wage to the average hourly wage actually suffered steady erosion beginning in 1968. From 1938 through the 1960s, the minimum wage hovered around at least 50 percent of the average hourly wage of production and nonsupervisory workers in the private sector. Since the late 1960s, the federal minimum wage lost more and more of its buying power, as it failed to keep up with inflation, productivity gains, or other relevant indicators (see Herzenberg, Alic, and Wial 1998: 152–3; Figart 2001: 114–15). The legislated "living" wage has become a starvation, not subsistence, wage.

Figure 9.1 tracks annual earnings in a full-time, year-round minimum wage job from 1968 through the end of the century. The line is flat during periods in which Congress did not increase the hourly rate. In order to show the widening gap between the minimum wage and a family-sustaining wage, the figure also maps the weighted average poverty thresholds for families of three and four persons. In 1969, a worker earning the minimum wage could support a family of four marginally above the federal poverty threshold for a family of that size. The minimum wage fell behind the poverty threshold for a family of four beginning in 1972, but managed to keep pace with the threshold for a family of three until 1980. Minimum wage earners who head families fell further and further behind these thresholds during the 1980s. The small increases in the wage floor in the early and mid-1990s did not close the gap.

One study estimates that the decline in the real value of the minimum

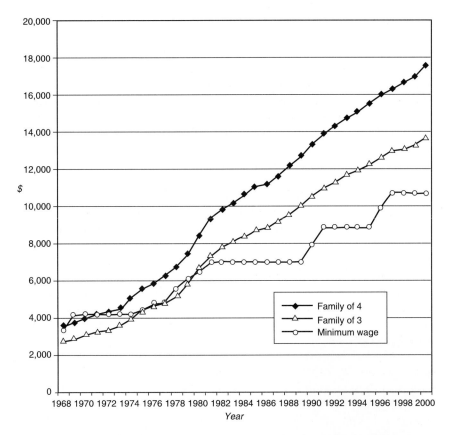

Figure 9.1 Annual minimum wage earnings compared with weighted average poverty
thresholds, 1968–2000

Sources: U.S. Census Bureau (2001b); Figart (2001: Table 6.1)

wage from 1979 to 1988 accounted for 30 percent of the rise in wage inequality *among* women (DiNardo, Fortin, and Lemieux 1996). The face of the
minimum wage has changed since 1938. Women workers and workers of
color, originally excluded from coverage because of the occupations and
industries in which they worked, now constitute the majority of minimum
wage workers. Roughly six out of ten minimum wage workers are women.
Compared with their representation in the U.S. labor force as a whole, minimum wage earners are disproportionately African American and Hispanic.
Nearly 40 percent are the sole breadwinners in their families (Figart 2001:
117).

Just as a living wage slipped through working-class women's fingers with
the declining real value of the minimum wage, so did the right to equal wages.
Despite passage of the first federal legislation enacted to correct the wage gap,
the Equal Pay Act of 1963, the female-to-male earnings ratio for full-time

workers remained relatively stable throughout the 1960s and 1970s. From 61 percent in 1960, it actually fell to 59 percent in 1975, increasing slightly to 60 percent in 1980. Enforcement of the Equal Pay Act permitted women to litigate the most egregious instances of overt unequal pay when performing essentially the same work. This primarily benefited the large numbers of women moving into nontraditional fields during the 1970s. However, the equal pay for equal work provision of the legislation did not address the portion of the wage gap that is attributable to the undervaluation of female-dominated jobs. Since the majority of working women were (and still are) employed in these occupations, the wage gap has persisted. It measured about 27 percent (or a gender-based wage ratio of 73 percent) for full-time workers at the close of the twentieth century. If weekly rather than annual earnings are measured, this gap falls by one cent. Either way, on average, a woman still earns fewer pennies for every dollar earned by a man, inspiring activists to create buttons and placards asking: "Where is my 26 cents?"

The new comparable worth movement

The "comparable worth" or "pay equity" movement brought together a familiar coalition of women's organizations and labor unions. In 1979, a

Plate 9.1 "Where Is My 26¢?" Activists rally for equal pay outside the State Capitol in Montpelier, Vermont, 1999

Source: courtesy of Albert C. Krawczyk, Member of Vermont House of Representatives, a speaker at the rally

national conference on pay equity was convened by a coalition calling itself the National Committee on Pay Equity (NCPE). Many of the same organizations that joined the 1953 National Committee for Equal Pay in support of the Equal Pay Act were members of the new coalition.[3]

The political and social context for discussing pay equity had changed. With deindustrialization, several of the largest unions in the U.S. were concentrated in the service and public sectors. Many other labor organizations who were losing members in manufacturing sought footholds in these feminized sectors. Women's groups had successfully elected some feminist politicians to state and local political offices or persuaded male politicians to appoint them to administrative positions. The college-educated women moving into managerial jobs often found the public sector more hospitable than the private sector. Finally, job classification systems in the public sector were explicit and public, facilitating a critical assessment of wage practices.

The pay equity movement shifted both its location and its strategy.[4] Pay equity activity during the 1980s was concentrated in the female-intensive public sector, in state and local governments. Coalitions of civil service unions, women's organizations, and feminist politicians and administrators inside state and local governments devoted enormous effort and energy to pressuring legislators and administrators to tackle wage discrimination against female-dominated jobs. State commissions on the status of women also took steps to introduce pay equity reform.

Several events crystallized the movement for equal value as a public policy. In 1981, a precedent-setting Supreme Court decision was issued in the case of *County of Washington, Oregon v. Gunther*. The case was brought by female prison guards who performed largely the same duties as male guards for considerably less pay. The plaintiffs made a claim of intentional sex discrimination in violation of Title VII of the Civil Rights Act of 1964. The Supreme Court ruled in their favor, rejecting Washington County's claim that the jobs were not identical. The decision prompted litigation elsewhere.

That same year, a pathbreaking report requested several years earlier by the Equal Employment Opportunity Commission (EEOC) was published by the National Academy of Sciences. The report, *Women, Work and Wages: Equal Pay for Work of Equal Value* (Treiman and Hartmann 1981), found strong evidence of gender-based wage discrimination. Specifically, using wage regression analysis, the report's authors determined that as the percentage female in an occupation rises, pay rates fall significantly. This key finding was used by comparable worth advocates to document the need for pay equity. Finally, in 1981, one of the first public sector strikes over pay equity occurred in San Jose, California. Because the pace of activity accelerated following these events, then-EEOC Director Eleanor Holmes Norton called comparable worth the major civil rights "issue for the 80s," and the phrase was adopted by many advocates.

Job evaluation as a feminist tool

Comparable worth job evaluation – job evaluation to uncover discrepancies in pay between men's and women's jobs – became one of the cornerstones of the new pay equity movement. Feminists and other advocates for working women attempted to wrest control of job evaluation from employers and managers. As noted in Chapter 7, these analysts exposed the biases in traditional job evaluation, and the uneven application of the principles of remunerating skill, effort, and responsibility and compensating for inferior working conditions (see, for example, Steinberg and Haignere 1987). Despite these flaws, job evaluation was viewed as a technique for reconstructing compensation practices. Reformed (gender-neutral) job evaluation systems could ensure that female-dominated jobs equivalent in value to male-dominated jobs within the same organization would be paid the same. Using job evaluation systems to rank jobs according to their value or worth, pay equity or comparable worth studies tested whether similarly ranked male and female job classes received comparable pay. Pay equity wage adjustments were given to workers in underpaid job classes to close identified gaps.[5] This technique underlay the slogan "equal pay for work of comparable value."

Another major lawsuit was filed in 1982, based on comparable worth job evaluation. The State of Washington commissioned the first so-called "comparable worth study" from a private consulting firm, Norman D. Willis and Associates. The 1974 study utilized job evaluation to indicate that jobs occupied predominantly by women were paid an average of 20 percent less than comparably valued male-dominated jobs. But the State refused to readjust pay, instead ordering further studies in 1976 and 1980, also to no effect.

When the State did nothing in response to the consistent findings in all of these studies, the American Federation of State, County and Municipal Employees (AFSCME) filed an internal complaint in 1981 and a lawsuit one year later. The lawsuit helped to put the struggle for comparable worth in the national spotlight. The 1983 District Court decision in *AFSCME v. State of Washington* was the first to impose remedies under Title VII for an employer's negligence in correcting wage discrimination uncovered by a pay equity study. In other words, failing to rectify identifiable pay discrepancies constituted illegal sex discrimination. The State appealed the decision. The legislature encouraged an out-of-court settlement, and passed a bill committing the State to the concept of pay equity and requiring full implementation within ten years. But it appropriated few funds to back up this ostensible commitment. AFSCME continued to press the issue. In 1986, the State and the union agreed upon pay equity raises for incumbents in undervalued, female-dominated jobs that were to be administered through the bargaining process. The settlement not only covered employees represented by AFSCME, it was binding on all state civil servants.

Subsequent to the favorable *Gunther* and *State of Washington* rulings, courts expressed conflicting opinions about the reach of Title VII. For example, the *AFSCME v. State of Washington* ruling was overturned on appeal in 1985. The threat of litigation, however, was key in motivating the reform of pay structures, at least until these reversals in the mid-1980s. In the states of Hawaii, Washington, Wisconsin, California, and Connecticut, lawsuits were dropped in exchange for a consultant's pay equity study or for funds being set aside for collectively bargained pay equity wage increases. This tactic was copied in several local jurisdictions.

Most of the cases of pay equity implementation followed a similar trajectory. The first phase of initiating pay equity involved the formation of a comparable worth commission (or task force) established by the legislature or the executive branch. The next stage (unless the first one was skipped) consisted of a comprehensive study of an employer's compensation system, most often performed under contract to private consultants. Some investigations were done by state commissions on the status of women, some were completed in-house by personnel or civil service staff, and a few were performed by legislative research bodies or other groups. The analysts reviewed where women and men were employed, what they were paid, and the extent to which "femaleness" artificially depressed the wages of historically female job classes. Where a study showed systemic wage discrimination, or female- and male-dominated jobs with equivalent value being remunerated differently, a remedy was debated and planned. However, the allocated remedy was usually less than the estimated wage disparity (see Gardner and Daniel 1998).

The social practice of unequal pay for comparable work

The successes and failures of this comparable worth movement have been extensively analyzed by feminist scholars. Many case studies of comparable worth implementation have concluded that the reliance upon job evaluation techniques had disadvantages as well as advantages (Acker 1989; Evans and Nelson 1989; Fudge and McDermott 1991; Figart and Kahn 1997). The process of constructing a pay equity study and negotiating the size of a fund for comparable worth wage adjustments was laden with decisions that affect the ultimate size of wage increases. The plurality of these decisions were delegated to consultants or retained by managers. The outcomes have been severely compromised. Nevertheless, legal scholar Michael McCann (1994) has argued that the comparable worth movement has been successful at mobilizing women in female-dominated occupations. Some of the benefits of this mobilization were less tangible than wage increases, but none the less important. They involved the ability of working women to provide a name for the type of injustice they experience: unequal pay for work of equal value.

In essence, the ambivalence of feminist scholars toward the strategy of comparable worth job evaluation exemplifies the tension between wages as a price and wages as a living as alternative understandings of wage setting.

Comparable worth job evaluation was predicated on the idea that it was scientifically feasible to compare disparate occupations using consistent compensable factors. Once freed of bias, the technique could be used to determine the proper relative value of jobs. While critiquing market wages for embodying the legacy of gender bias, comparable worth advocates' quest was to determine the correct gender-neutral rate for the job. Wages, as a price, could be set according to the productive value of the work for the employer. During a period in which neoclassical economics had become hegemonic and human capital theory was the dominant explanation for wage differentials, treating wages as a price resonated with comparable worth proponents and the public policy makers they hoped to sway. What they may have lost touch with was the vision of wages as a living. Although comparable worth campaigns also relied upon arguments about women's roles as providers, this discourse typically played a secondary role. Comparable worth discourse typically did not emphasize women's needs.

For example, a set of documents, essays, and testimony gathered as a result of the National Committee on Pay Equity's 1979 organizing conference affords an excellent glimpse into the arguments and rationales that guided the movement throughout the 1980s and early 1990s. This *Manual on Pay Equity*, the first publication of the National Committee on Pay Equity, continuously refers to "the undervaluation of women's work." Although there are many references to the types of women's jobs that are undervalued, there is only a brief mention that "achievement of pay equity will benefit millions of households, particularly the growing number headed by women" (Grune 1980: 5).

The undervaluation of women's work was frequently defended through job comparisons. Quoting *Washington Post* columnist Ellen Goodman, the *Manual on Pay Equity* noted: "Most bus drivers, for example, get paid more than a licensed practical nurse. Yet they are both jobs with physical labor, life-and-death decisions, and both take special training" (Grune 1980: 39). In another contribution to the manual, Eve Johnson of AFSCME compared the money earned by her son mowing lawns – about $6 for an hour's effort, minus the cost of gas – and her daughter's babysitting – $2 per hour (Johnson 1980: 46). A lawsuit in Denver compared registered nurses with higher-paid, male-dominated jobs such as tree trimmers and painters (Grune 1980: 49). Responding to a *Fortune* magazine article that referred to such arguments as comparing apples and oranges, the now long-standing practice of job evaluation was used to argue that "apples" and "oranges" were compared all the time (see, for example, Krucoff 1980 [1979]: 49–50).[6] After all, just as apples and oranges can be compared in terms of calories and vitamin content, the skills, effort, responsibilities, and working conditions of disparate jobs could be compared.

The comparable movement did evoke a critique of one aspect of wages as a price in articulating the ways in which men's and women's wages were socially constructed, reflecting gendered assumptions about the relative value of different types of work. In particular, advocates contested the assertion that wages set by supply and demand would reflect the productive contribution of the employee. Joy Ann Grune, the editor of the 1979 pay equity manual, maintained that "Community wage rates, on which employers frequently base their pay schedules, are a product in part of discriminatory practices by other employers. Supply and demand as a justification is . . . suspect" (Grune 1980: 39). Day Creamer, Executive Director of the Chicago-based organization Women Employed, suggested that "profit and prejudice" block the operation of market forces and assign a lower value to women's jobs. She observed that "Apparently, the law of supply and demand operates to raise wages when shortages occur in male-dominated fields, but not in female-dominated fields" (Creamer 1980: 51, 52). Wages should reflect the relative productivity of individuals in different jobs, however the market did not assure such an outcome.

Instead, pay equity advocates noted that "the undervaluation of women's work is rooted in history, culture, economics, and psychology" (Grune 1980: 39). The heart and soul of pay equity discourse was the assertion that market wages and wages set by traditional job evaluation systems are a gendered social practice. In fact, the chapter of the *Manual on Pay Equity* on "Raising Wages for Women's Work" began by listing "practices" that resulted in low wages for women. These included unequal pay for equal work; denial of promotions and transfer opportunities into men's occupations; inappropriate classification of duties performed by women into lower-paying grades; short career ladders in female-dominated occupations; entry requirements not integrally connected to job performance that block women from higher-paying jobs; the low level of minimum wages and continued exemption of some women's occupations; and the depression of wage rates for female-dominated occupations and occupational classes (Grune 1980: 37). The pay equity movement thereby articulated an alternative theory of wages, based upon the idea that institutions, norms, and expectations affect the wage-setting process at the same time that the movement's use of comparable worth job evaluation embraced the ideal of setting prices according to productivity. This theoretical ambivalence – embracing wages as a price while asserting that they are also a social practice – helps explain why the pay equity movement could seem at once potentially radical and also a modest reform.

Victories and setbacks

By the end of the 1980s, every state except five – Alaska, Arkansas, Delaware, Georgia, and Idaho – had at least investigated gender differentials in their civil service pay scales.[7] Many reformed their classification systems or provided targeted wage increases to underpaid job classes (Hartmann and Aaronson 1994). Over fifty municipalities, twenty-five counties, sixty school districts, and nearly two hundred public colleges and universities were the focus of campaigns to raise wages in low-paid female-dominated occupations (NCPE 1989). Virtually all of the public sector pay equity activity occurred at unionized workplaces, where collective bargaining was a successful tool for pay equity wage increases. Since litigation is an expensive strategy, most class action lawsuits on behalf of incumbents in female-dominated occupations were filed by their unions.

Ultimately, however, the movement has had difficulty in translating the gains made in the public sector into a broader movement affecting substantial numbers of working women. In contrast with this wave of activity on behalf of public sector workers, gains in the private sector have been relatively sparse. Most have also been as a result of collective bargaining. Surveying the newsletters of the National Committee on Pay Equity reveals a scattering of private sector bargaining agreements, especially with newspapers organized by the Newspaper Guild. Universities have also been targeted because of their large clerical and technical staffs. Indeed, the first major private sector strike over the issue of pay equity led to wage adjustments for clerical and technical workers at Yale University in 1984/5 (Gilpin *et al.* 1987).

Further, the comparable worth movement has not yet translated its gains into federal action. Efforts to broaden the Equal Pay Act through additional federal legislation, or even a comparable worth study of federal employees, have stalemated. Several sessions of the United States Congress have witnessed the introduction of bills titled "The Fair Pay Act," but no real movement of the legislation. The Fair Pay Act would outlaw discrimination in pay for female-dominated jobs that are equal in skill, effort, responsibility, and working conditions to comparable male-dominated jobs (for a discussion, see Figart and Hartmann 2000).

The spread of the comparable worth movement was undermined by some of the same forces that gave it life, though unintentionally. We can refer to these forces as "the five D's": deindustrialization, de-unionization, defensive posture by the women's movement, "DLC" (to stand for the rightward turn of the Democratic Party), and delegitimation of the state. First, deindustrialization, while expanding women's jobs, also divided workers' interests along gender lines. The loss of male breadwinner jobs in manufacturing drew attention away from the problem of women's low wages, especially in the industrial Midwest. Similarly, the decline in union density due to employment losses of these same male breadwinners divided the labor movement along gender lines according to membership, as unions in male-dominated sectors focused their resources on job security, leaving only a few to fight for equal pay. Third, the assault on abortion rights by conservative political groups in the 1980s diverted the efforts and resources of much of the women's movement away from pay equity toward defending women's reproductive rights. At the same time, the Democratic Party, led by a caucus called the Democratic Leadership Council, shifted to the right, especially on economic issues. Democratic politicians campaigned on the issue of reproductive choice rather than labor market issues to secure women's votes.

Finally, the public sector, both at the national and state levels, lost its mandate. Rather than being viewed as an economic stabilizer and guarantor of social justice, government was portrayed by conservative, and even moderate, politicians as an inefficient alternative to market mechanisms. Social services, and the tax base to support them, were pared. Some government functions were privatized, resulting in further job loss among unionized workers, but this time in the public sector.[8] These factors, especially privatization of public services, weakened the comparable worth movement at the same time that they also contributed to the shape of subsequent efforts to reinvigorate a living wage movement.

Why a contemporary living wage movement?

The 1990s saw a return to the discourse of wages as a living. The contemporary living wage movement – actually a relatively decentralized collection of local movements – once again transcends minimum notions of subsistence. The phrase "living wage" is used to express the idea that wages should provide a modest but decent standard of living, given current social norms. Current living wage campaigns, like those in the earlier part of the twentieth century, involve discussions of fairness. One difference is that contemporary campaigns reflect recent changes in family structure and attitudes. The goal is to enable a single earner to support a family, whether that earner is female or male, married or not. Perhaps this is one reason why economist Robert Kuttner, in 1997, called the living wage campaign "the most interesting (and under-reported) grass-roots enterprise to emerge since the civil rights movement" (1997: G3).

Living wage campaigns fall into two categories: (1) campaigns to establish a minimum wage for contractors doing business with local (city or county), government; and (2) state-wide efforts to raise the minimum wage above the federal threshold. We focus on the local campaigns, relatively new strategies to assist low-wage workers.[9] In particular, coalitions of community groups, faith-based activists, and labor unions have worked to pass legislation called municipal "living wage ordinances," mandating that private businesses receiving public funds (through supplier contracts, tax incentives, cash grants, subsidies, loans or development bonds, enterprise zone aid, and/or use of publicly owned land) should pay their own workers a living wage. The dollar threshold typically chosen is the hourly rate equivalent for one full-time earner to keep a family of three or a family of four above the federal poverty line.

Living wage activists have revived arguments, discussed in Chapter 5, that employers whose employees are among the working poor are parasitic, linking this argument to the rise in what has been called corporate welfare. If private sector employers receive tax subsidies and other benefits from state and local government, then those same employers have a social obligation to pay employees a family-sustaining wage. Organizers point to skyrocketing pay and perks for executives and administrators while low- and middle-income earnings stagnate or decline. An implicit or explicit ethical argument in many of the local living wage campaigns is that corporate America has a responsibility to treat their employees decently, in addition to piling up quarterly dividends for owners/shareholders. In this guise, living wage ordinances are a response to increased income inequality.

The growing concentration of low-wage jobs in cities as a result of publicly subsidized downtown revival projects is another catalyst for living wage activism. Many jobs in new city convention centers, sports stadiums, hotels, restaurants, and airports are minimum wage or near-minimum wage jobs. The ordinances are also a response to reductions in the relative size of the public sector, specifically the push to privatize government services. Privatization has consisted of the outright sale of public sector assets and especially the contracting out of services once provided by public employees. Inspired by Reaganomics (and Thatcherism in Great Britain), conservative politicians, economists, and businesspeople promoted privatization as a means of enlarging the domain of market forces. By the mid-1980s, there were tangible advances in the outsourcing of physical and commercial services in state and local government (Starr 1987; Donohue 1989; Gormley 1991). Some localities have stripped themselves of public assets such as water, waste water treatment, and electrical utility operations. Others have hired out services such as trash collection, recycling, and cleaning government buildings and parks to the private sector. Private firms are administering health services such as Medicare, absorbing public hospitals, managing educational institutions including public and charter schools, directing and staffing correctional facilities, and overseeing public assistance (welfare) case loads.

With public sector downsizing, unionization rates in the public sector began to fall during the 1980s. This was a dual blow to the labor movement. Private sector union density had already begun to decline in the 1960s and 1970s, precipitated by the relative decline in manufacturing and the more aggressive challenge by management to union organizing campaigns (see Goldfield 1987; Yates 1998). At first, union organization in state and local government was able to hold off labor's decline, as state governments passed legislation authorizing collective bargaining in state and municipal government. Momentarily, public sector union organizing outpaced private sector membership growth; but privatization began to take a toll on the newly unionized public sector labor force, especially women and people of color. Privatization was pitched as a cost-saving mechanism because it often replaced union workers with nonunion workers.

As a result, community organizations, labor unions, and religious groups have spearheaded local living wage campaigns. Through its state affiliates, a national clearinghouse of community groups, the Association of Community Organizations for Reform Now (ACORN), has been active in a majority of living wage campaigns in the U.S. The AFL-CIO and its affiliates, especially public sector unions such as the American Federation of State, County and Municipal Employees (AFSCME) and service sector unions such as the Service Employees International Union (SEIU), have been involved. Social services providers, including religious organizations, are ardent supporters of living wages because they are serving more and more clients under a shrinking social safety net. A joint statement by the bishops of Catholic, Episcopal, and Lutheran congregations in Cleveland, Ohio, read: "Basic justice compels us to advocate for the creation of a floor of material well-being on which all members of our community can stand" (quoted in Quinn 2000: 4B). Reverend Eugene Winkler, pastor of Chicago Temple First United Methodist Church related "It's an economic issue, but it's also a moral issue" (Herrmann 1996: 19).

Campaigns from coast to coast

The first living wage campaign in the U.S. is believed to have started in Baltimore, Maryland. Volunteers in many of the city's shelters and soup kitchens began to notice that more and more families were hungry, and that often at least one member of the family was employed in the labor market. One of the justifications for the downtown revival project in Baltimore's Inner Harbor was the promise of good jobs for city residents, many of whom are people of color (60 percent of Baltimore's population is African American). Reverend Vernon B. Dobson, minister of the Union Baptist Church in rundown East Baltimore, mobilized black voters to approve a referendum to allow construction of the first Inner Harbor buildings on city-owned land. The optimism that prompted this support ultimately faded. As reported in *The New York Times*, "And the jobs have indeed come, by the tens of thousands, but they are for maintenance workers, cleaning people, janitors, gardeners, store clerks, restaurant and hotel workers, and ticket takers and hawkers at Orioles games – all low-wage jobs" (Uchitelle 1996: A1). Baltimore's living wage effort was also aimed at privatization, as private firms received contracts for serving food in school cafeterias, cleaning municipal buildings, and driving city vans. The workers in the private sector did the same work for half of the pay of formerly municipal employees. One exceptional janitor's story is telling because of the reverse: Lonnie Howard, once a $4.25-per-hour employee of Broadway Services, Inc., a Baltimore-area cleaning contractor, managed to find work as a municipal janitor in an elementary school for $8.50 per hour (Thompson 2000: 1B).

Baltimore passed a living wage ordinance in December 1994, defining a "living wage" as an hourly wage rate of $6.10 in 1995, increasing to $7.70 by 1999.[10] The movement accelerated geometrically during its first years of growth. The one ordinance, Baltimore, was followed a year later by two ordinances, Santa Clara County, California, and the city of Milwaukee, Wisconsin; the number doubled to four in 1996 and doubled again to eight in

1997. A list of the localities and years of passage of their living wage ordinance appears in Table 9.1. Between 1994 and December 2000, a total of fifty-two separate living wage ordinances were approved across the United States.

Although the majority of ordinances were passed in city governments, ten counties, one school board, one township, and one university are also on the list. Regionally, the ordinances reach from the Northeast (Boston, Massachusetts) to the West (Portland, Oregon) and through the central states (Minneapolis, Minnesota; Chicago, Illinois; Omaha, Nebraska; and San Antonio, Texas) to the Southwest (Los Angeles, California, and Tucson, Arizona). The Southeast is not represented, with the exception of Alexandria, Virginia, a suburb of Washington, DC. The ordinances require wages

Table 9.1 Living wage ordinances in order of their passage, 1994–2000

1994	1 Baltimore, Maryland	1999	25 Hudson County, New Jersey
			26 Dane County, Wisconsin
1995	2 Santa Clara County, California		27 Madison, Wisconsin
	3 Milwaukee, Wisconsin		28 Hayward, California
			29 Cambridge, Massachusetts
1996	4 Milwaukee School Board		30 Miami-Dade County, Florida
	5 Portland, Oregon		31 Somerville, Massachusetts
	6 Jersey City, New Jersey		32 Ypsilanti Township, Michigan
	7 New York City, New York*		33 Ypsilanti, Michigan
			34 Los Angeles County, California
1997	8 St Paul, Minnesota		35 Buffalo, New York
	9 Minneapolis, Minnesota		36 Tucson, Arizona
	10 Los Angeles, California		37 Kankakee County, Illinois
	11 New Haven, Connecticut		38 Hartford, Connecticut
	12 Milwaukee County, Wisconsin		39 Corvallis, Oregon
	13 Boston, Massachusetts		
	14 Duluth, Minnesota	2000	40 Warren, Michigan
	15 West Hollywood, California		41 Denver, Colorado
			42 San Fernando, California
1998	16 Durham, North Carolina		43 Omaha, Nebraska
	17 Oakland, California		44 Wesleyan University, Connecticut
	18 San Antonio, Texas*		45 Toledo, Ohio
	19 Chicago, Illinois		46 Alexandria, Virginia
	20 Cook County, Illinois		47 Cleveland, Ohio
	21 Pasadena, California		48 St Louis, Missouri
	22 Multnomah County, Oregon		49 San Francisco, California
	23 Detroit, Michigan		50 Eau Claire County, Wisconsin
	24 San Jose, California		51 Berkeley, California and Marina
			52 Santa Cruz, California

Source: Association for Community Organizations for Reform Now (ACORN), http://www.livingwagecampaign.org

Note
*Denotes an extension of a prevailing wage law; Milwaukee, Portland, and Boston later amended their ordinances.

ranging from $6.25 per hour (County of Milwaukee, Wisconsin, in May 1997) to $11.00 per hour (Santa Cruz, California, in October 2000). Most require some amount of health benefits, or a slightly higher wage without benefits (for example, $12.00 in Santa Cruz). Others mandate vacations or sick leave.

Because they are local and do not cover the entire low-wage labor market, living wage ordinances do not reach as many workers as minimum wage laws.[11] Ordinances define coverage and eligibility either through dollar-value thresholds for public contracts and/or lists of occupations or jobs to be included under the ordinance. The Baltimore ordinance, for instance, requires service and professional contractors to pay employees enough to keep a family of four above poverty. Those receiving raises as a result of the ordinance (about 1,500 workers) have included female-concentrated occupations such as cleaners, stenographers, food service employees as well as janitors, carpet cleaners, laborers, and bus drivers. Unfortunately, a contract dollar threshold or a listing of narrow occupations covered can and has excluded many contracts and many employees. For instance, small contracts covering laundry services, food services, and security in the city of Buffalo, New York, fall below the dollar threshold of coverage (Williams 2000). Additionally, municipalities have exempted businesses already under contract. In Berkeley, California, pre-existing leases between the city and some businesses on city-owned land near the marina will not expire until between 2005 and 2015. As a result, more than 200 workers employed near the waterfront were not covered in the initial ordinance (Holtz 2000). It was quickly amended to include the city-owned and privately developed "Marina Zone," creating what ACORN, on its living wage web site, calls "the first area-based living wage policy in the nation." Coverage has yet to extend to an auditorium concessionaire in Omaha, Nebraska, who has a long-term contract that will not expire until 2009 (Ruggles 2000).

Opposition to living wage ordinances

The opponents of living wage campaigns utilize the analysis of wages as a price to try to defeat living wage ordinances. If the wage is raised, opponents contend, then the costs of doing business will rise and employment will fall. Adversaries thus make the same arguments in opposition to a living wage that they make about increases in the minimum wage and equal pay. Across the U.S., opposition has been launched by local-area Chambers of Commerce; in some localities, the Chamber was joined by restaurant lobby associations and/or hotels, other large private contractors, and developers. These critics point to potential loss of jobs if businesses leave the city, higher costs of municipal contracts and thereby higher tax rates, unnecessary regulation and more bureaucracy to ensure compliance, and (wage-push) inflation. In several cities with existing living wage ordinances – Chicago, New York, Los Angeles, and Omaha, for example – such arguments resonated and the ordinances were vetoed by the sitting mayor, only to be overridden by the city council.

A leading national "think tank" fighting to defeat living wage ordinances is the Employment Policies Institute in Washington, DC. Its promotional materials refer to the Institute as "the entry-level employment think tank," meaning a research association that assesses policies regarding low-waged workers. This "EPI" is not to be confused with the Economic Policy Institute, supported by organized labor. Instead, this Orwellian-named organization is backed by business. The living wage debate is articulated by a battle between these two EPIs. Economists have also lined up on both sides of the issue.[12]

The Employment Policies Institute is very concerned about the rapid spread of living wage ordinances. The Institute charges that the Economic Policy Institute, along with Robert Pollin, a political economist from the University of Massachusetts and co-author (with Stephanie Luce) of *The Living Wage: Building a Fair Economy* (1998), are ultimately promoting a national living wage (Employment Policies Institute 2000: section 2). With an extensive section of their internet site devoted to the living wage, along with a publication titled *Living Wage Policy: The Basics* (2000), this EPI aims to, in their words, "help lawmakers, the media and the public better understand the living wage movement by weighing the emotional rhetoric of living wage proponents against the economic realities" (EPI 2000:1). As in the debate over comparable worth, opponents assert that wage regulation would repeal a so-called natural law – the law of supply and demand. The Executive Director of the Employment Policies Institute, Richard Berman, published an editorial in the *Capital Times* of Madison, Wisconsin, as Dane County considered its living wage ordinance. In his argument, he cites research by neoclassical economists in opposition to minimum wage increases and offers that a living wage would hurt the lowest-skilled workers: "By forcing employers to pay inflated minimum wages for entry-level jobs, 'living wage' mandates encourage employers to hire only applicants with entry-level skills to match those wages. No amount of political grandstanding is going to repeal that economic law" (Berman 1997: 11A; see also Mac Donald 1996).

The Employment Policies Institute commissioned a national survey of professional labor economists to solicit their opinions on the living wage movement. The mailing list was obtained from the American Economic Association (AEA). The results show that 69 percent of labor economists responding to the survey believe that a living wage negatively affects employment, specifically in the hiring of entry-level employees. Ninety-three percent agreed that employment would drop once a living wage policy was introduced (EPI 2000: 47–8).

Living wage proponents counter

Competing research by the Economic Policy Institute, Robert Pollin, and other progressive scholars has found that job loss and other hypothesized negative economic and fiscal consequences have not happened. These backers assert that a living wage helps lift families out of poverty or near-poverty and opens up possible job training and retraining to the working poor. Compared with the extensive literature on the minimum wage, there is little empirical evidence about the impact of living wage ordinances *ex post*, a year or so after passage. The first impact study for the nation's first living wage ordinance, Baltimore, by the Washington-based Preamble Center for Public Policy (Weisbrot and Sforza-Roderick 1996) found no negative effects. A follow-up study by the Economic Policy Institute echoed these findings, pointing out that the ordinance itself has negligible negative or positive effects (Niedt *et al.* 1999).[13] While using neoclassical modeling tools, these studies note that the elasticity of employers' demand for labor is low, meaning that an increase in wages is absorbed rather than resulting in employment reductions.[14]

Proponents also address the issue of needs. Workers are quoted to demonstrate that they cannot live on the minimum wage, that they cannot feed their children, and that their jobs keep them in poverty. A newspaper article about the Duluth living wage campaign focuses on the story of Melissa Wright, a 29-year-old single mother of three working two secretarial jobs that pay the minimum wage; by the time she has paid for day care, she complains, "My two jobs weren't even enough" (Oakes 1997). Another article provides anecdotal evidence from employees who have been affected by the Los Angeles ordinance. Jose Morales is described as an airport janitor at Los Angeles International Airport. As a result of the 1997 Los Angeles living wage ordinance, he and some 2,000 other workers received a 36 percent wage boost, about $2.00 per hour to $7.25 during the first year of the ordinance. According to the reporter's account, Morales, who shares a small, converted garage with his sister, her husband, and their two children, used his raise to trade the flattened cardboard boxes that he slept on for a double bed. He was also able to purchase a used car that significantly cut his commuting time and some furniture for the garage apartment. Other beneficiaries of the living wage were Morales' coworkers, including a single mother who was able to quit her second job and spend more time with her children, a newlywed and his wife who were able to move from shared housing into their own apartment, and an older gentleman who could begin to pay off an outstanding hospital debt (Cleeland 1999).

These stories evoke the position that wages provide appropriate living standards based on social norms. The range of family types indicates the broader focus of contemporary living wage campaigns. Equality discourse has joined with living wage discourse to support equal access to a living wage.

A living wage ordinance: one case study

The city of Jersey City, New Jersey, is sometimes refereed to as the City of New York's "sixth borough" because so many New York commuters are settling across the Hudson River. According to the 2000 decennial census, Jersey City is the second-largest city in the state, with a population of over 240,000. (Newark was New Jersey's most populous city with almost 274,000 residents.) The population of Jersey City had grown by 5 percent since the 1990 census, while Newark's population declined. The enactment of a living wage ordinance in Jersey City, New Jersey, brought to the surface attitudes toward privatization and market forces, the problems of the working poor, the relative value of different jobs and the relative needs of different groups of workers. By focusing on the story of this small campaign, we were able to interview the participants and ascertain their implicit understandings of the role of public policy in wage-setting processes.

Despite its growing population and the influx of relatively prosperous commuters, Jersey City was a prime target for a living wage campaign. Not having enough income to afford their own homes, the majority of city residents live in renter-occupied housing. According to the City of Jersey City web site, households average 3.41 people, the approximate size targeted for family-sustaining wages by living wage ordinances. Almost one-third of the city's labor force is employed in technical, sales, and administrative support occupations. The number employed in service occupations and lower-skilled laborer jobs outnumbers those in management and professional positions. The city itself employs roughly 3,000 workers, at least half of whom are police and firefighters. The largest share of Jersey City residents are high school graduates with no college. Almost two-thirds are nonwhite. Specifically, the 2000 census indicates that 28 percent of the city's residents are African American and 28 percent are Hispanic and Latinos of any race (overlapping categories). It is therefore not surprising that Jersey City residents have a lower median income than residents in their larger neighbor across the river, New York City (especially Manhattan).

The campaign begins

In 1995, the Interfaith Community Organization (ICO) approached a member of the City Council, Jaime Vazquez, about proposing a living wage ordinance. The council has nine persons, including the Council President, elected every four years in a non-partisan election. The ICO is a coalition of religious groups, acting as a local civic organization. Since 1986, the ICO had been involved in local issues such as education, community-based policing, and environmental contamination. This is how they came to know Vazquez, one of the more liberal members of the predominantly Democratic city council. Vazquez recalls:

To me, this was a no-brainer. To me, it was easy to say "yes" because it was the right thing to do. When you have people who live around you who have children, who can't afford to buy them food or clothing, but yet are working people, there's something wrong and something had to be done about that. And I believe that if it's not done by the private sector, which it's not, then local government or the public sector has to become involved.

(Vazquez 2000)

Because the ICO was affiliated with the Industrial Areas Foundation (IAF), ICO activists were supported by staffers whose salaries were paid by the national organization. IAF is a national network of groups committed to community organizing strategies developed by Saul Alinsky. Through IAF networks, the Jersey City activists were aware of the early living wage campaigns in Baltimore, Maryland, and Santa Clara County, California. The IAF hoped to bring a living wage movement to the New York-New Jersey metropolitan region. In fact, during the same period, city council members in New York City were also considering a living wage ordinance.

Living wage ordinances base wages on socially-defined living standards (wages as a living). In order to determine what constitutes a living wage, organizers in many cities have assembled what they considered to be a "basic needs budget" for families. The concept of a basic needs budget derives from feminist critiques of the federal poverty line and academic research on alternative income thresholds (see, for example, Ruggles 1990; Renwick and Bergmann 1993). Some campaigns drew upon this academic research and local scholarly communities while others simply calculated the costs of housing and other key necessities in their communities. Activists in Jersey City, only the sixth jurisdiction to pass a living wage ordinance, worked with Rutgers University faculty to develop some preliminary calculations. Based upon the estimated local cost of living for a single adult with two children, the initial proposal would have required a company bidding for a city contract to offer wages no lower than $12.50 per hour (plus benefits for full-time workers). Vazquez (2000) characterized this figure as based upon a "no frills" budget, a basic needs budget of about $19,500 per year to live in Jersey City without luxuries. He indicated that it was similar to the figure being used by living wage activists in New York City.

The Jersey City living wage ordinance was first introduced in November of 1995. There was some support on Council, but not enough, and certainly not enough to block an anticipated veto by the Republican Mayor Bret Schundler (Wilson 1996: 4). Council President Thomas A. DeGise and others were clear and vocal in their opposition. According to Jaime Vazquez (2000), the position of DeGise was that the ordinance would make the running of government more expensive. DeGise (2000) admitted he had many questions: "How much was it going to cost? What services were to be covered? . . . I was pretty much booed at the time for doing that." The original

$12.50 proposal was tabled to allow time for public hearings to gather information and community reaction. Public hearings were held on January 16 and 30, 1996 (Donohue 1996). Although local activists came out to the hearings, Vazquez saw that he lacked support in Council for the ordinance as written. It was clear that there was going to be some serious opposition.

A negotiated compromise

As a result of the resistance, representatives of the Interfaith Community Organization met regularly with City Council members to hammer out a compromise. Specifically, the ICO began a series of negotiations with Council President DeGise. According to Vazquez, they preferred a compromise to defeat. DeGise remembers these negotiations as eye-opening. Everyone knew that some jobs, even with the city, were low-paid, but he did not realize how low-paid. DeGise recalled in the year 2000: "I was only elected in 1993, so I was not as wise as I am now, and I said, 'Jeez, that's all these people make?!'" These meetings resulted in a new proposal, supported by the ICO and DeGise, that set the living wage at $7.50 per hour. Activists accepted the lower amount, knowing that $7.50 was 50 percent higher than the state minimum wage at the time. Yet, by doing so, they compromised the vision of a family-sustaining wage. According to Reverend George Ligos, pastor of St. Paul de Cross Roman Catholic Church in Jersey City, "This is a start toward raising the standard of living of more and more people in the area so that they can raise families" (quoted in Keller 1997).

Like other early living wage ordinances and proposals, the Jersey City ordinance mandated minimum hourly rates of pay, vacation benefits, and health insurance benefits to certain entities entering into contract with the city. Employers who contracted with the city were required to pay their own employees, employed either full-time or part-time, at least $7.50 per hour, to give them at least five days of paid vacation for the first six months of continuous employment (and another five days for the second six months of continuous employment), and to provide them with no less than $2,000 each for health and major medical insurance. Although there was no dollar threshold for the value of a city contract, there were limitations. Coverage was limited to a contractor's employees who were under contract in specific job categories: clerical workers, food service workers, janitorial workers, and unarmed security guards. The largest groups who would be affected by the ordinance were janitors and security guards, primarily male. Both cleaning and security services were privatized at the time. Several private companies bid annually for cleaning contracts. About forty security guard jobs were also subcontracted; those jobs paid between $6.00 and $6.60 per hour with no health benefits. The city also had a relatively small contract for food services in summer food programs, providing lunches for children in summer camp.

Although contemporary living wage proponents have stressed the equality of needs among categories of workers and families, traditional gender norms persist. In the negotiations between the ICO and Council President DeGise on a compromise, there was some lively discussion about whether the city's part-time crossing guards, who were women, should be paid at least $7.50 per hour. (Even though they were municipal, not subcontracted, employees, the discussions also focused on city salaries that violated the spirit of the proposed ordinance.) DeGise's sense was that these women were not breadwinners so they did not need to be paid a living wage, either by the city or by a private contractor should those jobs be privatized. He argued:

> There was some fuss made about crossing guards, because crossing guards are not very well paid. However, crossing guards get the same benefits as [we] get. So a lot of the women who do the crossing guard work don't do it necessarily for the larger paycheck but because it provides them with an excellent health benefit package.
>
> (DeGise 2000)

Vazquez countered at the time that the guards were paid so little that they could not feed their children (Vazquez 2000).

Council President DeGise also asserted that the arguments for a living wage did not necessarily hold for primarily male security workers: "For many security people, it is their second job. They do something else during the daytime" (DeGise 2000). Further, teenagers hired as summer locker room attendants did not need to earn $7.50 an hour. After making a reference to the fast food restaurant leader McDonalds, he stated, "There should be a segment of jobs, of lower-paying jobs, for kids, second jobs, etc." These arguments demonstrate unease with interference with existing social practice. Some jobs had been constructed on the assumption that certain workers – women, teens, and some working-class men, primarily men of color – neither required nor were seeking a breadwinner wage. As DeGise's quote suggests, the social practice then became naturalized and seen as normal and desirable. Nevertheless, he agreed to support the compromise version of the ordinance.

There was a "first reading" of the new living wage ordinance (City Ordinance 96–063) on May 22, 1996; a first reading allows a proposal to be officially discussed and debated. However, by the first reading of the ordinance, all the hard work had been done. Council was unanimously behind the measure, introduced and moved in the first reading by an 8–0 vote. Several community activists also testified at the council meeting where the first reading took place. One was Walter Blenman, a city resident and leader of the ICO who had worked extensively with DeGise to forge a compromise. Some of the motivations for a living wage are apparent in Blenman's testimony:

> When we met it was something that came out of the need to see what's going on in our city, what's happening with our families, what's happening

with downsizing and privatization and leaving these poor families out there with no benefits, no real wages to suffer.

(City of Jersey City Municipal Council 1996a: 23)

The year of the first reading of the ordinance, 1996, was also an election year. The mayor and the entire city council were up for re-election. In May, sensing a popular issue, Mayor Schundler enacted an executive order setting the living wage ordinance at $7.00 per hour, just as the city council was ready to vote on the compromise proposal. One ICO representative accused the mayor of "stealing" the idea (Wilson 1996: 1). Council President DeGise said the mayor did not want to be outdone. It was a bit of "showmanship" on the mayor's part:

> I think he realized it was going to pass; he was being perceived by the people who wanted it as being against it, and so I guess he figured it was better for me [the mayor] to get the headline than them [Council] to get the headline.

(DeGise 2000)

The nonwage provisions were identical to the bill under consideration by City Council.

"How you can live": unanimous passage of the ordinance

At the second reading of the Jersey City living wage ordinance on June 12, 1996, some community activists turned out once again to support the measure. One was Lee Barile, a local housing activist. Barile spoke about the living wage (or, interchangeably, the minimum wage) as an historically changing social construct:

> It is not something that is static, so the minimum wage of yesterday is not the minimum wage of today. We have to look at it in its historical context because, in fact, the necessity and needs of minimum wages and living wages are very much dependent upon the conditions in which we live. . . . There was a time when we fought for everybody to have a radio. Then we fought for everybody to have televisions. Shouldn't everybody have a computer today? How can children live without computers today if, in fact, they're going to be able to compete in the job market? Well, that's what the meaning of minimum and living wage is. It's not abject poverty and how you can just get by, but how you can live.

(City of Jersey City Municipal Council 1996b: 34–5)

The measure was also viewed as a means of setting boundaries for privatization initiatives. The real enemy, according to citizen advocate and retiree Chester Jankowski, was outsourcing public functions. Referring to a decision to displace the city's security guards with private contractors, he noted: "[T]hey're saying we're going to save money and put them into this minimum wage bracket. So what are we really doing? You know, these people were under the auspices of city government receiving a decent salary, not a crazy salary" (City of Jersey City Municipal Council 1996b: 32–3).[15] The ordinance might not halt privatization or unionize subcontract employees, but it was portrayed as a means of cushioning its effects. According to DeGise, privatization would continue:

> I'm not never going to vote for privatization initiative again because I probably will, but we have to level the playing field and you can't compete against somebody who's going to win a bid contract by paying their people the absolute minimum with no vacations, no holiday pay, no health benefit, that's an unfair competition for public employees.
>
> (City of Jersey City Municipal Council 1996a: 35)

After hearing from those who spoke to the ordinance, the City Council unanimously (8–0) passed the living wage ordinance negotiated by the ICO and DeGise, thereby establishing a $7.50 threshold. This June 12, 1996, ordinance superseded the mayor's executive order. Following passage, the city's major newspaper, *The Jersey Journal*, endorsed the ordinance on its editorial page, largely because privatization was a steadily growing trend in government and the living wage would help smooth the transition for workers ("'Living Wage' a Fair One" 1996).

After the vote, Councilperson Vazquez reiterated that this ordinance was only a beginning; he calculated out loud that $7.50 an hour for a forty-hour work week only amounted to about $900 a month after taxes. The next step has not been taken. Nor was the ordinance officially monitored, according to Vazquez. Although living wage language is supposed to be part of the bid specification process, there is no staff person or office overseeing the pay and benefits of workers covered by the ordinance who are employed by private sector companies. Council members see only a vendor list, not a list of employees and what they earn. The Jersey City living wage ordinance provided a temporary effect on people's consciousness, but the tangible results, even anecdotal, are more difficult to discern. This confirms a finding by Bruce Nissen (2000) in an analysis of the living wage campaign in Miami, Florida. Political opportunities and mobilizing structures have been more intangible outcomes than empirical measures of wage increases and poverty reductions.

Conclusion: lessons from two social movements

Women's wages, and specifically the need by a broad range of women to support their families, are an integral part of pay equity and living wage campaigns. Wages, and wage regulations, reflect and construct the living arrangements and activities deemed appropriate in a particular time and place. They serve as a social practice. From the 1970s through the end of the twentieth century, wages as a social practice had to confront the reality of women's changing economic roles. The two movements have not had substantive impacts on wages thus far. But they have advanced a discourse that values the economic contributions of marginalized workers and mobilized them to insist that these contributions be recognized.

The movement to expand the basis for equal wages to incorporate female-dominated jobs found its greatest success in the public sector. In the 1980s, explicit job classification systems, high levels of both union density and female employment, and sympathetic women in executive and legislative positions on the employer's side of the bargaining table were conducive conditions for reevaluating gendered pay scales. Activists hoped that these public sector initiatives could serve as models for private sector organizing. However, this occurred on a very limited scale. And unlike the Fair Labor Standards Act and the Equal Pay Act, state-level initiatives have not yet translated into federal action. There are efforts to enact a federal policy, spurred on by the importance working women continue to place on this issue. In fact, the AFL-CIO's annual "Ask a Working Woman" survey has consistently found that equal pay is cited as working women's number one priority.

Ironically, it was the delegitimation of state functions that undermined the public sector-based comparable worth movement and paved the way for living wage ordinances. Cutbacks in public sector workforces and privatization of government functions put the unions that spearheaded pay equity on the defense. New conditions emerged between public sector/service sector unions and community organizations, this time focused on the problems of the working poor and the inadequacy of the federal minimum wage. Living wage campaigns since the 1990s targeted the subset of private sector employers who performed privatized functions or received government subsidies, mandating a family-sustaining wage floor in exchange for public funds. Although women's organizations have not been the prime movers of the campaigns for local ordinances, many of the occupations affected are the female-dominated jobs designated by pay equity policies. Further, living wage campaigns in urban areas have mobilized minority communities and workers in minority-concentrated jobs that were generally overlooked in comparable worth job evaluation studies.[16] Yet until there is a national living wage with broader coverage, the local ordinances will continue to have limited impact.

These two movements also illuminate the ongoing tension between wages as a living and wages as a price. Feminists and labor activists centered much of their arguments for comparable worth job evaluation on the need for objective, bias-free wage-setting mechanisms. Feminist scholars have noted that the technocratic nature of comparable worth strategies partly undermined the viability of pay equity as a social movement. In contrast, contemporary living wage campaigns have emphasized grassroots mobilization around the rhetoric of wage fairness and living standards. Technical evidence has been used to bolster claims about adequate wage levels or to respond to ability-to-pay arguments, but tends to play a secondary role at the local level. The revival of this living wage discourse is a positive harbinger for political and economic change and should serve as a lesson for wage theorists. The waning of living wages as a movement and a theoretical idea in the latter part of the twentieth century ought to be reversed in the twenty-first century.

10 Applying feminist political economy to wage setting

Two recurring themes in the public policy debates over wages discussed in this book have been the relative weight given to profit considerations versus needs, and the centrality of cultural struggles over how people should live. In evaluating the economic success of the United States, we must pay attention to the issues of needs and of choices. A primary measure of the success of an economy is whether it provides for human well-being. Well-being requires that all members of the community be enabled to achieve a decent living. But in addition, as Amartya Sen has argued, well-being requires that all community members be allowed a voice, and significant choices about how to live their lives – what Sen describes as good choices they can really make (see, for example, Sen 1999). Well-being requires both a living and choices. Wages, in a market economy, are an important means of attaining the resources that facilitate well-being. Through the enactment of labor market policies designed to raise wages, working women and men have attempted to enhance their material livelihoods and widen their ability to choose how to live.

As the account in the previous chapters illustrates, understanding the movements to regulate wages requires a heterodox approach to economic theorizing as opposed to an approach that privileges the market over other institutions involved in wage setting. Markets matter but so do the relative power of contending interests and cultural understandings of what constitutes a living. Mainstream economists talk about the "magic of the market," but, as our discussion has emphasized, markets are human-constructed, culturally embedded institutions whose outcomes are neither infallible nor beyond challenge. The "law" of supply and demand is nothing of the sort. Economic activity is undertaken through the construction of institutions, practices, and regulations that reflect cultural values and relations of power in society at a point in time. As cultural institutions, then, markets are not value-free. Normative judgements are an inherent part of economic analysis, and should be made explicit.

If economic theory is going to be a positive force in the twenty-first century, in our collective struggle for human well-being within the United States and across the globe, it must replace its emphasis on mechanistic modeling with a holistic, humanistic, and (for economists used to tidy models) frighteningly messy and nondeterministic methodology. Economists can find inspiration in their classical nineteenth-century roots, in the works of institutionalist economists, and in the writings of feminist theorists and progressive social scientists for this challenging and exciting enterprise. This is why, from the outset, our project has been interdisciplinary. It is also important that scholars in other countries compile similar inductive accounts of wage setting and wage policies to further elaborate the conceptual framework we present here.

Implications for theory

To develop a feminist political economy framework, we have relied upon the groundwork established by institutionalist and radical economists and by feminist theorists. Our multidimensional approach not only allows us to tell a richer and less deterministic story, it also highlights the differing experiences of wage earners by gender, race-ethnicity, and other salient characteristics. The three faces of wage setting identified at the outset of our journey through twentieth century wage policies and practices are meant to call attention to these dynamics. They are not intended as necessarily competing frameworks, but as different dimensions of the wage-setting process that economic actors have chosen to underscore to greater or lesser degrees. In our view, each of these dimensions – wages as a living, wages as a price, and wages as a social practice – captures important elements that interact with each other in a given place and time. Figure 10.1 illustrates these interactions, providing a framework for understanding wage-setting processes.

Wages as a living refers to the concept of setting wages according to socially defined appropriate living standards in order to maintain the reproduction of the labor force and macroeconomic growth. Classical political economists such as Marx emphasized that the relative bargaining power of capitalists and workers at the level of the economy as a whole determined how these living standards were defined. Systemic needs, for social reproduction and sustainable growth, also influence living standards. Therefore, in our diagram, bargaining power and macroeconomic dynamics are depicted as factors determining the level of appropriate living standards. Bargaining power itself is influenced by many factors, including the level of employment, the degree of unionization, and technology.

As the price of an input to the production process, wages are a cost that must be offset by an at least equal benefit to the individual employer purchasing labor services – the equality of exchange. This benefit is the revenue gained by selling labor's product. Market mechanisms, specifically adjustments in the quantity of labor supplied and demanded, are hypothesized to regulate wages until costs and benefits are equalized. Labor markets are therefore depicted in the figure as factors determining *wages as a price*. Demand for

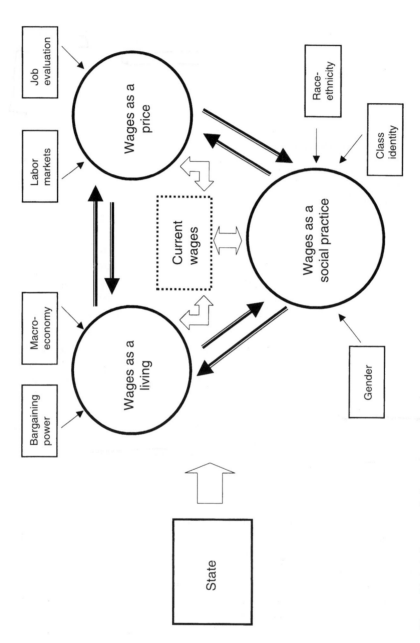

Figure 10.1 A framework for understanding wage setting

labor, for example, in neoclassical analysis, is primarily based upon the marginal productivity of workers and the structure of product markets that influences the revenue earned by selling labor's product. Job evaluation systems can also be used to set relative wages within firms; however, as we saw in Chapter 7, these are often designed in a way that replicates market wages outside the firm.

We have identified *wages as a social practice* because they are a means of reinforcing or redefining how women and men of different classes, races, and ethnicities should live. Factors influencing social practice therefore include gender, race-ethnicity, and class identity. During much of the twentieth century, the male breadwinner family was a hegemonic archetype and institution for situating not only one's gender, but also one's race-ethnicity and class identity as well. Social practices are organized by gender, class, and race-ethnicity in the workplace, the union hall, the welfare office, and other locations in addition to the family.

All three dimensions of wages – living, price, and social practice – influence the level of workers' current wages (the center of the diagram). Since there are feedback effects between current wage levels and the three dimensions, the arrows are bi-directional. The state is positioned on the left side of the diagram as an institution influencing the seven factors we have identified. The type of market system, for example *laissez-faire* or welfare state capitalism, is structured in part by the state. Specifically, labor markets are constructed through a political process that is aided and abetted by government policies and programs. As we have seen in our analysis of wage regulations in the twentieth century, the state affects workers' and employers' bargaining power and the macro economy. Its actions influence social practices that define living standards. Through entities such as the National War Labor Board, the state has also influenced administrative procedures within firms such as job evaluation. Other institutions – unions, employer organizations, families, for instance – impact these processes, though we highlight the state because of our focus on wage regulation.

Discrimination: interactions with the price of labor

Figure 10.1 also indicates that none of the three dimensions of wage setting exists in isolation from the others. In contrast with neoclassical models that isolate the price dimension of wages, our framework places labor markets within a larger context. For example, the economics literature on discrimination, like the implicit wage theories used by advocates of pay equity, can be seen as constructing an argument that the wages of certain groups are not set at the appropriate price. (For an overview of labor market discrimination theories, see Figart 1999.) Because wages are a social practice as well as a price, other considerations besides a rational economic calculus of costs and benefits enter into the process. According to mainstream economists, discrimination interferes with fair wage setting by violating the equivalency of productivity and remuneration. Gary Becker has proposed that individuals (either employers or coworkers) may have an irrational "taste for discrimination," developed outside the labor market, that causes the employers who have or cater to such tastes to pay a wage premium for desirable workers. Uninhibited market forces should punish such discriminators, according to Becker, since nondiscriminating firms that do not pay a premium would be more competitive.

The theory of statistical discrimination, attributed to economists Edmund Phelps and Kenneth Arrow, suggests that discrimination may, in fact, be rational and therefore profitable. Because employers have imperfect information about potential employees, it may be cost-effective to judge individuals using generalizations about groups of employees. If employers *believe* most women quit when they get pregnant, follow their husbands when transferred, call in sick more frequently, and/or are not candidates for promotions, this will influence hiring and wage decisions about individuals who may not engage in any of these behaviors. In fact, employers who testified against the Equal Pay Act made such generalizations about working women (see Chapter 8). Both of these stories about discrimination focus, without using these terms, on the interaction between wages as a price and the organization of social practices by gender and race-ethnicity. In the diagram, an arrow from social practice to price could indicate discrimination against individuals whose position in social hierarchies are defined by gender, race-ethnicity, and class.

Structural theories of discrimination, both within institutionalist economics and within radical political economy, focus on the interaction between market forces and the factors that determine bargaining power. The left-to-right arrow from wages as a living to wages as a price captures this process. Neoinstitutionalist economists, in their work on wage contours and internal labor markets, emphasize the multiplicity of labor markets and wage rates defined in relation to each other. The "crowding hypothesis," adapted by Barbara Bergmann, observes that working women, by virtue of their limited bargaining power (as well as gender ideology), are concentrated in a relatively small subset of occupations. An oversupply in the labor markets for these jobs drives down women's wage rates. If the markets for men's work and women's work are institutionally separated, the forces of supply and demand will not correct wage imbalances.

Segmentation theory within radical political economy also evokes the concept of separable (or segmented) labor markets, in this case characterized by firm size and structure as well as the gender and race-ethnicity of the labor supply. Wage differentials are partly explained by men's concentration in unionized jobs in oligopolistic firms where wage increases can be passed on to consumers; women, in contrast, work in industries such as textiles, apparel, and services where, for much of the postwar period, domestic and then global competition maintained downward pressure on wages. However, as Rhonda Williams has added, wage differentials are also explained by employers' and white male workers' interest in maintaining divisions among workers. Such divisions may reduce workers' bargaining power and therefore their ability to raise their socially defined living standard.

In Figure 10.1, therefore, both social practice and the struggle over living standards influence the process of setting wages as a price. The limitation of both mainstream and heterodox accounts of discrimination, however, is that they treat discriminatory wage differentials as simply distortions of market wages. Wages as a price remains the primary focus. Instead, our framework treats the organization of gender, race-ethnicity, and class segments as well as structural features of labor markets as integral to the development of wages as a price.

Other interactions

Because price mechanisms have been at the core of recent economic theory, there is an extensive literature on the disruptions to market processes. Other types of interactions have received less attention. Yet living wages are also affected by the other two dimensions. Appropriate living standards have historically been based upon family structure, gender, race-ethnicity, segments within classes, and many other factors (as seen in Chapters 5 and 6). This is the arena of social practice directly influencing the delineation of a multiplicity of living wages; it is shown by the arrow from "social practice" to "living" in the diagram. And the economic actors engaged in the bargaining process over definitions of a living have to be mindful of the price dimension of wages, symbolized by the right-to-left arrow. For example, the relative supply and demand of a given category of labor affects the unemployment rate in an industry, and an increase in the level of unemployment diminishes the workers' bargaining power. Market structures in which employers operate (a facet of labor markets) also help determine bargaining power. Ironically, employers in oligopolistic industries may be in a position to share their profits with their employees, while competitive industries tend to be low-waged. To compensate for this diminished bargaining power, employees in competitive industries such as textiles were targeted as beneficiaries of a federal minimum wage in the 1930s (Chapter 6). In contrast, during the *laissez-faire* 1980s increased competition from foreign automakers was allowed to undermine manufacturing wages (Chapter 9).

Finally, Figure 10.1 stresses that wages as both a living and a price influence the ways in which wages also serve as a social practice. These dynamics are depicted by the arrows pointing towards the bottom circle. When wages define appropriate living standards, they circumscribe not only someone's material standard of living, but also the ability to choose with whom to live and how to allocate one's time. As a price, wages are a marker of value. When market wages for women's work – for example, child-care workers – are low, this signals the social devaluation of caregiving and other activities that have been gendered as female. Comparable worth advocates, as argued in

Chapter 9, have emphasized both the material and symbolic aspects of low wages for women's work.

Cumulative causation and historical transformations

From the outset, we have asserted the need for a dynamic analysis of wages, including relative wages, that focuses on both rigidity and change. We treat wages, in the words of institutional economist John Commons, as "a *process* and not an *attribute*" (1923: 111, emphases in original). This is not an equilibrium-based framework. The wage-setting process depicted in Figure 10.1 is an outgrowth of the cumulative causation among the three faces of wages. This cumulative causation can lead to inertia in relative wages, especially given the feedback effects between current wage levels and the three faces. However, there have been major transformations in women's and men's economic lives and the meaning of this economic activity in their lives. A disruption in any of the underlying factors in wage-setting processes – bargaining power, labor markets, job evaluation, or the organization of gender, race-ethnicity, and class identity – interrupts the cycle, facilitating social change.

Throughout the twentieth century, changes in the political economy and in the organization of families created major disruptions in these factors. The political movements for different forms of wage regulations and policies were one response to these disruptions. The state, through its actions and inactions, can readjust bargaining power (influencing wages as a living), modify the structure of product and labor markets and the relative supply of and demand for labor (influencing wages as a price), and sanction particular models of gender, class, and racial-ethnic relations (influencing wages as a social practice). The issue is not whether or not the state will intervene in wage setting, but how.

Let us review each of the wage policies described in the previous chapters in light of the framework in Figure 10.1. We began our story of wage regulations in Chapter 5 with state-level minimum wages for women. The policy was clearly an effort to establish a socially defined living wage. During the Progressive Era, business concentration combined with mass immigration and macroeconomic fluctuations placed many workers, especially recent immigrants in sweatshops, in a weak position to negotiate a fair price for their labor. Social activists called attention to this lack of bargaining power. Gendered social practices came to define women in these work places as the key group with inadequate bargaining power. Male workers were deemed able to rely upon market mechanisms (despite the long-term goal of some social reformers for a broader policy covering both sexes) to set the price for their labor. Social practices also influenced the definition of a living wage for women, since wage boards were careful to set levels that reinforced appropriate living situations and women's status as future mothers. Race-ethnicity helped circumscribe which mothers were to be protected. The demise of gender-specific minimum wage laws following the *Adkins* decision is partially attributable to the emergence of an alternative concept of gender – one based on equality – embedded in the attainment of suffrage. Closing the doors to further immigration and the perception of the 1920s as a time of prosperity also led to the state's retrenchment from labor market intervention.

The federal minimum wage (described in Chapter 6) also emanates primarily from wages as a living. Macroeconomic factors are crucial, as the Great Depression rendered millions of workers unable to garner a living for their families. Gender was destabilized, as men lost the jobs that defined them as breadwinners and some women became "added workers," finding jobs gendered as female in less cyclically sensitive industries. Once again, minimum wage regulations were structured to define certain groups as possessing inadequate bargaining power and other groups as able to negotiate their own wage (individually or through collective bargaining). Skilled male workers in unions could use their bargaining power to define acceptable living standards and labor markets to ensure a share of productivity gains. But unorganized workers in manufacturing and related industries were given a legislated wage floor. African Americans concentrated in agriculture and domestic service had neither bargaining power nor state protection. Multiple wage earners, rather than a male breadwinner, was the logical implication. Gender, class, and race-ethnicity therefore combined during this period to define a multiplicity of living wages and different means to attain them. As movements for gender and racial-ethnic equality progressed over the course of the century, new groups became included under the federal statute, yet the real value of the minimum wage diminished.

In Chapter 7, we turned to the practice of job evaluation. Job evaluation attempts to set wages according to their value to the firm and is therefore concerned with wages as the price of labor power. The emergence of mass-production industry (along with policies to foster mass consumption of the products of these industries) created large firms with bureaucratic management and diminished skill and autonomy for workers. Internal labor markets and personnel practices began to augment external labor markets in setting wages and other conditions of employment. Job evaluation was adopted by employers to stabilize class relations and undermine union power. Gender, however, was destabilized. Job evaluation posited the principle of equal pay for equal work, regardless of living situation or needs. Feminists therefore embraced the practice of paying the rate for the job. The principle of equal pay for equal work was ratified by the decisions of the National War Labor Board during World War II. But during the postwar period this principle became narrowly defined to exclude comparisons between jobs, reasserting gender and racial-ethnic hierarchies.

Feminists unsuccessfully attempted to broaden the basis for pay comparisons in their early attempts to pass equal pay legislation after the war (see Chapter 8). During this period, the male breadwinner family began to lose its grip on peoples' consciousness. As discussed in Chapter 2, women's labor force participation and attachment over the life cycle grew due to a combination of supply-side and demand-side factors. Families increased their consumption standards by adding a second earner, while the female-intensive service sector was growing. New social practices regarding gender thus combined with changes in labor markets (affecting wages as a price) and increased bargaining power (affecting wages as a living). Opponents of legislating equal pay still diminished women's value as employees based on their gender. Although less overt about women's different natures and needs than they had been in the past, the interaction of social practice and price can be discerned in opponents' arguments that (married) women's family responsibilities lowered their human capital and made them less productive than men performing similar work. The Equal Pay Act of 1963 institutionalized the idea that justice and fairness consisted of treating workers objectively and basing the wage rate on the productive value of the work to the employer. It also implicitly asserted that some women were breadwinners, at the same time that it privileged women in male-dominated and integrated fields over women in female-dominated job classes.

Chapter 9 discussed two recent policies that assert new social practices by valuing the work of those excluded by previous policies. The comparable worth movement of the 1980s developed as women's bargaining power increased, especially within the public sector. The growth of public service unions along with the election of women into administrative and legislative positions in state government during the 1970s laid the foundation for reform efforts. Job evaluation was revived as a tool for comparing female-dominated job classes to those containing a high percentage of male workers. Feminists portrayed this as a mechanism for establishing the right price, unaffected by discrimination. However, this pay equity movement was undermined by macroeconomic instability. As the recession of the early 1980s evolved into massive restructuring of manufacturing industries, the wage cuts and job losses faced by male workers in the private sector took center stage. Further, as the public sector lost legitimacy and tax cuts led to job cuts, pay equity advocates lost their foothold. The living wage movement that emerged in the 1990s took off at the point where pay equity was stymied. Privatization of public sector services had become a widespread practice. Macroeconomic indicators, however, had become more favorable, leading to public sympathy for those left out of the economic boom. The ultimate impact and effectiveness of this new movement is still inconclusive.

The evolution of living wages and equal wages

As we look back over the movements to regulate wages during the twentieth century, we can also glean a clear evolution in the implicit wage theories articulated by public policy advocates. Early in the century, that employers had a moral responsibility to pay their workers a living wage was a widespread ideal, if not a practice. Employers who paid less than a living were viewed as harming not only their workers' health and morals but the health of the community as well. When John Bates Clark, an eminent early neoclassical economist, said that the inability of hardworking Americans to earn a living was "an indictment of civilization" (1913: 289), and labor organizer Maud Swartz said of the charge that paying living wages would force some employers out of business "God speed the day!" (Swartz in Women's Bureau 1923b: 81), they were reflecting the belief that wages should first and foremost provide a living.

Thinkers across the theoretical and political spectrums in the early twentieth century understood economic activity as a process of provisioning, that is, producing and reproducing human material life. An economy could be judged by its ability to provide economic well-being, what Adam Smith had termed the "necessaries and conveniences of life" (Smith 1937 [1776]: 78). As we have seen, while the role of market forces in setting wages had been long understood, market outcomes were not seen as infallible or untouchable. The market could be judged by its ability to provide a living, and could be regulated when it failed to do so. In this context, it is understandable that the first two major initiatives on wages, state-level minimum wages for women and a gender-neutral minimum wage enacted in the Fair Labor Standards Act of 1938, were both based on the primacy of wages as a living.

Nevertheless, social practice of the time created ambivalence about the meaning of living wages for women, since they were expected to rely upon fathers and husbands for their primary support. Women's entitlement to minimum wages came not on the basis of their identity as workers but on the basis of their identity as mothers. Health and morality of future mothers (or, at least, white mothers) had to be guaranteed for the larger social and economic good. In contrast, when the federal minimum wage was enacted, it covered white male workers whose claim was based on their role as breadwinners and providers. The concept of living wages took on multiple meanings for different constituencies, serving as a social practice organized by gender and race-ethnicity. The dominant model, legitimated by labor market and social welfare policies, was the white male breadwinner family, with subordinated groups attempting to gain access to such family arrangements.

Redefining fairness

By mid-century, stories about wages increasingly emphasized the necessary equivalence of exchange between the value of the work performed and the wage received. Fairness was defined purely in terms of commutative justice, that is, an equal exchange between two parties. For neoclassical economists and those endorsing their worldview, market mechanisms – the laws of supply and demand – were the most efficient and objective means of ensuring the equivalence of exchange. However, management consultants and neo-institutional economists looked to job evaluation systems and other wage-setting practices within firms to determine the relative value of different jobs and compensate them fairly. In the context of these two versions of wages as a price, fairness became separated from measures of well-being. The understanding of economic activity as provisioning gradually faded into the background.

The shift from "living wages" to "equal wages" discourse within reform movements reflected this emerging standard of fairness. Challenging the neutrality of market mechanisms, feminists nevertheless adapted to the constraints imposed by market discourse by strategically adopting the language of productivity and fairness in exchange. Reformers advocating higher wages for women had to explain why the wages women received did not conform to their true productive value. They focused on the concept of discrimination, defined as pay less than the value (in monetary terms) of the marginal product of labor or as different pay for identically productive workers; these definitions hinged on the quest for a gender-neutral (or racially neutral) price for labor. Noting imperfections in market mechanisms, working women's advocates endorsed job evaluation as a means of rectifying market-generated wage inequality. The rate for the job and equal pay for equal work became the focus.

The Equal Pay Act of 1963 that resulted from the movement for equal wages was utilized to make improvements in some women's economic position. Under this legislation, it was women's identity as workers alongside men, rather than their differential status within the family, that was the basis for state intervention. Yet, despite the rigid rules of the discourse that allowed only for arguments based on wages as a price, it is clear that feminists and labor activists did not forget the roles of wages as a living and a social practice. Equal pay advocates continued to use these forms of arguments, while the opponents of the Equal Pay Act focused primarily on productivity and prices. The very assertion of equal wages by feminists and labor activists was predicated upon changes in family structure, in the nature and organization of work, and in gender norms that called for a new set of social practices in setting wages – including the recognition that women did not, by choice as well as by circumstance, rely upon male breadwinners for their living.

Responding to market hegemony

As the century waned, the primacy of market mechanisms increasingly dominated other stories. The movement for equal wages had to settle for partial victories, as it faced increasing obstacles to extending pay equity policies from the state government to the private sector or federal legislation. By focusing on job evaluation as a technique and gender-neutral prices as a discourse, pay equity advocates partly lost touch with the grassroots mobilization based upon needs that marked living wage movements in the early part of the century. Pay equity was also undermined by the delegitimation of the state and fragmentation of its potential political base wrought by the rise of free market ideology.

Current living wage initiatives can be seen as attempts to reassert the provisioning view of economic activity, and to give community interests and well-being primacy over market forces. These movements bring "living wages" and "equal wages" discourse into harmony, by asserting both the needs and the contributions of workers who were neglected by previous wage policies. A true commitment to living wages is not impossible, but it would require political courage and the willingness to face down vested interests that adamantly oppose even modest increases in the minimum wage. It would also require challenging the mystified vision of the market that has become hegemonic since the 1980s.

One example is illustrative. Writing in the *Boston Globe*, N. Gregory Mankiw, a leading neoclassical economist, critiqued the efforts of student activists at Harvard University (where Mankiw teaches) to demand that the university pay a living wage to its workers. While the students' hearts were in the right place, Mankiw argued, their strategy was flawed because, in the words of the article title, "We can't ignore [the] law of supply and demand" (Mankiw 2001: D8). Repeating the postwar orthodoxy, Mankiw depicted markets as impersonal and well-tuned machines rewarding productivity without reference to the personal characteristics of workers: "The major difference between high-wage workers and low-wage workers is not that the former are better organized or better liked by their employers – it's that their higher productivity enhances the demand for their services" (2001: D8). Many decades of repetition of the importance of an unobstructed market, and the dangers of interference, make this struggle difficult to bring to the national level.

Voicing alternative theories about how political-economic institutions can serve to foster well-being is an essential task facing feminist scholars. So is seeking to impact policy debates. We believe that the two broad principles that we have identified in the twentieth century – living wages and equal wages – can also serve as a guideline for policy in the twenty-first. To establish the principle that work should earn a socially defined appropriate living standard, we need to strengthen current minimum wage laws by instituting a mechanism (such as indexing) that regularly raises the wage floor. Living wage ordinances that require a family-sustaining wage in exchange for government subsidies or contracts provide an interesting model for federal policy makers if they are well monitored, but only a beginning. To ensure equal wages, the first step is better enforcement of the existing Equal Pay Act (as well as Title VII of the Civil Rights Act). Beyond this, it is time to legislate the principle of pay equity for undervalued job categories, both female-dominated and minority concentrated. Each of these policies should be constructed to provide workers with both needs and choices, the essential elements of well-being.

This book has focused on regulations that affect wages. We do not mean to suggest, however, that remuneration for labor services is the only way to secure economic needs. In provisioning for society's well-being, wages are one key element of a multifaceted agenda. The state has a role in supplying essential services such as health care and child and dependent care. Income support programs, either targeted to specific groups or universally guaranteed, are another ongoing policy concern. In other words, many policies to help families and individuals attain appropriate living standards should be adopted on the national level.

Final thoughts

As feminist political economists, we wish to illuminate the experiences of women and men who are struggling to provide a living for themselves and their families. Rather than an impersonal narrative of demand functions and supply functions, wage setting is a human story. The agency of human actors attempting to steer the interaction of the state, economic relations including markets, and families in order to produce certain defined outcomes is at the heart of the process of wage setting.

Notes

1 Introduction: living wages, equal wages, and the value of women's work

1 See May (1982), Roediger (1991), Fraser and Gordon (1994), and Glickman (1997) for analyses of breadwinning in the United States during the nineteenth and twentieth centuries.

2 Protective legislation commonly established maximum hours, restrictions on night work, and limits on heavy lifting; some laws also barred women from specific occupations ostensibly for reasons of health and safety. In the short run, these laws benefited working-class women in sweatshops and other substandard workplaces. In the long run, such measures reinforced gender inequality by creating barriers that limited women's ability to work in some highly paid manual jobs.

3 In 1918, the War Labor Administration created an office called Women in Industry Service, a precursor to the Women's Bureau. Congress established the Women's Bureau within the Department of Labor in June 1920.

4 Most of what follows, including direct quotes, is drawn from the transcript of the conference, which was published as one of the Women's Bureau bulletins (see Women's Bureau 1923b).

5 Kessler-Harris (1987) describes the rift between "social feminists," those with strong ties to the labor movement who favored protective legislation to ameliorate the conditions for factory workers, and feminist supporters of the newly proposed Equal Rights Amendment, many of them middle class, who viewed protective legislation as an obstacle to equality.

6 Burroughs, whose mother was a domestic, had founded the National Association of Wage Earners, a union for domestics, in 1920. She was a longtime activist on behalf of African American women, particularly through the Woman's Convention, an auxiliary of the National Baptist Convention, and the first president of the National Training School for Women and Girls (Higginbotham 1993).

7 For several discussions of the relationship between feminism and political economy, see Waller and Jennings (1990), Emami (1993), Peterson and Brown (1994), and Matthaei (1996).

8 Thorstein Veblen (1993 [1898]) articulated this critique of mainstream economic theory in his essay "Why is Economics Not an Evolutionary Science?"

9 The assertion that economic theory is culturally constructed is central to recent work in feminist economics (see Jennings 1993; Strassmann 1994; Figart 1997; Waller 1999a).

2 Waged work in the twentieth century

1 Some farm girls also used these earnings to create an independent life for themselves, or even to pay for college (Dublin 1979: 35–8).

2 Connell (1993, 1995) argues that multiple forms of masculinity coexist in a particular time and place, although some forms are deemed culturally superior (hegemonic) and others are subordinate.

3 This phrase is derived from an 1897 pamphlet about the National Association of Colored Women entitled "The Awakening of Afro-American Woman" and is cited in Landry (2000: 73). Nevertheless, Landry does note that the image of black women as co-breadwinners "was not reached without ambivalence and debate" (2000: 79).

4 Gender did not become a consistent measurement category for federally gathered statistics until 1948, when a monthly sampling technique was utilized in the Current Population Survey.

5 The labor force includes everyone who is working or willing and able to work. The indicator counts both employed and unemployed persons. Someone who is unemployed is different than retired persons or others who are not actively looking for work.

6 For example, in describing the "economic emergence of women," Barbara Bergmann (1986) claims that higher wages pulled women into the labor force, an increase in labor supply. In economic terms, the "opportunity cost" of not working increased. Higher wages were the result of productivity growth that began with the industrial revolution. Juanita Kreps and Robert Clark (1975) offer a similar account of changes in women's labor supply, modeling a lifetime utility function.

7 For example, when the expansion of public relations led to the hiring of women, the job was redefined as requiring people skills. As real estate firms hired women agents, their familiarity with homes overcame their supposed lack of financial skills (Reskin and Roos 1990).

8 The literature on consumerism draws inspiration from institutionalist economist Thorstein Veblen's *Theory of the Leisure Class* (1994, first published in 1899). Although Veblen's emphasis was on class and not gender, his idea is that emulating the consumption patterns of the leisure class is a motivating force in labor market behavior, specifically in the decision to supply a certain number of hours to the market.

9 Clair Brown (1987), for example, traces shifts in consumption norms and their impact on women's increased labor force attachment.

10 Note that there was a substantial decline in single women's labor force participation during the depression decade of the 1930s. With jobs tight, there was a backlash against women's employment and employers favored hiring men. Many young women dropped out of the labor force rather than appearing in the unemployment statistics (see Kessler-Harris 1990).

11 A segregation index (or the Duncan index of dissimilarity) is another statistical measure designed to evaluate degree of occupational segregation in the labor market as a whole. The values of the index range from zero to one, with zero being perfect integration and one being perfect segregation. Therefore, the higher the index, the greater the degree of occupational segregation. The index has declined since 1960, but the decrease was most rapid in the 1970s (see, for example, Burris and Wharton 1982; Beller 1984).

3 Two faces of wages within the economics tradition: wages as a living, wages as a price

1 The relative emphasis placed on economic, cultural, and ideological factors has become a point of contention among Marxist political economists. This dispute could be oversimplified as a disagreement between orthodox economic determinists and postmodern overdeterminists. For a discussion of this distinction in

Marxian economics, see the 1999 symposium on "Anti-essentialist Marxism and Radical Institutionalism" in the *Journal of Economic Issues* (DeMartino 1999).

2 The phrase "peculiar commodity-owners" refers to Marx's characterization of workers as people who owned and sold their own labor power because they did not own capital (the means of producing their own subsistence).

3 This, of course, is a naturalized explanation, focusing on physical differences, in which women and children are collectively seen as people whose "bodily development is incomplete, but whose limbs are all the more supple" (Marx 1967: v. I, 394). In reference to women, Marx's discussion is more than a little contradictory in this respect, since he had just completed a description of the use of women rather than horses to haul canal boats.

4 Nancy Folbre has pointed out, however, that there was an existing socialist literature, particularly the writings of William Thompson and Anna Wheeler, that developed a less traditionally gendered analysis of women's roles (Folbre 1993: 98–100).

5 "Sweated industries" (or sweatshops) referred to establishments in which the wages, working conditions, and pace of work were appallingly bad. Often small and labor-intensive, these establishments remained in business by cutting costs through low pay, long hours, and neglect for the health and safety of their workers. Women workers were particularly likely to work in sweatshops, especially if they were recent immigrants or African American. Public indignation was aroused by the existence of sweatshops, and they became the impetus for campaigns for protective legislation limiting hours, raising wages, and improving conditions, as discussed in Chapter 5. The use of the term "sweated" trades, and the public response, suggest that the notion of a living wage (as well as acceptable working conditions) had wide societal acceptance. It must be noted, however, that sweatshops still exist, particularly in the garment industry in this country, and in garment and a range of other industries in poor countries.

6 Pigou also argued for a guaranteed minimum income in his text *Economics of Welfare*, which was originally written in 1932.

7 The term *"laissez-faire"* refers to free market economic doctrines that assert the beneficence of market forces and the undesirability of state regulations, labor unions, or other institutions deemed to interfere with the market mechanism.

8 According to Ely, a small group of economists (fewer than fifty) met in Saratoga, New York, in conjunction with the recently constituted American Historical Association, to discuss formation of the American Economic Association. A few women were among the early members, including Florence Kelley whose pioneering role in labor regulation is described in subsequent chapters (Ely 1938).

9 Paul McNulty views medieval Catholic economic thought as resting on the obligation to act justly in all spheres of activity, including the economic realm. From this, Aquinas derived the concept of a "just price" (McNulty 1984: 16).

10 Neoclassical economics commonly employs this technique of examining the effects of small, marginal changes in economic variables, while holding the rest of the economic environment constant. The rise of neoclassical economics in the late nineteenth century is, as a result, sometimes referred to as the "marginalist revolution" (see, for example, Hunt 1992; Screpanti and Zamagni 1993). Neoclassical economics differs significantly in this respect from Smithian, Marxian, and institutionalist economics, which theorize wages as historically determined, dynamic social relations, determined very differently from other prices.

11 Ironically, Hicks recanted the microeconomic wage gospel he was so influential in spreading. Shortly after *The Theory of Wages* was published in 1932, Hicks read the work of John Maynard Keynes and he subsequently became one of the prime advocates of postwar Keynesianism. When he finally permitted a second edition of his book on wages to be published in 1963, he wrote that it was only with

great reluctance, given how much his own ideas had changed (Hicks 1963 [1932]: v–vii).

12 Neoclassical economists in the 1960s and 1970s did confront the "theoretically embarrassing" issue of wage differentials based on factors besides productivity (Boyer and Smith 2001: 212). The two most common defenses were the existence of short-run disequilibria and omitted variables.

13 Neoinstitutionalists are also referred to as "neoclassical revisionists" (Boyer and Smith 2001). Neoinstitutionalism, however, is to be differentiated from a newer strand of theory called "new institutionalism" that relies on Austrian and/or game-theoretic frameworks (Rutherford 1996).

14 Two exceptions to the relative neglect of institutionalism in labor texts are *The Economics of Labor Markets* by Bruce Kaufman and Julie Hotchkiss (2000) and *Labor Economics and Labor Relations* by Lloyd Reynolds, Stanley Masters, and Colletta Moser (1998). For example, in their opening chapter, Kaufman and Hotchkiss contend that three forces determine wage rates: (1) markets, (2) institutions, and (3) sociological forces.

4 The third face: wages as a social practice

1 Folbre (1987, 1994) has offered a variation on dual systems theory, by suggesting that patriarchy can be viewed as a mode of production rather than a system.

2 Epistemology is the study of the nature of knowledge. Epistemological theories offer explanations of how knowledge is obtained and verified, and what limits there are to human knowledge and understanding. The eighteenth-century historical period referred to as the "Enlightenment" emphasized humanity's capacity for expanding understanding through the use of reason and the scientific method; it was a secular and humanistic approach to epistemology.

3 For example, the acquisition and presentation of scientific, including economic, knowledge depends on measurement. Using the examples of comparable worth and labor supply, feminist institutional economist Ann Jennings (2001) has argued that measurement is itself a social construction.

4 Children born as hermaphrodites or with genitalia that does not fit into the preconceived distinction between male and female are surgically "fixed." Until recently, psychology reinforced biological categories by labeling gender-inappropriate behavior (especially by women) as a form of deviance.

5 Again, de Beauvoir foreshadows contemporary feminist thought with her analysis of women in alternative circumstances: the married woman, the mother, the lesbian, the narcissist, the woman in love, the independent woman, and others.

6 Hawkesworth (1997) identifies and describes these alternative gender theories in the late 1990s.

7 Joya Misra and Frances Akins (1998) provide an excellent treatment of the tension between structure and agency in feminist research on the welfare state.

8 Wilkinson (1999) has written a review of this literature.

9 ADC was later renamed Aid to Families with Dependent Children or AFDC. The Personal Responsibility and Work Opportunity Act of 1996 replaced AFDC with Temporary Assistance for Needy Families (TANF).

10 For an analogous critique of neoclassical and Marxist theories with respect to race, see Williams (1987, 1995).

5 An experiment in wage regulation: minimum wages for women

1 The *Lochner* ruling prohibited legislation limiting hours of work for bakers in New York on the grounds that such legislation interfered with the workers' freedom of contract. The *Muller* ruling upheld a gender-specific hours limitation for

women in Oregon on the grounds that the state had an overriding interest in protecting the health of future mothers, so as to preserve future generations. Reformers generally interpreted the *Muller* ruling as allowing protective legislation for women workers, while prohibiting it for men. The *Adkins* ruling that threw out the District of Columbia's minimum wage for women constituted a rejection of protective legislation for women as well, and effectively ended the gender-specific reform strategy.

2 The states with viable minimum wage laws for women, according to the Women's Bureau, were Massachusetts, California, Minnesota, Oregon, Washington, Wisconsin, Arkansas, Kansas, Washington, DC, and North Dakota. In addition, Utah, Arizona, Puerto Rico, and South Dakota established inflexible flat rate minimums, which quickly became irrelevant in the high inflation of the period. Colorado, Nebraska, and Texas passed laws but never implemented them; Nebraska and Texas repealed their laws in 1919.

3 The eight industrialized states without minimum wage laws used in the Women's Bureau's calculations were Illinois, Indiana, Michigan, New Hampshire, New Jersey, New York, Ohio, and Pennsylvania.

4 An excellent treatment of the history of the National Consumers' League through the New Deal era can be found in Storrs (2000). Florence Kelley, a socialist, led the organization from the 1890s to 1932.

5 The Consumers' League of New York united with branches in three other states to form the National Consumers' League in 1899. Their motto was "investigate, agitate, legislate" (Storrs 2000: 14–15).

6 Reformers were not, of course, uniformly in agreement about the lack of desirability of waged work for women. Many middle-class women in the reform movement were themselves unmarried, building their lives around their careers (paid or unpaid). However, most women did marry and have children, and the conviction that mothers should not engage in waged work was widespread and deeply held.

7 The Triangle Shirtwaist Company, located near Washington Square in New York City, long resisted unionization. It was located in the top three stories of a ten-story building with a single, poorly constructed fire escape that quickly collapsed during the fire on March 25, 1911. Some women jumped to their deaths and others burned inside the building, for a total loss of 145 women, most of whom were immigrants (Foner 1982: ch. 8).

8 Alice Kessler-Harris notes that reliable figures on union membership are difficult to find for this early period. However, it is clear that very few women were members of unions. Kessler-Harris estimates that, by 1920, women constituted nearly 21 percent of the labor force, but less than eight percent of organized workers (1982: 152). Lacking a union to negotiate on her behalf, each woman worker faced her employer alone, often with neither the bargaining power nor the information to effectively negotiate a living wage.

9 There was not unanimity among economists about the determination of a worker's "true worth." For some (such as John Bates Clark) it was a market-clearing wage; for others (such as C. E. Persons) the classical notion of a natural wage reflecting the costs of reproducing labor power remained the standard.

10 It is interesting to note that many states required that one or more members of the Wage Board be women (Women's Bureau 1928).

11 By the time the minimum wage for laundry workers was in effect, the court case which would end in the abolition of Washington, DC's minimum wage legislation (*Adkins v. Children's Hospital*) was working its way through the Court of Appeals. The Laundry Employers Association used this litigation as an excuse to disregard the wage order, and it was never successfully enforced (Hart 1992: 14).

12 For a discussion of the National Woman's Party and the campaign for the ERA, see Cott (1987), Chafe (1991), and Evans (1997).

6 A living for breadwinners: the federal minimum wage

1 Some historians have divided the New Deal into two or three distinct phases (see Jeffries 1996 for an overview of the pros and cons of periodization). However, from the perspective of wage and hour regulations, there was relative continuity.

2 Although the term "social worker" might seem inappropriate today because we think of it as a paid occupation, in fact, the women-run settlement houses that begat Perkins and her allies also led to the formation of social work as a profession. Martin's source is the transcript of Perkins' Oral History recorded in the early 1950s and housed at Columbia University's Oral History Research Office. He reports that Perkins said Kelley was actually moved to tears when told of the job offer the next day, saying "I never thought I would live to see the day when someone we had trained, who knew about industrial conditions, cared about women, cared to have things right, would have the chance to be an administrative officer" (Martin 1976: 144).

3 Tipaldo himself met with hostility and informal boycotts, eventually going broke – as did the Schechter brothers.

4 There were many "cooks" involved in putting the bill together and various scholars have attributed it to different authors.

5 The full text of Roosevelt's statement is in the report submitted when the Senate first passed an amended version of the bill (see U.S. Senate 1937: 1–3).

6 The description of events leading to passage of the Fair Labor Standards Act is culled from the following sources: U.S. Senate (1937), Douglas and Hackman (1938), Perkins (1946), Ingalls (1974), Grossman (1978), Hart (1994), Paulsen (1996), Nordlund (1997), and Storrs (2000).

7 Throughout this chapter, the testimony by individuals in the transcript of the hearings is cited under the institutional author as U.S. Congress (1937).

8 Agricultural exemptions were increased to include dairying, horticulture, forestry, truck gardening, raising livestock, bees, and poultry, and "any practice incident to farming" (quoted in Douglas and Hackman 1938: 504), including those involved in delivering to market and those preparing, packaging, or storing fresh fruits and vegetables for local distribution.

9 In the U.S. Congress, each bill needs its own set of "rules" (establishing the ground rules for debate) in order to be discussed and considered by the full body of each house. By issuing, or not issuing, a rule, the Rules Committee controls the agenda.

10 Kelley, who died in 1932, unfortunately did not live to see the Supreme Court's reversal in favor of minimum wage legislation or passage of the Fair Labor Standards Act. Lucy Randolph Mason was General Secretary until 1937, when she left to work for the newly formed Congress of Industrial Organizations.

11 For estimates of coverage by industry, see Weiss (1944).

12 The terms "unskilled" and "unorganized" were used virtually interchangeably. Although the term "unskilled" is problematic because the definition of what constitutes skill is gendered and racialized, we use the term as it was used during the period in question, to refer to manufacturing jobs with few prior training requirements and that were relatively unorganized.

13 The impact of a mass–production economy on labor-management relations is discussed in greater detail in the following chapter.

14 African American males were eventually granted inclusion in the FLSA and other welfare state policies due to changes in economic structures as well as a grassroots

political struggle to redefine their masculine identity (see Alston and Ferrie 1993; Palmer 1995).

15 Storrs (2000) documents the discussions within the National Consumers' League about whether to attempt to degender the state laws following FLSA passage. The organization's leadership decided that the strategy was too risky; amending the existing laws might lead to them being discarded altogether.

7 Job evaluation and the ideology of equal pay

1 For a summary of Taylorism and scientific management, see Anderson (1939) and Meyer (1947).

2 Gordon, Edwards, and Reich (1982) provide an excellent discussion of changes in the structure of labor relations as part of a Social Structure of Accumulation (SSA), but those authors do not address wage-setting practices as part of the evolving SSA.

3 While managers such as Henry Ford (1922) viewed the ideal assembly-line worker as a person devoid of intellect and/or creativity, repetitive labor was not necessarily unskilled. For example, workers who were considered "unskilled" typically fixed their own machines on the factory floor.

4 Drawing on the scholarship of earlier institutionalists, the pioneering work on internal labor market theory was by Peter Doeringer and Michael Piore (1971).

5 For a description of these and other plans, see Walters (1938). NMTA estimated that there were 500 users of their plan by 1950; NEMA estimated that 1200 to 1500 plants employed their plan (Patton and Smith 1950: 68). Other trade associations developed similar plans but they were not extensively adopted by individual employers (Benge, Burk, and Hay 1941: 178).

6 To broadly publicize and promote job evaluation, the National Industrial Conference Board in New York (what we know of as the Conference Board today) described in great detail some early, model, successful job evaluation plans in industry. Several companies in attendance at the University of Michigan had their job evaluation plans profiled in the Conference Board Report in 1940.

7 For descriptions of employers' unequal pay practices, including unequal pay for women and men performing identical work, see the following two job evaluation textbooks: Lytle (1946: appendix A) and Smyth and Associates and Murphy (1946: ch. 10).

8 This directly contradicts Nobel laureate economist Gary Becker's hypothesis in *The Economics of Discrimination* (1957). Becker argued that discriminatory tastes are unprofitable in the long run because employers pay a wage premium to attract preferred categories of workers. Nondiscriminating employers would have a cost advantage and be more profitable. However, competition among firms employing job evaluation served to maintain discrimination; in reality, nondiscriminating employers would be the ones paying higher wages. Therefore, discrimination is profitable when it is a generalized practice.

9 For more on the War Labor Board, see Dubofsky (1994) and Workman (2000).

10 In addition to job evaluation, the National War Labor Board used other methods to award wage increases. One case was the so-called "Little Steel formula" decision of July 12, 1942, resolving a dispute between the Little Steel companies and the United Steelworkers of America. The complicated formula awarded wage increases, but guaranteed that they would not surpass price increases. The Board's wage stabilization policies were set on a case-by-case basis, but the Little Steel formula was precedent-setting. For a discussion, see, for example, Levitan (1951), Lichtenstein (1982), and Dubofsky (1994).

11 The previous day, the Board issued a similar decision in a case involving Brown and Sharpe Manufacturing Company (NWLB n.d.: v. 1, 291).

12 The War Labor Board opinion also argued: "Economic and political discrimination on account of race or creed is in line with the Nazi program" (NWLB n.d.: v. 2, 340). They referred to equal pay for equal work as "one of those equal rights in the promise of American democracy" (NWLB n.d.: v. 2, 340).

13 The National War Labor Board during World War I also affirmed equal pay with an official declaration: "If it shall become necessary to employ women on work ordinarily performed by men, they must be allowed equal pay for equal work and must not be allotted tasks disproportionate to their strength" (Women's Bureau 1942: 18). During World War I, equal pay issues were raised most often in manufacturing industries, especially munitions, and services such as operating street cars and buses. But this declaration had little lasting impact after the war.

14 The Board still accepted the implausibility of women performing men's work up to equivalent standards, as can be seen in the following passage:

> If, for example, the replacement of men by women is accompanied by a dilution of the job requirements, General Order No. 16 applied only in modified form. . . . A wage differential on the basis of lower production or performance standards, however, is entirely compatible with the principle of equal pay for equal work.
>
> (NWLB n.d.: v. 2, 1015)

15 This is not meant to suggest that job evaluation was not sold prior to the end of World War II. In fact, in 1944, one prominent management consulting firm produced a pamphlet on job evaluation to sell their services. Its title was *Job Evaluation: A Simple, Scientific Answer to One of Industry's Greatest Problems* (Corrigan, Osburne and Wells, Inc. 1944).

16 Marlene Kim (1999) found similar rationales for lowering wages paid to historically female jobs in documents supporting a job evaluation system applied to California state public employees and implemented in the 1930s.

17 From reviewing job evaluation texts over the course of three decades, it appears that by 1963, the instructions on sample wage surveys did not include a place for indicating the sex of the job, as seen in Lanham (1963: 216–17). It was standard practice to include sex in the salary survey until the Equal Pay Act of 1963 and the Civil Rights Act of 1964. For a treatment of more subtle forms of bias in contemporary salary surveys, see Kim (2000).

18 Obtaining data for scholarly investigations of gender-based wage differentials within establishments is more difficult than broader-based measures of the wage gap. As a result, we have fewer studies from which to derive generalizations.

8 Legislating equal wages

1 A portion of Polinsky's thesis was reprinted in the transcripts of the 1945 Congressional hearings on equal pay, published in 1946. Throughout this chapter, we refer to individuals' testimony, statements, and other supporting documentation and cite the U.S. Senate or U.S. House of Representatives as institutional authors.

2 For example, in the essay in *A Woman's Wage* on "The Double Meaning of Equal Pay," Kessler-Harris treats the major changes in the bill in an endnote (1990: 151; see also Blankenship 1993). Harrison (1988) provides a fairly detailed legislative history, though her primary focus is the relationship between feminists supporting the Equal Rights Amendment and those advocating equal pay.

3 One exception is Cobble (1994), who documents activism by working-class feminists during the postwar period. She observes that women in trade unions were active supporters of equal pay legislation, as well as collective negotiations for pay equity.

4 There were two other clauses in the bill covering layoffs and discharges, and prohibiting retaliation against employees who file complaints.

5 Kessler-Harris (1990: 83) notes that the American Federation of Labor had voiced support for the slogan since the end of the nineteenth century. However, as in the debate over minimum wages discussed in Chapter 6, the AFL resisted legislation that it believed undermined the need for collective bargaining.

6 Another supporter of equal pay not listed in either table because it does not fit either category was the American Civil Liberties Union.

7 The following description of this legislative process is pieced together from U.S. House of Representatives (1963) and BNA (1963) as well as the transcripts of the Congressional hearings.

8 More hearings took place in an effort to increase support in May of 1950.

9 The five members of the Findings Committee included the bill's author Mary Anderson (at the time, a private citizen) and individuals associated with the National Council of Jewish Women, the International Ladies' Garment Workers' Union, East River Savings Bank, and Namm's Department Store.

10 Representative Frances Bolton, a Republican from Ohio, introduced weaker versions of equal pay legislation based on the BPW model throughout the rest of the 1950s.

11 The employer has remained generically "he" but the aggrieved employee can be of either sex.

12 Only the primary alternatives that led to the eventual wording of the Equal Pay Act are included in this discussion.

13 The Age Discrimination in Employment Act was passed separately in 1967. Title VII and all of its amendments exclude small employers, that is, employers with fourteen or fewer employees.

14 Some analysts do not believe that the amendment would have been successful if it had actually been sponsored by the advocates of gender equity and it has even been suggested that using Smith was a calculated strategy (Robinson 1979; Deitch 1996).

15 For an analysis of the Moynihan report, see Ann Jennings and Dell Champlin (1994).

16 Similar language was used by Joseph A. Beirne, President of the Communications Workers of America in his statement at the 1948 hearings.

17 Caroline Davis, Director of the UAW's Women's Department, wrote in a submitted statement that women were not the only group accused of poor work habits (U.S. Senate 1963: 153). Immigrants, African Americans, and indigenous populations of colonial countries were equally accused of the same traits. But absenteeism, tardiness, and other work interruptions reflected low morale on the job. Equal pay and equal opportunities would increase morale and alleviate these problems.

18 Of course, occupation segmentation by gender was not new to the postwar period. See Albelda and Tilly (1994) for an analysis of labor market segmentation by race and gender before and during the postwar era.

19 Feminist academic literature on the social construction of skill asserts that gender enters into the designation of what constitutes skill (see, for example, Steinberg 1990).

9 Living wages, equal wages revisited: contemporary movements and policy initiatives

1 These percentages are based on 1984 data and were taken from Bergmann (1986: Appendix A).

2 A simplified neoclassical model of supply and demand was used to argue that

wage increases necessarily led to employment losses. Widespread acceptance of this model over other theoretical approaches and empirical research rendered policy makers unwilling to raise the wage floor (see Card and Krueger 1995; Levin-Waldman 2001).

3 NCPE provided (and continues to provide) an important role in facilitating communication and supplying information and resources to local pay equity campaigns.

4 The details of the pay equity movement during this period are drawn from a number of sources including: NCPE (1989); Sorensen (1994); McCann (1994); Figart and Kahn (1997); and Gardner and Daniel (1998).

5 Note that all incumbents in an undervalued job receive the pay adjustments, even if some men work in a predominantly female job.

6 The discourse of comparable worth opponents is analyzed in Figart and Mutari (1997).

7 Gardner and Daniel (1998) provide an update on pay equity activity and note that these five states still have not pursued pay equity reform.

8 Figart and Kahn (1997) evaluate what they term a "contradictory moment" that both fostered and inhibited pay equity.

9 Efforts to increase state minimum wages are discussed in Figart (2001).

10 Some researchers include usage of "prevailing wage laws" to extend living wages to private sector workers as part of the early living wage movement. Federal and state prevailing wage laws require contractors to pay wages that reflect community standards, often union-scale wages, and even benefits, to employees working on publicly funded construction projects. This means that three municipalities that extended prevailing wages to some contractors outside the construction industry would precede Baltimore: Des Moines, Iowa (in 1988), Gary, Indiana (in 1991), and San Jose, California (in 1991) (see Pollin and Luce 1998: ch. 2).

11 Nationwide, current ordinances affect only about 100,000 workers, according to one estimate (Murray 2001).

12 For example, University of California-Berkeley economics professor Michael Reich endorsed living wage initiatives on the West Coast, including San Francisco, Oakland, and Santa Monica (see, for example, Reich 1999).

13 For an assessment of the impact in Los Angeles, see Zabin (1997).

14 Two labor economists from Michigan State University and the University of Michigan respectively, David Neumark and Scott Adams (2001), also estimated the impact of living wage ordinances in numerous cities on wages, urban poverty, and employment. They found a significant increase in earnings of low-wage workers, modest reductions in poverty, and minimal disemployment effects.

15 By July of 1999, the city shifted the unarmed security guards back to full-time municipal employees, leaving cleaning occupations as the only positions left covered by the ordinance.

16 For a discussion of the potential of pay equity policies for minority-concentrated occupations, see Figart and Lapidus (1998).

References

Abramovitz, Mimi. (1988) *Regulating the Lives of Women: Social Welfare Policy from Colonial Times to the Present*, Boston, MA: South End Press.

Acker, Joan. (1989) *Doing Comparable Worth: Gender, Class, and Pay Equity*, Philadelphia, PA: Temple University Press.

Acker, Joan. (1991) "Thinking About Wages: The Gendered Wage Gap in Swedish Banks," *Gender & Society* 5 (3): 390–407.

Adkins v. Children's Hospital of Washington, DC. (1923) United States Supreme Court, 261 U.S. 525.

Akerlof, George and Yellen, Janet. (1986) *Efficiency Wage Models of the Labour Market*, Cambridge, U.K.: Cambridge University Press.

Albelda, Randy. (1985) "'Nice Work If You Can Get It': Segmentation of White and Black Women Workers in the Post-war Period," *Review of Radical Political Economics* 17 (3): 72–85.

Albelda, Randy and Tilly, Chris. (1994) "Towards a Broader Vision: Race, Gender, and Labor Market Segmentation in the Social Structure of Accumulation Framework," in David M. Kotz, Terrence McDonough, and Michael Reich (eds) *Social Structures of Accumulation: The Political Economy of Growth and Crisis*, pp. 212–30, Cambridge, U.K.: Cambridge University Press.

Albelda, Randy and Tilly, Chris. (1997) *Glass Ceilings and Bottomless Pits*, Boston, MA: South End Press.

Aldridge, Delores P. (1999) "Black Women and the New World Order: Toward a Fit in the Economic Marketplace," in Irene Browne (ed.) *Latinas and African American Women at Work*, pp. 357–79, New York: Russell Sage Foundation.

Alston, Lee and Ferrie, Joseph. (1993) "Paternalism in Agricultural Labor Contracts in the U.S. South: Implications for the Growth of the Welfare State," *American Economic Review* 83 (4): 852–76.

Amott, Teresa and Matthaei, Julie. (1996) *Race, Gender, and Work: A Multi-cultural Economic History of Women in the United States*, revised edition, Boston, MA: South End Press.

Anderson, Edward Hutchings. (1939) "Production Economics and Scientific Management," *Southern Economic Journal* 5 (4): 511–26.

Andrews, Elmer. (1939) "Making the Wage-hour Law Work," *American Labor Legislation Review* 29 (2): 53–61.

Appelbaum, Eileen and Batt, Rosemary. (1994) *The New American Workplace: Transforming Work Systems in the United States*, Ithaca, NY: ILR Press.

Armstrong, Barbara Nachtrieb. (1932) *Insuring the Essentials: Minimum Wage,*

Plus Social Insurance – a Living Wage Program, New York: The Macmillan Company.

Backhouse, Roger E. (1998) "The Transformation of U.S. Economics, 1920–1960," in Mary S. Morgan and Malcolm Rutherford (eds) *From Interwar Pluralism to Postwar Neoclassicism*, pp. 85–107, Durham, NC: Duke University Press.

Badgett, M. V. Lee and Williams, Rhonda M. (1994) "The Changing Contours of Discrimination: Race, Gender, and Structural Economic Change," in Michael A. Bernstein and David E. Adler (eds) *Understanding American Economic Decline*, pp. 313–29, Cambridge, U.K.: Cambridge University Press.

Baker, Helen and True, John M. (1947) *The Operation of Job Evaluation Plans: A Survey of Experience*, Princeton, NJ: Princeton University, Industrial Relations Section.

Barrett, Michele. (1988) *Women's Oppression Today: The Marxist/Feminist Encounter*, London: Verso.

Beatty, Richard W. and Beatty, James R. (1984) "Some Problems with Contemporary Job Evaluation Systems," in Helen Remick (ed.) *Comparable Worth and Wage Discrimination: Technical Possibilities and Political Realities*, pp. 59–78, Philadelphia, PA: Temple University Press.

Becker, Gary S. (1957) *The Economics of Discrimination*, Chicago: University of Chicago Press.

Becker, Gary S. (1964) *Human Capital*, New York: National Bureau of Economic Research.

Beckley, Harlan R. (1996) "Introduction: Catholic Social Ethicist and Advocate for Reform," in John A. Ryan, *Economic Justice*. Selections from *Distributive Justice* and *A Living Wage*, edited and introduced by Harlan R. Beckley, Louisville, KY: Westminster John Knox Press.

Beller, Andrea H. (1984) "Trends in Occupational Segregation by Sex and Race, 1960–1981," in Barbara F. Reskin (ed.) *Sex Segregation in the Workplace: Trends, Explanations, Remedies*, pp. 11–26, Washington, DC: National Academy Press.

Benería, Lourdes. (1999) "Globalization, Gender and the Davos Man," *Feminist Economics* 5 (3): 61–83.

Benge, Eugene J., Burk, S. L. H., and Hay, Edward N. (1941) *Manual of Job Evaluation*, New York: Harper Brothers.

Benhabib, Seyla and Cornell, Drucilla (eds) (1987) *Feminism as Critique*, Minneapolis: University of Minnesota Press.

Bergmann, Barbara R. (1986) *The Economic Emergence of Women*, New York: Basic Books.

Berman, Richard. (1997, September 2) "'Living Wage' Would Make Low-skill Workers Worse Off," *Capital Times* (Madison, WI) [Online]. Available: http://web.lexis-nexis.com/universe [accessed 1999, May 26].

Bernstein, Michael A. (1987) *The Great Depression: Delayed Recovery and Economic Change in America, 1929–1939*, Cambridge, U.K.: Cambridge University Press.

Blackwelder, Julia Kirk. (1997) *Now Hiring: The Feminization of Work in the United States, 1900–1995*, College Station, Texas: A&M University Press.

Blankenship, Kim M. (1993) "Bringing Gender and Race In: U.S. Employment Discrimination Policy," *Gender & Society* 7 (2): 204–26.

Blau, Francine D., Simpson, Patricia, and Anderson, Deborah. (1998) "Continuing Progress? Trends in Occupational Segregation in the United States over the 1970s and 1980s," *Feminist Economics* 4 (3): 29–71.

Bluestone, Barry and Bluestone, Irving. (1992) *Negotiating the Future: A Labor Perspective on American Business*, New York: Basic Books.

Bluestone, Barry and Rose, Stephen. (2000) "The Enigma of Working Time Trends," in Lonnie Golden and Deborah M. Figart (eds) *Working Time: International Trends, Theory and Policy Perspectives*, pp. 21–37, London: Routledge.

Bond, James T., Galinsky, Ellen, and Swanberg, Jennifer E. (1998) *The 1997 National Study of the Changing Workforce*, New York: Families and Work Institute.

Boris, Eileen. (1993) "The Power of Motherhood: Black and White Activist Women Redefine the 'Political,'" in Seth Koven and Sonya Michel (eds) *Mothers of a New World: Maternalist Politics and the Origins of Welfare States*, pp. 213–45, New York: Routledge.

Boris, Eileen. (1994) *Home to Work: Motherhood and the Politics of Industrial Homework in the United States*, Cambridge, U.K.: Cambridge University Press.

Boris, Eileen. (1995) "The Racialized Gendered State: Constructions of Citizenship in the United States," *Social Politics* 2 (2): 160–80.

Boyer, George R. and Smith, Robert S. (2001) "The Development of the Neoclassical Tradition in Labor Economics," *Industrial and Labor Relations Review* 54 (2): 199–223.

Brandeis, Elizabeth. (1935) "Labor Legislation," in John R. Commons (ed.) *History of Labor in the United States, 1896–1932*, pp. 399–697, New York: The Macmillan Company.

Breckinridge, Sophonisba P. (1923) "The Home Responsibilities of Women Workers and the 'Equal Wage,'" *Journal of Political Economy* 31 (4): 521–43.

Brewer, Rose. (1999) "Theorizing Race, Class and Gender: The New Scholarship of Black Feminist Intellectuals and Black Women's Labor," *Race, Gender & Class* 6 (2): 29–47.

Brown, Clair. (1987) "Consumption Norms, Work Roles, and Economic Growth, 1918–80," in Clair Brown and Joseph A. Pechman (eds) *Gender in the Workplace*, pp. 13–49, Washington, DC: The Brookings Institution.

Brown, Doug. (1989) "Is Institutional Economics Existential Economics?" in William M. Dugger (ed.) *Radical Institutionalism: Contemporary Voices*, pp. 65–82, New York: Greenwood Press.

Bureau of National Affairs [BNA]. (1956) *Job Evaluation: Survey No. 40 of BNA's Personnel Policies*, Washington, DC: BNA, December.

Bureau of National Affairs [BNA]. (1963) *Equal Pay for Equal Work. Operations Manual*, Washington, DC: BNA.

Burris, Val. (1982) "The Dialectic of Women's Oppression: Notes on the Relation Between Capitalism and Patriarchy," *Berkeley Journal of Sociology* 27: 51–73.

Burris, Val and Wharton, Amy. (1982) "Sex Segregation in the U.S. Labor Force," *Review of Radical Political Economics* 14 (3): 43–56.

Burstein, Paul. (1985) *Discrimination, Jobs, and Politics: The Struggle for Equal Employment Opportunity in the United States since the New Deal*, Chicago: University of Chicago Press.

Butler, Judith and Scott, Joan W. (eds) (1992) *Feminists Theorize the Political*, New York: Routledge.

Cancian, Francesca M. (1992) "Feminist Science: Methodologies that Challenge Inequality," *Gender & Society* 6 (4): 623–42.

Card, David and Krueger, Alan B. (1995) *Myth and Measurement: The New Economics of the Minimum Wage*, Princeton, NJ: Princeton University Press.

Carter, Michael J. and Carter, Susan Boslego. (1981) "Women's Recent Progress in the

Professions Or, Women Get a Ticket to Ride After the Gravy Train Has Left the Station," *Feminist Studies* 7 (3): 477–504.

Chafe, William H. (1991) *The Paradox of Change: American Women in the 20th Century*, New York: Oxford University Press.

Chambers, John W. (1969) "The Big Switch: Justice Roberts and the Minimum-wage Cases," *Labor History* 10 (1): 44–73.

Cherry, Robert. (2001) *Who Gets the Good Jobs? Combating Race and Gender Disparities*, New Brunswick, NJ: Rutgers University Press.

City of Jersey City Municipal Council. (1996a) Transcript of Proceedings, Regular Meeting, May 22.

City of Jersey City Municipal Council. (1996b) Transcript of Proceedings, Regular Meeting, June 12.

Clark, John Bates. (1913) "Minimum Wage," *Atlantic Monthly* 112 (September): 289–97.

Clark, John Bates. (1965 [1899]) *The Distribution of Wealth*, New York: Augustus M. Kelley.

Cleeland, Nancy. (1999, February 7) "Lives Get a Little Better on a Living Wage," *Los Angeles Times* [Online]. Available: http://web.lexis-nexis.com/universe [accessed 1999, May 26].

Cobble, Dorothy Sue. (1994) "Recapturing Working-class Feminism: Union Women in the Postwar Era," in Joanne Meyerowitz (ed.) *Not June Cleaver: Women and Gender in Postwar America, 1945–1960*, pp. 57–83, Philadelphia, NJ: Temple University Press.

Cockburn, Cynthia. (1991) *In the Way of Women: Men's Resistance to Sex Equality in Organizations*, Ithaca, NY: ILR Press.

Cohn, Samuel. (1985) *The Process of Occupational Sex-typing: The Feminization of Clerical Labor in Great Britain*, Philadelphia, PA: Temple University Press.

Commons, John R. (1923) "Wage Theories and Wage Policies," *American Economic Review* 13 (1, supplement): 110–17.

"Conference of Trade-union Women Under Auspices of U.S. Department of Labor." (1918) *Monthly Labor Review* 7 (5): 1340–2.

Connell, R. W. (1987) *Gender and Power*, Stanford, CA: Stanford University Press.

Connell, R. W. (1993) "The Big Picture: Masculinities in Recent World History," *Theory and Society* 22: 597–623.

Connell, R. W. (1995) *Masculinities*, Berkeley: University of California Press.

Corrigan, Osburne, and Wells, Inc. (1944) *Job Evaluation: A Simple, Scientific Answer to One of Industry's Greatest Problems*, New York: Author.

Cott, Nancy F. (1987) *The Grounding of Modern Feminism*, New Haven, CT: Yale University Press.

Creamer, Day. (1980) "Organizing Strategies: Closing the Wage Gap between Men and Women," in Joy Ann Grune (ed.) *Manual on Pay Equity: Raising Wages for Women's Work*, pp. 51–3, Washington, DC: Conference on Alternative State and Local Policies.

Dale, Ernest. (1950) "How to Conduct a Wage Survey," in Joseph M. Dooher and Vivienne Marquis (eds) *The AMA Handbook of Wage and Salary Administration: Tested Compensation Methods for Factory, Office and Managerial Personnel*, pp. 89–105, New York: American Management Association.

Davies, Gareth and Derthick, Martha. (1997) "Race and Social Welfare Policy: The Social Security Act of 1935," *Political Science Quarterly* 112 (2): 217–35.

de Beauvoir, Simone. (1974 [1952]) *The Second Sex*, New York: Vintage Books.

DeGise, Thomas A. (2000) Council President, City of Jersey City, New Jersey. Interview, Jersey City, NJ, August 14.

Deitch, Cynthia. (1996) "Gender, Race, and Class Politics and the Inclusion of Women in Title VII of the 1964 Civil Rights Act," in Esther Ngan-Ling Chow, Doris Wilkinson, and Maxine Baca Zinn (eds) *Race, Class, & Gender: Common Bonds, Different Voices*, pp. 288–307, Thousand Oaks, CA: Sage Publications.

DeMartino, George. (1999) "Anti-Essentialist Marxism and Radical Institutionalism: Introduction to the Symposium," *Journal of Economic Issues* 33 (4): 797–800.

Deslippe, Dennis A. (2000) *"Rights, Not Roses": Unions and the Rise of Working-class Feminism, 1945–80*, Urbana: University of Illinois Press.

Dickinson, Z. Clark. (1943) "Men's and Women's Wages in the United States," *International Labour Review* 47 (6): 693–720.

DiNardo, John, Fortin, Nicole, and Lemieux, Thomas. (1996) "Labor Market Institutions and the Distribution of Wages, 1973–1992: A Semiparametric Approach," *Econometrica* 64 (5): 1001–44.

Doeringer, Peter B. and Piore, Michael J. (1971) *Internal Labor Markets and Manpower Analysis*, Lexington, MA: D. C. Heath and Company.

Donohue, Brian. (1996) "'Living Wage' Bill Hearing Tonight," *The Jersey Journal*, January 16, p. 2.

Donohue, John D. (1989) *The Privatization Decision: Public Ends, Private Means*, New York: Basic Books.

Dooher, M. Joseph and Marquis, Vivienne (eds) (1950) *The AMA Handbook of Wage and Salary Administration*, New York: American Management Association.

Douglas, Dorothy W. (1920) "The Cost of Living for Working Women: A Criticism of Current Theories," *Quarterly Journal of Economics* 34 (1): 225–59.

Douglas, Paul H. and Hackman, Joseph. (1938) "The Fair Labor Standards Act of 1938 I," *Political Science Quarterly* 53 (4): 491–515.

Dublin, Thomas. (1979) *Women at Work: The Transformation of Work and Community in Lowell, Massachusetts, 1826–1860*, New York: Columbia University Press.

DuBoff, Richard B. (1989) *Accumulation and Power*, Armonk, NY: M. E. Sharpe.

Dubofsky, Melvyn. (1994) *The State and Labor in Modern America*, Chapel Hill, NC: University of North Carolina Press.

Dugger, William M. (ed.) (1989) *Radical Institutionalism: Contemporary Voices*, Westport, CT: Greenwood Press.

Dugger, William M. and Waller, William T. (eds) (1992) *The Stratified State: Radical Institutionalist Theories of Participation and Duality*, Armonk, NY: M. E. Sharpe.

Dunlop, John T. (1964) "The Task of Contemporary Wage Theory," in John T. Dunlop (ed.) *The Theory of Wage Determination*, pp. 3–27, New York: Augustus M. Kelley.

Dunlop, John T. (1966 [1944]) *Wage Determination Under Trade Unions*, New York: Augustus M. Kelley.

Edwards, Richard. (1979) *Contested Terrain: The Transformation of the Workplace in the Twentieth Century*, New York: Basic Books.

Ehrenberg, Ronald G. and Smith, Robert S. (2000) *Modern Labor Economics: Theory and Public Policy*, seventh edition, Boston, MA: Addison-Wesley.

Eisenstein, Zillah R. (1979) *Capitalist Patriarchy and the Case for Socialist Feminism*, New York: Monthly Labor Review.

Elder, Peyton K. and Miller, Heidi D. (1979) "The Fair Labor Standards Act: Changes of Four Decades," *Monthly Labor Review* 102 (7): 10–16.

Ely, Richard T. (1938) *Ground Under Our Feet: An Autobiography*, New York: Macmillan.

Emami, Zohreh. (1993) "Challenges Facing Social Economics in the Twenty-first Century: A Feminist Perspective," *Review of Social Economy* 52 (4): 416–25.

Employment Policies Institute [EPI]. (2000) *Living Wage Policy: The Basics*, Washington, DC: Employment Policies Institute.

England, Paula. (1982) "The Failure of Human Capital Theory to Explain Occupational Sex Segregation," *Journal of Human Resources* 17 (3): 358–70.

England, Paula. (1992) *Comparable Worth: Theories and Evidence*, New York: Aldine de Gruyter.

England, Paula. (1993) "The Separative Self: Androcentric Bias in Neoclassical Assumptions," in Marianne A. Ferber and Julie A. Nelson (eds) *Beyond Economic Man: Feminist Theory and Economics*, pp. 37–53, Chicago: University of Chicago Press.

Evans, Sara M. (1997) *Born for Liberty: A History of Women in America*, New York: The Free Press.

Evans, Sara M. and Nelson, Barbara J. (1989) *Wage Justice: Comparable Worth and the Paradox of Technocratic Reform*, Chicago: University of Chicago Press.

Fair Labor Standards Act of 1938. (1938) Public Laws – CH. 676 – June 25, 1938.

Families and Work Institute. (1995) *Women: The New Providers*, New York: Author.

Ferber, Marianne A. and Nelson, Julie A. (eds) (1993) *Beyond Economic Man: Feminist Theory and Economics*, Chicago: University of Chicago Press.

Figart, Deborah M. (1997) "Gender as More Than a Dummy Variable: Feminist Approaches to Discrimination," *Review of Social Economy* 55 (1): 1–32.

Figart, Deborah M. (1999) "Discrimination, Theories of," in Janice Peterson and Margaret Lewis (eds) *The Elgar Companion to Feminist Economics*, pp. 107–12, Cheltenham, U.K.: Edward Elgar.

Figart, Deborah M. (2001) "Raising the Minimum Wage and Living Wage Campaigns," in Mary C. King (ed.) *Squaring Up: Policies to Raise Women's Incomes in the United States*, pp. 111–35, Ann Arbor: University of Michigan Press.

Figart, Deborah M. and Hartmann, Heidi I. (2000) "Broadening the Concept of Pay Equity: Lessons for a Changing Economy," in Ron Baiman, Heather Boushey, and Dawn Saunders (eds) *Political Economy and Contemporary Capitalism: Radical Perspectives on Economic Theory and Policy*, pp. 285–93, Armonk, NY: M. E. Sharpe.

Figart, Deborah M. and Kahn, Peggy. (1997) *Contesting the Market: Pay Equity and the Politics of Economic Restructuring*, Detroit, MI: Wayne State University Press.

Figart, Deborah M. and Lapidus, June. (1998) "Will Comparable Worth Reduce Race-Based Wage Discrimination?" *Review of Radical Political Economics* 30 (3): 14–24.

Figart, Deborah M. and Mutari, Ellen. (1997) "Markets, Flexibility, and Family: Evaluating the Gendered Discourse Against Pay Equity," *Journal of Economic Issues* 31 (3): 687–705.

Fisher, Marguerite J. (1948) "Equal Pay for Equal Work Legislation," *Industrial and Labor Relations Review* 2 (1): 50–7.

Fogarty, Michael P. (1957) "The Catholic Theory of the Family Living Wage," *Review of Social Economy* 15 (2): 91–103.

Folbre, Nancy. (1987) "A Patriarchal Mode of Production," in Randy Albelda,

Christopher Gunn, and William Waller (eds) *Alternatives to Economic Orthodoxy*, pp. 323–38, Armonk, NY: M. E. Sharpe.

Folbre, Nancy. (1993) "Socialism, Feminist and Scientific," in Marianne A. Ferber and Julie A. Nelson (eds) *Beyond Economic Man: Feminist Theory and Economics*, pp. 94–110, Chicago: University of Chicago Press.

Folbre, Nancy. (1994) *Who Pays for the Kids? Gender and the Structures of Constraint*, London: Routledge.

Foner, Philip S. (1982) *Women and the American Labor Movement: From the First Trade Unions to the Present*, New York: The Free Press.

Ford, Henry. (1922) *My Life and Work*, Garden City, NY: Garden City Publishing.

Frankel, Noralee and Dye, Nancy S. (eds) (1991) *Gender, Class, Race and Reform in the Progressive Era*, Lexington: The University Press of Kentucky.

Fraser, Nancy and Gordon, Linda. (1994) "A Genealogy of 'Dependency': Tracing a Keyword of the U.S. Welfare State," *Signs* 19 (2): 309–36.

Fudge, Judy and McDermott, Patricia. (1991) *Just Wages: A Feminist Assessment of Pay Equity*, Toronto: University of Toronto Press.

Gardner, Susan E. and Daniel, Christopher. (1998) "Implementing Comparable Worth/Pay Equity: Experiences of Cutting-edge States," *Public Personnel Management* 27 (4): 475–89.

Gearty, Patrick W. (1953) *The Economic Thought of Monsignor John A. Ryan*, Washington, DC: The Catholic University of America Press.

Giddings, Paula. (1984) *When and Where I Enter . . . : The Impact of Black Women on Race and Sex in America*, New York: William Morrow and Co.

Gilpin, Toni, Isaac, Gary, Letwin, Dan, and McKivigan, Jack. (1987) *On Strike for Respect: The Yale Strike of 1984–85*, Chicago: Charles H. Kerr.

Gimble, Daniel E. (1991) "Institutionalist Labor Market Theory and the Veblenian Dichotomy," *Journal of Economic Issues* 25 (3): 625–48.

Glenn, Evelyn Nakano. (1998) "Gender, Race, and Class: Bridging the Language–Structure Divide," *Social Science History* 22 (1): 29–38.

Glickman, Lawrence B. (1993) "Inventing the 'American Standard of Living': Race, Gender, and Working-Class Identity, 1880–1925," *Labor History* 34 (2/3): 221–35.

Glickman, Lawrence B. (1997) *A Living Wage: American Workers and the Making of Consumer Society*, Ithaca, NY: Cornell University Press.

Goldfield, Michael. (1987) *The Decline of Organized Labor in the United States*, Chicago: University of Chicago Press.

Goldin, Claudia. (1990) *Understanding the Gender Gap: An Economic History of American Women*, New York: Oxford University Press.

Gomberg, William. (1947) *A Labor Union Manual on Job Evaluation*, Chicago: Labor Education Division, Roosevelt College.

Goodwin, Crauford G. (1998) "The Patrons of Economics in a Time of Transformation," in Mary S. Morgan and Malcolm Rutherford (eds) *From Interwar Pluralism to Postwar Neoclassicism*, supplement to vol. 30 of *History of Political Economy*, pp. 53–81, Durham, NC: Duke University Press.

Gordon, David M., Edwards, Richard, and Reich, Michael. (1982) *Segmented Work, Divided Workers: The Historical Transformation of Labor in the United States*, Cambridge, U.K.: Cambridge University Press.

Gordon, Linda. (1994) *Pitied But Not Entitled: Single Mothers and the History of Welfare*, New York: The Free Press.

Gormley, William T., Jr. (1991) "The Privatization Controversy," in William T.

Gormley, Jr (ed.), *Privatization and Its Alternatives*, Madison: University of Wisconsin Press, 3–16.

Grossman, Jonathan. (1978) "Fair Labor Standards Act of 1938: Maximum Struggle for a Minimum Wage," *Monthly Labor Review* 101 (6): 22–30.

Grune, Joy Ann. (ed.) (1980) *Manual on Pay Equity: Raising Wages for Women's Work*, Washington, DC: Conference on Alternative State and Local Policies.

Gunderson, Morley. (1989) "Male–Female Wage Differentials and Policy Responses," *Journal of Economic Literature* 27 (1): 46–72.

Harding, Sandra. (1986) *The Science Question in Feminism*, Ithaca, NY: Cornell University Press.

Harding, Sandra. (ed.) (1987) *Feminism and Methodology: Social Science Issues*, Bloomington: Indiana University Press.

Harrison, Cynthia. (1988) *On Account of Sex: The Politics of Women's Issues, 1945–1968*, Berkeley: University of California Press.

Hart, Vivien. (1992) "Feminism and Bureaucracy: The Minimum Wage Experiment in the District of Columbia," *Journal of American Studies* 26 (Part 1): 8–17.

Hart, Vivien. (1994) *Bound by Our Constitution: Women, Workers, and Minimum Wage Laws in the United States and Britain*, Princeton, NJ: Princeton University Press.

Hartmann, Heidi. (1976) "Capitalism, Patriarchy, and Job Segregation by Sex," *Signs* 1 (3): 137–69.

Hartmann, Heidi. (1981 [1979]) "The Unhappy Marriage of Marxism and Feminism: Towards a More Progressive Union," in Lydia Sargent (ed.) *Women and Revolution: A Discussion of the Unhappy Marriage of Marxism and Feminism*, pp. 1–41, Boston, MA: South End Press.

Hartmann, Heidi I. and Aaronson, Stephanie. (1994) "Pay Equity and Women's Wage Increases: Success in the States, A Model for the Nation," *Duke Journal of Gender Law and Policy* 1: 69–87.

Hawkesworth, Mary. (1997) "Confounding Gender," *Signs* 22 (3): 649–713.

Hay, Edward N. (1940) "The Right Pay for the Job," *Banking* (March): 22–3.

Heath, Julia A. and Bourne, David W. (1995) "Husbands and Housework: Parity or Parody," *Social Science Quarterly* 76 (1): 195–202.

Heath, Julia A., Ciscel, David H., and Sharp, David C. (1998) "The Work of Families: The Provision of Market and Household Labor and the Role of Public Policy," *Review of Social Economy* 56 (4): 501–21.

Herrmann, Andrew. (1996, December 21) "Religious Leaders Regroup in Push for City Wage Law," *Chicago Sun-Times* [Online], p. 19. Available: http://web.lexis-nexis.com/universe [Accessed 1998, June 24].

Herzenberg, Stephen A., Alic, John A., and Wial, Howard. (1998) *New Rules for a New Economy: Employment and Opportunity in Postindustrial America*, Ithaca, NY: Cornell University Press.

Hewitson, Gillian J. (1999) *Feminist Economics: Interrogating the Masculinity of Rational Economic Man*, Cheltenham, U.K.: Edward Elgar.

Hicks, John R. (1963 [1932]) *The Theory of Wages*, London: Macmillan.

Higginbotham, Evelyn Brooks. (1993) *Righteous Discontent: The Women's Movement in the Black Baptist Church, 1880–1920*, Cambridge, MA: Harvard University Press.

Holcombe, A. N. (1912) "The Legal Minimum Wage in the United States," *American Economic Review* 2 (1): 21–37.

Holtz, Debra Levi. (2000, May 25) "Berkeley Gives the Go-Ahead for Draft of Living-

Wage Law," *The San Francisco Chronicle* [Online], p. A17. Available: http://web.lexis-nexis.com/universe [accessed 2000, October 11].

Humphries, Jane. (1976) "Women: Scapegoats and Safety Valves in the Great Depression," *Review of Radical Political Economics* 8 (1): 98–121.

Hunnicutt, Benjamin Kline. (1988) *Work Without End: Abandoning Shorter Hours for the Right to Work*, Philadelphia, PA: Temple University Press.

Hunt, E. K. (1992) *History of Economic Thought: A Critical Perspective*, New York: Harper-Collins.

Hunter, Tera W. (1997) *To 'Joy My Freedom: Southern Black Women's Lives and Labors After the Civil War*, Cambridge, MA: Harvard University Press.

Hutchinson, Emilie Josephine. (1919) *Women's Wages: A Study of the Wages of Industrial Women and Measures Suggested to Increase Them*, New York: Longmans, Green, & Company.

Hutner, Frances C. (1986) *Equal Pay for Comparable Worth*, New York: Praeger.

Ingalls, Robert P. (1974) "New York and the Minimum-Wage Movement, 1933–1937," *Labor History* 15 (2): 179–98.

International Labour Office. (1960) *Job Evaluation*, Geneva: ILO.

International Labour Office. (1986) *Job Evaluation*, Geneva: ILO.

Jacobs, Jerry A. (1989) "Long-term Trends in Occupational Segregation by Sex," *American Journal of Sociology* 95 (1): 160–73.

Jeffries, John W. (1996) "A 'Third New Deal'? Liberal Policy and the American State, 1937–1945," *Journal of Policy History* 8 (4): 387–409.

Jennings, Ann L. (1993) "Public or Private? Institutional Economics and Feminism," in Marianne A. Ferber and Julie A. Nelson (eds) *Beyond Economic Man: Feminist Theory and Economics*, pp. 111–29, Chicago: University of Chicago.

Jennings, Ann. (2001) "Social Constructions of Measurement: Three Vignettes from Recent Events and Labor Economics," *Journal of Economic Issues* 35 (2): 365–71.

Jennings, Ann and Champlin, Dell. (1994) "Cultural Contours of Race, Gender, and Other Class Distinctions: A Critique of Moynihan and Other Functionalist Views," in Janice Peterson and Doug Brown (eds) *The Economic Status of Women under Capitalism*, pp. 95–110, Aldershot, U.K.: Edward Elgar.

Johnson, Eve. (1980) "Teenagers' Summer Jobs," in Joy Ann Grune (ed.) *Manual on Pay Equity: Raising Wages for Women's Work*, p. 46, Washington, DC: Conference on Alternative State and Local Policies.

Johnson, Forrest Hayden, Boise, Robert W., and Pratt, Dudley. (1946) *Job Evaluation*, New York: John Wiley & Sons.

Jones, Jacqueline. (1986) *Labor of Love, Labor of Sorrow: Black Women, Work, and the Family from Slavery to the Present*, New York: Vintage Books.

Kabeer, Naila. (1994) *Reversed Realities: Gender Hierarchies in Development Thought*, London: Verso.

Kaufman, Bruce E. and Hotchkiss, Julie L. (2000) *The Economics of Labor Markets*, fifth edition, Fort Worth, TX: Dryden Press.

Keller, Susan Jo. (1997, November 27) "New Jersey Daily Briefing; Ordinance Would Raise Wages," *The New York Times*, p. B1.

Kelley, Florence. (1912) "Minimum Wage Laws," *Journal of Political Economy* 20 (December): 999–1010.

Kerr, Clark. (1954) "The Balkanization of Labor Markets," in Edward Wight Bakke (ed.) *Labor Mobility and Economic Opportunity*, pp. 92–110, New York: John Wiley.

Kerr, Clark and Fisher, Lloyd H. (1950) "Effect of Environment and Administration on Job Evaluation," *Harvard Business Review* 38 (3): 77–96.

Kessler-Harris, Alice. (1982) *Out to Work*, Oxford: Oxford University Press.

Kessler-Harris, Alice. (1987) "The Debate Over Equality for Women in the Workplace: Recognizing Differences," in Naomi Gerstel and Harriet Engel Gross (eds) *Families and Work*, pp. 520–39, Philadelphia, PA: Temple University Press.

Kessler-Harris, Alice. (1990) *A Woman's Wage: Historical Meanings and Social Consequences*, Lexington: The University Press of Kentucky.

Keynes, John Maynard. (1964 [1936]) *The General Theory of Employment, Interest, and Money*, New York: Harcourt.

Kim, Marlene. (1999) "Inertia and Discrimination in the California State Civil Service," *Industrial Relations* 38 (1): 46–68.

Kim, Marlene. (2000) "Employers' Estimates of Market Wages: Implications for Wage Discrimination in the U.S.," *Feminist Economics* 6 (2): 97–114.

King, L. J. (1938) "Job Evaluation," *The Society for the Advancement of Management Journal* III (3): 93–8.

King, Mary C. (1992) "Occupational Segregation by Race and Sex, 1940–88," *Monthly Labor Review* 115 (4): 30–6.

Koven, Seth and Michel, Sonya. (eds) (1993) *Mothers of a New World: Maternalist Politics and the Origins of Welfare States*, New York: Routledge.

Kreps, Juanita and Clark, Robert. (1975) *Sex, Age, and Work: The Changing Composition of the Labor Force*, Baltimore, MD: The Johns Hopkins University Press.

Kress, A. L. (1939) "How to Rate Jobs and Men," *Factory Management and Maintenance* XCVII (October): 59–70.

Krucoff, Carol. (1980 [1979]) "MONEY: The Question of Men, Women and 'Comparable Worth,'" in Joy Ann Grune (ed.) *Manual on Pay Equity: Raising Wages for Women's Work*, pp. 49–50, Washington, DC: Conference on Alternative State and Local Policies.

Kuiper, Edith and Sap, Jolande. (eds) (1995) *Out of the Margin: Feminist Perspectives on Economics*, London: Routledge.

Kuttner, Robert. (1997, August 17) "Making Sure Workers Live Decently," *The San Diego Union-Tribune* [Online], p. G3. Available: http://web.lexis-nexis.com/universe [accessed 1999, May 26].

Landry, Bart. (2000) *Black Working Wives: Pioneers of the American Family Revolution*, Berkeley: University of California Press.

Landry, Donna and MacLean, Gerald. (1993) *Materialist Feminisms*, Cambridge, MA: Blackwell.

Lanham, Elizabeth. (1963) *Administration of Wages and Salaries*, New York: Harper & Row.

Laslett, Barbara and Brenner, Johanna. (1989) "Gender and Social Reproduction: Historical Perspectives," *Annual Review of Sociology* 15: 381–404.

Laughlin, Kathleen A. (2000) *Women's Work and Public Policy: A History of the Women's Bureau, U.S. Department of Labor, 1945–1970*, Boston, MA: Northeastern University Press.

Leete, Laura and Schor, Juliet B. (1994) "Assessing the Time-squeeze Hypothesis: Hours Worked in the United States, 1969–89," *Industrial Relations* 33 (1): 25–43.

Leo XIII. (n.d. [1891]) *Rerum Novarum. Encyclical Letter of Pope Leo XIII on the Condition of Labor*, New York: The Paulist Press.

Lester, Richard A. (1946a) "Shortcomings of Marginal Analysis for Wage-employment Problems," *American Economic Review* 36 (1): 63–82.

Lester, Richard A. (1946b) "Wage Diversity and Its Theoretical Implications," *Review of Economics and Statistics* 28 (3): 152–9.

Levin-Waldman, Oren M. (2001) *The Case of the Minimum Wage: Competing Policy Models*, Albany: State University of New York Press.

Levitan, Sar. A. (1951) "Union Attitudes toward Job Evaluation and Ingrade Progression," *Industrial and Labor Relations Review* 4 (2): 268–74.

Levy, Frank. (1998) *The New Dollars and Dreams: American Incomes and Economic Change*, New York: The Russell Sage Foundation.

Lewchuk, Wayne A. (1993) "Men and Monotony: Fraternalism as a Managerial Strategy at the Ford Motor Company," *Journal of Economic History* 53 (4): 824–56.

Lewis, Jane. (1992) "Gender and the Development of Welfare Regimes," *Journal of European Social Policy* 2 (3): 159–73.

Lichtenstein, Nelson. (1982) *Labor's War at Home: The CIO in World War II*, New York: Cambridge University Press.

Lieberman, Jacob Andrew. (1971) "Their Sisters' Keepers: The Women's Hours and Wages Movement in the United States, 1890–1925," Ph.D. thesis, Columbia University.

Lieberman, Robert C. (1998) *Shifting the Color Line: Race and the American Welfare State*, Cambridge, MA: Harvard University Press.

Lipschultz, Sybil. (1996) "Hours and Wages: The Gendering of Labor Standards in America," *Journal of Women's History* 8 (1): 114–36.

Livernash, E. Robert. (1957) "The Internal Wage Structure," in George W. Taylor and Frank C. Pierson (eds) *New Concepts in Wage Determination*, pp. 140–71, New York: McGraw-Hill.

"'Living Wage' a Fair One." (1996, June 15) *The Jersey Journal*, p. B10.

Livy, Bryan. (1975) *Job Evaluation: A Critical Review*, London: Allen & Unwin.

Lorber, Judith. (1994) *Paradoxes of Gender*, New Haven, CT: Yale University Press.

Lytle, Charles Walter. (1946) *Job Evaluation Methods*, New York: Ronald Press.

Mac Donald, Heather. (1996) "'Living Wages,' Fewer Jobs," *The New York Times* [Online], p. A31. Available: http://web.lexis-nexis.com/universe [accessed 1998, June 23].

McCann, Michael W. (1994) *Rights at Work: Pay Equity Reform and the Politics of Legal Mobilization*, Chicago: University of Chicago Press.

McConnell, Campbell R., Brue, Stanley L., and Macpherson, David A. (1999) *Contemporary Labor Economics*, fifth edition, Irwin/McGraw-Hill.

Macdonald, Martha. (1995) "Feminist Economics: From Theory to Research," *Canadian Journal of Economics* 28 (1): 159–75.

Macek, Steve. (1997, June) "New Party Report: Making Work Pay," *Z Magazine* [Online]. Available: http://www.lbbs.org/ZMag/articles/june97macek.htm [accessed 1998, September 12].

McLoughlin, William G. (1978) *Revivals, Awakenings, and Reform: An Essay on Religion and Social Change in America, 1607–1977*, Chicago: University of Chicago Press.

McNulty, Paul J. (1984) *The Origins and Development of Labor Economics*, Cambridge, MA: MIT Press.

Mankiw, N. Gregory. (1997) *Principles of Economics*, Fort Worth, TX: The Dryden Press.

Mankiw, N. Gregory. (2001) "We Can't Ignore Law of Supply and Demand," *Boston Globe*, June 24, p. D8.

Manning, Robert D. (2000) *Credit Card Nation: The Consequences of America's Addiction to Credit*, New York: Basic Books.

Margo, Robert A. (1993) "Employment and Unemployment in the 1930s," *Journal of Economic Perspectives* 7 (2): 41–59.

Martin, George. (1976) *Madam Secretary: Frances Perkins*, Boston, MA: Houghton Mifflin.

Marx, Karl. (1967 [1867]) *Capital*, vols I–III, New York: International Publishers.

Matthaei, Julie A. (1982) *An Economic History of Women in America*, New York: Schocken Books.

Matthaei, Julie A. (1996) "Why Feminist, Marxist, and Anti-Racist Economists Should Be Feminist-Marxist-Anti-Racist Economists," *Feminist Economics* 2 (1): 22–42.

May, Martha. (1982) "The Historical Problem of the Family Wage: The Ford Motor Company and the Five Dollar Day," *Feminist Studies* 8 (2): 399–424.

Meyer, Julie. (1947) "Hierarchy and Stratification of the Shop," *Social Research* 14 (2): 168–90.

Meyerowitz, Joanne J. (1988) *Women Adrift: Independent Wage Earners in Chicago, 1880–1930*, Chicago: University of Chicago Press.

Michel, Sonya. (1993) "The Limits of Maternalism: Policies Toward American Wage-earning Mothers during the Progressive Era," in Seth Koven and Sonya Michel (eds) *Mothers of a New World: Maternalist Politics and the Origins of Welfare States*, pp. 277–320, New York: Routledge.

Milkman, Ruth. (1987) *Gender at Work: The Dynamics of Job Segregation by Sex during World War II*, Urbana: University of Illinois Press.

Mincer, Jacob and Polachek, Solomon. (1974) "Family Investments in Human Capital: Earnings of Women," *Journal of Political Economy* 82 (2): S76-S108.

Mink, Gwendolyn. (1995) *The Wages of Motherhood: Inequality in the Welfare State, 1917–1942*, Ithaca, NY: Cornell University Press.

Mishel, Lawrence, Bernstein, Jared, and Schmitt, John. (1999) *The State of Working America, 1998–99*, Ithaca, NY: ILR Press.

Misra, Joya and Akins, Frances. (1998) "The Welfare State and Women: Structure, Agency, and Diversity," *Social Politics* 5 (3): 259–85.

Moody, Kim. (1988) *An Injury to All: The Decline of American Unionism*, New York: Verso.

Moore, Geoffrey H. (1980) "Business Cycles, Panics, and Depression," in Glenn Porter (ed.) *Encyclopedia of American Economic History*, pp. 151–6, New York: Charles Scribner's Sons.

Morgan, Mary S. and Rutherford, Malcolm. (eds) (1998) *From Interwar Pluralism to Postwar Neoclassicism*, supplement to vol. 30 of *History of Political Economy*, Durham, NC: Duke University Press.

Murolo, Priscilla. (1997) *The Common Ground of Womanhood*, Urbana: University of Illinois Press.

Murray, Bobbi. (2001) "Living Wage Comes of Age," *The Nation* 273 (4), July 23/30: 24–8.

Mutari, Ellen. (1996) "Women's Employment Patterns During the U.S. Inter-war Period: A Comparison of Two States," *Feminist Economics* 2 (2): 107–27.

Mutari, Ellen. (2000) "Feminist Political Economy: A Primer," in Ron Baiman,

Heather Boushey, and Dawn Saunders (eds) *Political Economy and Contemporary Capitalism: Radical Perspectives on Economic Theory and Policy*, pp. 29–35, Armonk, NY: M. E. Sharpe.

Nathan, Maud. (1926) *The Story of an Epoch-Making Movement*, New York: Doubleday, Page, & Company.

National Association of Manufacturers [NAM], Employee Relations Department. (1957) "Fundamentals of Job Evaluation," Information Bulletin #25, New York, NY: NAM.

National Association of Manufacturers, Law Department. (1963) "Summary Analysis of the Equal Pay Act of 1963," Washington, DC: NAM, June 13.

National Committee on Pay Equity [NCPE]. (1989) *Pay Equity in the Public Sector, 1979–1989*, Washington, DC.

National Industrial Conference Board. (1940) *Job Evaluation: Formal Plans for Determining Basic Pay Differentials*, New York: National Industrial Conference Board, Studies in Personnel Policy, no. 25.

National War Labor Board [NWLB]. (n.d.) *The Termination Report of the National War Labor Board. Volume I: Industrial Disputes and Wage Stabilization in Wartime, January 12, 1942 – December 31, 1945*. 3 vols, Washington, DC: U.S. Government Printing Office.

Nelson, Julie A. (1993) "The Study of Choice or the Study of Provisioning? Gender and the Definition of Economics," in Marianne A. Ferber and Julie A. Nelson (eds) *Beyond Economic Man: Feminist Theory and Economics*, pp. 23–36, Chicago: University of Chicago Press.

Nelson, Julie A. (1996) *Feminism, Objectivity and Economics*, London: Routledge.

Neumark, David and Adams, Scott. (2001) "Do Living Wage Ordinances Reduce Urban Poverty?" unpublished.

Nicholson, Linda J. (ed.) (1990) *Feminism/Postmodernism*, New York: Routledge.

Niedt, Christopher, Ruiters, Greg, Wise, Dana, and Schoenberger, Erica. (1999) *The Effects of the Living Wage in Baltimore*, Working Paper no. 119, Washington, DC: Economic Policy Institute.

Nissen, Bruce. (2000) "Living Wage Campaigns from a 'Social Movement' Perspective: The Miami Case," *Labor Studies Journal* 25 (3): 29–50.

Nordlund, Willis J. (1997) *The Quest for a Living Wage: The History of the Federal Minimum Wage Program*, Westport, CT: Greenwood Press.

Oakes, Larry (1997, July 16) "Duluth Council Backs Ordinance on 'Living Wage,'" *Star Tribune* (Minneapolis) [Online]. Available: http://web.lexis-nexis.com/universe [accessed 1998, June 24].

O'Hara, Phillip Anthony. (1995) "The Association for Evolutionary Economists and the Union for Radical Political Economics: General Issues of Continuity and Integration," *Journal of Economic Issues* 29 (1): 137–59.

Omi, Michael and Winant, Howard. (1994 [1986]) *Racial Formation in the United States: From the 1960's to the 1980's*, second edition. New York: Routledge.

O'Neill, June. (1985) "The Trend in the Male–Female Wage Gap in the United States," *Journal of Labor Economics* 3 (1), pt. 2: S91–S116.

Oppenheimer, Valerie K. (1979) *The Female Labor Force in the United States: Demographic and Economic Factors Governing Its Growth and Changing Composition*, Westport, CT: Greenwood Press.

Orloff, Ann. (1996) "Gender in the Welfare State," *Annual Review of Sociology* 22: 51–78.

Ortner, Sherry B. (1996) *Making Gender: The Politics and Erotics of Culture*, Boston: Beacon Press.

Palmer, Phyllis. (1995) "Outside the Law: Agricultural and Domestic Workers Under the Fair Labor Standards Act," *Journal of Policy History* 7 (4): 416–40.

Parrish, John B. (1948) "Impact of World War II on Internal Wage Rate Structures," *Southern Economic Journal* 15 (October): 134–51.

Patton, John A. (1961) "Job Evaluation in Practice: Some Survey Findings," in *AMA Management Report no. 54, Industrial Relations Forum*, pp. 73–7, New York: American Management Association.

Patton, John A. and Littlefield, C. L. (1957) *Job Evaluation: Text and Cases*, Homewood, IL: Richard D. Irwin.

Patton, John A. and Smith, Reynold S., Jr. (1950) *Job Evaluation*, Chicago: Richard D. Irwin.

Paulsen, George E. (1996) *A Living Wage for the Forgotten Man: The Quest for Fair Labor Standards 1933–1941*, Selinsgrove, PA: Susquehanna University Press.

Perkins, Frances. (1946) *The Roosevelt I Knew*, New York: Viking Press.

Persons, Charles E. (1915) "Women's Work and Wages in the United States," *Quarterly Journal of Economics* 29 (1): 201–34.

Petersen, Trond and Morgan, Laurie A. (1995) "Separate and Unequal: Occupation-establishment Sex Segregation and the Gender Wage Gap," *American Journal of Sociology* 101 (2): 329–65.

Peterson, Agnes L. (1929) *What the Wage-earning Woman Contributes to Family Support*, Washington, DC: United States Department of Labor, Women's Bureau, Bulletin no. 75.

Peterson, Janice and Brown, Doug. (eds) (1994) *The Economic Status of Women under Capitalism: Institutionalist Economics and Feminist Theory*, Aldershot, U.K.: Edward Elgar.

Phelps, Orme W. (1957) "A Structural Model of the U.S. Labor Market," *Industrial and Labor Relations Review* 10 (3): 402–23.

Phelps Brown, E. H. (1962) *The Economics of Labor*, New Haven, CT: Yale University Press.

Pidgeon, Mary Elizabeth. (1936) *The Employed Woman Homemaker in the United States: Her Responsibility for Family Support*, Washington, DC: United States Department of Labor, Women's Bureau, Bulletin no. 148.

Pidgeon, Mary Elizabeth. (1938) *Differences in the Earnings of Women and Men*, Washington, DC: United States Department of Labor, Women's Bureau, Bulletin no. 152.

Pidgeon, Mary Elizabeth and Mettert, Margaret Thompson. (1939) *Employed Women and Family Support*, Washington, DC: United States Department of Labor, Women's Bureau, Bulletin no. 168.

Pierson, Frank C. (1957) "An Evaluation of Wage Theory," in George W. Taylor and Frank C. Pierson (eds) *New Concepts in Wage Determination*, pp. 3–31, New York: McGraw-Hill.

Pigou, A. C. (1913) "Principle of the Minimum Wage," *Nineteenth Century* 73 (March): 644–58.

Pigou, A. C. (1960 [1932]) *The Economics of Welfare*, London: Macmillan.

Pinchbeck, Ivy. (1969) *Women Workers and the Industrial Revolution 1750–1850*, London: Virago.

Pius XI. (n.d. [1931]) *Quadragesimo Anno. Encyclical Letter of Pope Pius XI on Reconstructing the Social Order*, New York: The Paulist Press.

Piven, Frances Fox and Cloward, Richard A. (1971) *Regulating the Poor: The Functions of Public Welfare*, New York: Vintage Books.

Pollin, Robert and Luce, Stephanie. (1998) *The Living Wage: Building A Fair Economy*, New York: The New Press.

Power, Marilyn. (1983) "From Home Production to Wage Labor: Women as a Reserve Army of Labor," *Review of Radical Political Economics* 15 (1): 71–91.

Power, Marilyn. (1999) "Parasitic-industries Analysis and Arguments for a Living Wage for Women in the Early Twentieth-century United States," *Feminist Economics* 5 (1): 61–78.

Power, Marilyn and Rosenberg, Sam. (1995) "Race, Class, and Occupational Mobility: Black and White Women in Service Work in the United States," *Feminist Economics* 1 (3): 40–59.

Quadagno, Jill. (1994) *The Color of Welfare: How Racism Undermined the War on Poverty*, New York: Oxford University Press.

Quaid, Maeve. (1993) *Job Evaluation: The Myth of Equitable Assessment*, Toronto: University of Toronto Press.

Quinn, Christopher. (2000, May 12) "Three Bishops Endorse Local "Living Wage' Law," *Plain Dealer* [Online], Metro, p. 4B. Available: http://web.lexis-nexis.com/ universe [accessed 2000, October 11].

Reich, Michael. (1981) *Racial Inequality: A Political-economic Analysis*, Princeton, NJ: Princeton University Press.

Reich, Michael. (1999, January 19) "True Benefits of a Living Wage Figured," *San Francisco Chronicle* [Online]. Available: http://web.lexis-nexis.com/universe [accessed 1999, May 26].

Renwick, Trudi J. and Bergmann, Barbara R. (1993) "A Budget-based Definition of Poverty," *The Journal of Human Resources* 28 (1): 1–24.

Reskin, Barbara F. and Roos, Patricia A. (eds) (1990) *Job Queues, Gender Queues: Explaining Women's Inroads into Male Occupations*, Philadelphia, PA: Temple University Press.

Reynolds, Lloyd G. (1971 [1951]) *The Structure of Labor Markets: Wages and Labor Mobility in Theory and Practice*, Westport, CT: Greenwood Press [reprint].

Reynolds, Lloyd G., Masters, Stanley H., and Moser, Colletta H. (1998) *Labor Economics and Labor Relations*, eleventh edition, Upper Saddle River, NJ: Prentice Hall.

Riegel, John W. (1937) *Wage Determination*, Ann Arbor: Bureau of Industrial Relations, University of Michigan.

Riegel, John W. (1940) *Salary Determination: Common Policies and Selected Practices in Forty American Corporations*, Ann Arbor: Bureau of Industrial Relations, University of Michigan.

Robinson, Donald Allen. (1979) "Two Movements in Pursuit of Equal Opportunity," *Signs: Journal of Women in Culture and Society* 4 (3): 413–33.

Roediger, David R. (1991) *The Wages of Whiteness: Race and the Making of the American Working Class*, London: Verso.

Romer, Christina D. (1993) "The Nation in Depression," *Journal of Economic Perspectives* 7 (2): 19–39.

Roosevelt, Franklin D. (1967a [1937]) "Fourth Annual Message," in Fred L. Israel (ed.) *The State of the Union Messages of the Presidents, 1790–1966*, Volume III (1905–66), pp. 2827–33, New York: Chelsea House Publishers.

Roosevelt, Franklin D. (1967b [1938]) "Fifth Annual Message," in Fred L. Israel (ed.)

The State of the Union Messages of the Presidents, 1790–1966, Volume III (1905–66), pp. 2833–41, New York: Chelsea House Publishers.

Rubin, Gayle. (1975) "The Traffic in Women: Notes on the 'Political Economy' of Sex," in Rayna Reiter (ed.) *Toward an Anthropology of Women*, pp. 157–210, New York: Monthly Review Press.

Ruggles, Patricia. (1990) *Drawing the Line: Alternative Poverty Measures and Their Implication for Public Policy*, Washington, DC: Urban Institute Press.

Ruggles, Rick. (2000, April 28) "Wage Costs Elusive," *Omaha World-Herald* [Online]. Available: http://web.lexis-nexis.com/universe [accessed 2000, October 11].

Rutherford, Malcolm. (1996) *Institutions in Economics: The Old and the New Institutionalism*, Cambridge, U.K.: Cambridge University Press.

Rutherford, Malcolm. (1997) "American Institutionalism and the History of Economics," *Journal of the History of Economic Thought* 19 (3): 178–95.

Ryan, John A. (1906) *A Living Wage: Its Ethical and Economic Aspects*, New York: Macmillan Company.

Sanborn, Henry. (1964) "Pay Differences Between Men and Women," *Industrial and Labor Relations Review* 17 (4): 534–50.

Sargent, Lydia (ed.) (1981) *Women and Revolution: A Discussion of the Unhappy Marriage of Marxism and Feminism*, Boston, MA: South End Press.

Scharf, Lois. (1980) *To Work and To Wed: Female Employment, Feminism and the Great Depression*, Westport, CT: Greenwood Press.

Schor, Juliet B. (1998) *The Overspent American: Upscaling, Downshifting, and the New Consumer*, New York: Basic Books.

Schulman, Bruce J. (1991) *From Cotton Belt to Sunbelt: Federal Policy, Economic Development, and the Transformation of the South, 1938–1980*, New York: Oxford University Press.

Schultz, Theodore W. (1961) "Investment in Human Capital," *American Economic Review* 51 (1): 1–17.

Schwab, Donald P. (1980) "Job Evaluation and Pay Setting: Concepts and Practices," in Robert E. Livernash (ed.) *Comparable Worth: Issues and Alternatives*, pp. 49–77, Washington, DC: Equal Employment Advisory Council.

Scott, Joan W. (1988) *Gender and the Politics of History*, New York, Columbia University Press.

Screpanti, Ernest and Zamagni, Stefano. (1993) *An Outline of the History of Economic Thought*, Oxford: Clarendon Press.

Seager, Henry R. (1913) "The Theory of the Minimum Wage," *American Labor Legislation Review* 3 (February): 81–115.

Seligman, Edwin R. A. (1926) *Principles of Economics*, ninth edition, New York: Longmans, Green, & Company.

Sen, Amartya. (1999) *Development As Freedom*, New York: Alfred A. Knopf.

Sibson, Robert E. (1960) *Wages and Salaries: A Handbook for Line Managers*, New York: American Management Association.

Sieling, Mark S. (1984) "Staffing Patterns Prominent in Female–Male Earnings Gap," *Monthly Labor Review* 107 (6): 29–33.

Sklar, Kathryn Kish. (1995) "Two Political Cultures in the Progressive Era: the National Consumers' League and the American Association for Labor Legislation," in Linda K. Kerber, Alice Kessler-Harris, and Kathryn Kish Sklar (eds) *U.S. History as Women's History*, pp. 36–62, Chapel Hill: University of North Carolina Press.

Slichter, Sumner H. (1950) "Notes on the Structure of Wages," *Review of Economics and Statistics* 32 (1): 80–91.

Slichter, Sumner H., Healy, James J., and Livernash, Robert E. (1960) *The Impact of Collective Bargaining on Management*, Washington, DC: The Brookings Institution.

Smith, Adam. (1937 [1776]) *The Wealth of Nations*, New York: The Modern Library.

Smith, Ralph E. (ed.) (1979) *The Subtle Revolution: Women at Work*, Washington, DC: The Urban Institute.

Smyth, Richard C. and Associates, and Murphy, Matthew J. (1946) *Job Evaluation and Employee Rating*, New York: McGraw-Hill.

Society for the Advancement of Management, Detroit Chapter. (1945) *Job Evaluation, Time and Motion Study, Wage Incentives*, 1945 Lecture Series, Detroit, MI: Society for the Advancement of Management.

Sorensen, Elaine. (1990) "The Crowding Hypothesis and Comparable Worth," *Journal of Human Resources* 25 (1): 55–89.

Sorensen, Elaine. (1994) *Comparable Worth: Is It a Worthy Policy?* Princeton, NJ: Princeton University Press.

Squires, Judith. (1999) *Gender in Political Theory*, Cambridge, U.K.: Polity Press.

Starr, Paul. (1987) "The Case for Skepticism," in William T. Gormley, Jr (ed.) *Privatization and Its Alternatives*, pp. 25–36, Madison: University of Wisconsin Press.

Steinberg, Ronnie. (1982) *Wages and Hours: Labor and Reform in Twentieth-Century America*, New Brunswick, NJ: Rutgers University Press.

Steinberg, Ronnie J. (1984) "'A Want of Harmony': Perspectives on Wage Discrimination and Comparable Worth," in Helen Remick (ed.) *Comparable Worth and Wage Discrimination: Technical Possibilities and Political Realities*, pp. 2–27, Philadelphia, PA: Temple University Press.

Steinberg, Ronnie. (1990) "Social Construction of Skill: Gender, Power, and Comparable Worth," *Work and Occupations* 17 (4): 449–82.

Steinberg, Ronnie J. (1992) "Gendered Instructions: Cultural Lag and Gender Bias in the Hay System of Job Evaluation," *Work and Occupations* 19 (4): 387–432.

Steinberg, Ronnie J. (1999) "Emotional Labor In Job Evaluation: Redesigning Compensation Practices," *Annals of the American Academy of Political and Social Science* 561 (January): 143–57.

Steinberg, Ronnie and Haignere, Lois. (1987) "Equitable Compensation: Methodological Criteria for Comparable Worth," in Christine Bose and Glenna Spitze (eds) *Ingredients for Women's Employment Policy*, pp. 157–82, Albany: State University of New York Press.

Storrs, Landon R. Y. (2000) *Civilizing Capitalism: The National Consumers' League, Women's Activism, and Labor Standards in the New Deal Era*, Chapel Hill: University of North Carolina Press.

Strassmann, Diana L. (1994) "Feminist Thought and Economics; Or, What Do the Visigoths Know?" *American Economic Review* 84 (2): 153–58.

Strober, Myra H. (1994) "Rethinking Economics Through a Feminist Lens," *American Economic Review* 84 (2): 143–47.

Taussig, Frank W. (1916) "Minimum Wages for Women," *Quarterly Journal of Economics* 30 (2): 411–42.

Tax, Meredith. (1980) *The Rising of the Women: Feminist Solidarity and Class Conflict, 1880–1917*, New York: Monthly Review Press.

Tentler, Leslie Woodcock. (1979) *Wage-earning Women: Industrial Work and Family Life in the United States, 1900–1930*, New York: Oxford University Press.

Thompson, Neal. (2000, May 24) "Hopkins Arm Facing Protests; Living Wage Sought for Janitors at For-Profit Subsidiary," *The Baltimore Sun* [Online], p. 1B. Available: http://web.lexis-nexis.com/universe [accessed 2000, October 11].

Treiman, Donald J. (1979) *Job Evaluation: An Analytic Review*, Washington, DC: National Academy of Sciences.

Treiman, Donald J. and Hartmann, Heidi I. (eds) (1981) *Women, Work, and Wages: Equal Pay for Jobs of Equal Value*, Washington, DC: National Academy Press.

Tyson, James L. (1996, April 10) "'Living Wage' Drive Accelerates in Cities." *The Christian Science Monitor* [Online], p. 1. Available: http://www.csmonitor.com/cgi-bin/getasciiarchive?tape/96/apr/day10/10012 [accessed 1998, September 17].

United Electrical, Radio & Machine Workers of America [UE]. (1943) *UE Guide to Wage Payment Plans, Time Study, and Job Evaluation*, New York: UE.

Uchitelle, Louis. (1996, April 9) "Some Cities Flexing Muscle To Make Employers Raise Wages." *The New York Times* [Online], p. A1. Available: http://web.lexis-nexis.com/universe [accessed 1999, May 26].

U.S. Census Bureau. (1975) *Historical Abstracts of the United States: Colonial Times to 1970*, Washington, DC: U.S. Government Printing Office.

U.S. Census Bureau. (1999) *Statistical Abstract of the United States: 1999*, 119th edition, Washington, DC: U.S. Government Printing Office.

U.S. Census Bureau. (2000) *Statistical Abstract of the United States: 2000*, 120th edition, Washington, DC: U.S. Government Printing Office.

U.S. Census Bureau. (2001a) *Money Income in the United States: 2000*, P60–213, Washington, DC: U.S. Government Printing Office.

U.S. Census Bureau. (2001b) Poverty Thresholds [Online]. Available: http://www.census.gov/hhes/poverty/histpov/hstpov1.html [accessed 2001, September 26].

U.S. Congress, Joint Hearings Before the Committee on Education and Labor, U.S. Senate, and the Committee on Labor, House of Representatives [U.S. Congress]. (1937) *Fair Labor Standards Act of 1937*. 75th Congress, Washington, DC: Government Printing Office.

U.S. Congress, Hearings Before the Subcommittee of the Committee on Education and Labor, U.S. Senate [U.S. Senate]. (1946) *Equal Pay for Equal Work for Women*. 79th Congress, October 29, 30, and 31, 1945, Washington, DC: U.S. Government Printing Office.

U.S. Congress, Hearings Before Subcommittee No. 4 of the Committee on Education and Labor, U.S. House of Representatives [U.S. House of Representatives]. (1948) *Equal Pay for Equal Work for Women*. 80th Congress, February 9, 10, 11, and 13, 1948, Washington, DC: U.S. Government Printing Office.

U.S. Congress, Hearings Before the Subcommittee on Labor of the Committee on Labor and Public Welfare, U.S. Senate [U.S. Senate]. (1963) *Equal Pay Act of 1963*. 88th Congress, April 2, 3, and 16, 1963, Washington, DC: U.S. Government Printing Office.

U.S. Congress, House of Representatives, Committee on Education and Labor [U.S. House of Representatives]. (1963) *Legislative History of the Equal Pay Act of 1963*. Miscellaneous Committee Reprints, no. 7, Washington, DC: U.S. Government Printing Office.

U.S. Department of Labor, Bureau of Labor Statistics [BLS]. (1980) *Perspectives on Working Women: A Databook*, Washington, DC: U.S. Government Printing Office.

U.S. Department of Labor, Bureau of Labor Statistics [BLS]. (1989) *Handbook of Labor Statistics*, Washington, DC: U.S. Government Printing Office.

U.S. Department of Labor, Bureau of Labor Statistics [BLS]. (2001) *Employment and Earnings*, 48 (1), Washington, DC: U.S. Government Printing Office.

U.S. Department of Labor, Women's Bureau [Women's Bureau]. (1923a) *The Share of Wage-Earning Women in Family Support*, Bulletin no. 30, Washington, DC: Women's Bureau.

U.S. Department of Labor, Women's Bureau [Women's Bureau]. (1923b) *Proceedings of the Women's Industrial Conference*, Bulletin no. 33, Washington, DC: Women's Bureau.

U.S. Department of Labor, Women's Bureau [Women's Bureau]. (1928) *The Development of Minimum Wage Laws in the U.S., 1912 to 1927*, Bulletin no. 61, Washington, DC: Women's Bureau.

U.S. Department of Labor, Women's Bureau [Women's Bureau]. (1938) *The Negro Woman Worker*, Bulletin no. 165, Washington, DC: U.S. Government Printing Office.

U.S. Department of Labor, Women's Bureau [Women's Bureau]. (1942) *"Equal Pay" for Women in War Industries*. Bulletin no. 196, Washington, DC: U.S. Government Printing Office.

U.S. Department of Labor, Women's Bureau [Women's Bureau]. (1952) *Report of the National Conference on Equal Pay: March 31 and April 1, 1952*. Bulletin no. 243, Washington, DC: U.S. Government Printing Office.

U.S. Department of Labor, Women's Bureau [Women's Bureau]. (1955) *Equal-pay Primer: Some Basic Facts*, Washington, DC: U.S. Government Printing Office.

U.S. Department of Labor, Women's Bureau [Women's Bureau]. (1963) *Economic Indicators Relating to Equal Pay*, Washington, DC: U.S. Government Printing Office.

U.S. Department of Labor, Women's Bureau [Women's Bureau]. (1998) *Equal Pay: A Thirty-Five Year Perspective*, Washington, DC: U.S. Department of Labor.

U.S. Senate. (1937) *Fair Labor Standards Act: Report to Accompany S. 2475*, Report no. 884, July 6, Washington, DC: Government Printing Office.

Van Kleeck, Mary. (1919) "Federal Policies for Women in Industry," *Annals of the American Academy of Political and Social Science* 81: 87–94.

Vazquez, Jaime. (2000) Former Councilperson, 1985–99, City of Jersey City, New Jersey. Interview, Jersey City, NJ, September 6.

Veblen, Thorstein. (1993 [1898]) "Why is Economics Not an Evolutionary Science?" in Rick Tilman (ed.) *A Veblen Treasury*, pp. 129–43, Armonk, NY: M. E. Sharpe.

Veblen, Thorstein. (1994 [1899]) *The Theory of the Leisure Class*, New York: Penguin Books.

Vogel, Lise. (1993) *Mothers on the Job*, New Brunswick, NJ: Rutgers University Press.

Vogel, Lise. (1995) *Woman Questions: Essays for a Materialist Feminism*, London: Pluto Press.

Vogel, Lise. (2000) "Domestic Labor Revisited," *Science & Society* 64 (2): 151–70.

Wagman, Barnet and Folbre, Nancy. (1988) "The Feminization of Inequality: Some New Patterns," *Challenge* 31 (6): 56–9.

Walby, Sylvia. (1986) *Patriarchy at Work: Patriarchal and Capitalist Relations in Employment*, Minneapolis: University of Minnesota Press.

Walby, Sylvia. (1997) *Gender Transformations*, New York: Routledge.

Wallace, Phyllis A. (1982) "Increased Labor Force Participation of Women and

Affirmative Action" in Phyllis A. Wallace (ed.) *Women in the Workplace*, pp. 1–24, Boston, MA: Auburn House Publishing.

Waller, William. (1999a) "Institutional Economics, Feminism, and Overdetermination," *Journal of Economic Issues* 33 (4): 835–44.

Waller, William. (1999b) "Institutional Political Economy: History," in Phillip Anthony O'Hara (ed.) *Encyclopedia of Political Economy*, pp. 523–28, London: Routledge.

Waller, William and Jennings, Ann. (1990) "On the Possibility of a Feminist Economics," *Journal of Economic Issues* 24 (2): 613–22.

Walters, J. E. (1938) "Job Evaluation: An Analysis of the Several Plans in Use Today," *Mechanical Engineering* (December): 921–30.

Webb, Sidney and Webb, Beatrice. (1920) *Industrial Democracy*, London: Longmans, Green, & Company.

Weber, Lynn and Higginbotham, Elizabeth. (1997) "Black and White Professional-Managerial Women's Perceptions of Racism and Sexism in the Workplace," in Elizabeth Higginbotham and Mary Romero (eds) *Women and Work: Exploring Race, Ethnicity, and Class*, pp. 153–75, Thousand Oaks, CA: Sage Publications.

Weedon, Chris. (1987) *Feminist Practice and Poststructuralist Theory*, Oxford, U.K.: Basil Blackwell.

Weiner, Lynn Y. (1985) *From Working Girl to Working Mother: The Female Labor Force in the United States, 1820–1980*, Chapel Hill: University of North Carolina Press.

Weisbrot, Mark and Sforza-Roderick, Michelle. (1996) *Baltimore's Living Wage Law: An Analysis of the Fiscal and Economic Costs of Baltimore City Ordinance 442*, Washington, DC: The Preamble Center for Public Policy.

Weiss, Harry. (1944) "Economic Coverage of the Fair Labor Standards Act," *Quarterly Journal of Economics* 58 (2): 460–81.

Wells, David R. (1998) *Consumerism and the Movement of Housewives into Wage Work*, Aldershot, U.K.: Ashgate Publishing.

West Coast Hotel v. Parrish. (1937) 57 S.Ct. 578, 300 U.S. 379, (U.S. Wash. 1937).

Wikander, Ulla, Kessler-Harris, Alice, and Lewis, Jane. (eds) (1995) *Protecting Women: Labor Legislation in Europe, the United States, and Australia, 1880–1920*, Urbana: University of Illinois Press.

Wilkinson, Patrick. (1999) "The Selfless and the Helpless: Maternalist Origins of the U.S. Welfare State," *Feminist Studies* 25 (3): 571–97.

Williams, Fred O. (2000, July 21) "City's Living Wage Law Languishes Year After Passage," *The Buffalo News* [Online], p. 6B. Available: http://web/lexis-nexis.com/universe [accessed 2000, October 11].

Williams, Rhonda. (1987) "Capital, Competition, and Discrimination: A Reconsideration of Racial Earnings Inequality," *Review of Radical Political Economics* 19 (2): 1–15.

Williams, Rhonda M. (1995) "Consenting to Whiteness: Reflections on Race and Marxian Theories of Discrimination" in Antonio Callari, Stephen Cullenberg, and Carole Biewener (eds) *Marxism in the Postmodern Age: Confronting the New World Order*, pp. 301–08, New York: Guilford Press.

Wilson, Greg. (1996) "Living Wage Ordered: Schundler Beats Opponents to Punch," *The Jersey Journal*, May 15, pp. 1, 5.

Woodbury, Stephen A. (1987) "Power in the Labor Market: Institutionalist Approaches to Labor Problems," *Journal of Economic Issues* 21 (4): 1781–807.

Woolley, Frances R. (1993) "The Feminist Challenge to Neoclassical Economics," *Cambridge Journal of Economics* 17: 485–500.

Workman, Andrew A. (2000) "Creating the National War Labor Board: Franklin Roosevelt and the Politics of State Building in the Early 1940s," *Journal of Policy History* 12 (2): 233–64.

Yates, Michael D. (1998) *Why Unions Matter*, New York: Monthly Review Press.

Zabin, Carol. (1997, January 7) "Assessing the Costs and Benefits of the 'Living Wage Ordinance': A Review of the Evidence," Policy Brief. Los Angeles: Center for Labor Research and Education, University of California – Los Angeles.

Zieger, Robert H. (1995) *The CIO, 1935–1955*, Chapel Hill: University of North Carolina Press.

Zimmerman, Joan. (1991) "The Jurisprudence of Equality: The Women's Minimum Wage, the First Equal Rights Amendment, and *Adkins v. Children's Hospital*, 1905–1923," *Journal of American History* 78 (1): 188–225.

Index

References for figures, plates, and tables are in *italics*